# SHAKESPEARE
# AND THE LAWYERS

# SHAKESPEARE
# AND THE LAWYERS

O. Hood Phillips
QC DCL

METHUEN & CO LTD
LONDON

*First published* 1972
*by Methuen & Co Ltd*
11 *New Fetter Lane London EC4*
© 1972 *O. Hood Phillips*
*Printed in Great Britain by*
*T & A Constable Ltd Edinburgh*

SBN 416 76020 1

*Distributed in the USA by*
HARPER & ROW PUBLISHERS, INC.
BARNES & NOBLE IMPORT DIVISION

# Contents

v

*Preface*

In the quatercentenary year of 1964 I contributed two
articles to the *Law Quarterly Review* under the title 'The
Law Relating to Shakespeare'. My purpose was to give a
broad survey of what Shakespeare wrote about the law and
lawyers, and what had been written, especially by lawyers,
about Shakespeare in relation to the law, and the light which
all this has been supposed to throw on the legal learning, or
even the identity, of the poet and playwright. It was afterwards suggested to me that if these articles were rewritten
and expanded into the form of a book, the result would be of
interest to a wider circle of readers. Some of the material
has also been used for a talk given at the Shakespeare Institute on 17 June 1965, and an address read to the Gray's Inn
Historical Society in Gray's Inn Hall on 7 July 1970, and
published in *Graya*, Michaelmas 1970.

The title of the original articles was a kind of pun and
only doubtfully conveyed its meaning. 'Shakespeare and
the Law', besides being overworked, sounded too technical
for the way I have approached the subject. Also it is too
narrow, because I am concerned with what lawyers have
written about the non-legal as well as the legal aspects of
Shakespeare. The most precise title would probably be
'Shakespeare, the Law and the Lawyers', as the background
must be filled in by the researches of Shakespeare scholars
who are or were laymen, but this would be cumbersome. So
I have chosen 'Shakespeare and the Lawyers', which in spite

of its imperfection gives the right emphasis. A liberal interpretation has been given to the term 'lawyer', so as to include
a number of authors – of whom Malone was the greatest –
who obtained legal qualifications but abandoned the practice
of law for literary scholarship.

The result of the first rewriting and expansion would have
made the book too long, and the publishers asked me to
reduce it appreciably. This I have now done partly by prun-
ing the remaining chapters, but chiefly by omitting three
chapters on the question whether William Shakespeare,
actor and house-owner of Stratford-on-Avon, really was the
author of the plays and poems attributed to him. It was with
regret that I omitted the authorship question from this book,
as it is a controversy in which lawyers have taken a prominent
and enthusiastic part, although it may be taboo among
Shakespeare scholars. However, I hope the material excised
may form the subject of a separate book to be published
later. It was not practicable to cite in the text all the materials
read for the purpose of writing the present book, but a
Bibliography has been added, consisting mainly of the
writings of lawyers and articles published in legal periodicals,
though excluding works dealing with the authorship
question unless otherwise relevant. Quotations are from
*The Oxford Shakespeare.*

How can lawyers most usefully contribute to Shakespeare
studies in the future? We are unlikely to find lawyers with
private means, like Malone, who can afford to devote
much time to literary pursuits. A survey of what lawyers
have written on their favourite Shakespearean topic, *The
Merchant of Venice* (chapter 8), may lead to the conclusion,
*quot jurisprudentes tot sententiae.* From Shakespeare scholars
there seems to come an insatiable demand for more technical
knowledge of legal terms, principles and procedure, presumably of English law of the Elizabethan and Jacobean
period. I am inclined to think that this demand is misguided.
If the poet and playwright was not himself a legal expert (as

is the better opinion among lawyers themselves) then it is not clear how an exact knowledge of the law – English law or any other – of his time can bring us much closer to his meaning and intentions. Poets share with lawyers a common interest in the precise use of words, but the effect that the poet seeks to produce by his use of words is often the direct opposite of the aim that the lawyer hopes to achieve. However, if this demand of the scholars is to be satisfied the most hopeful way seems to be, not to leave the lawyers to their own devices which are liable to descend to trivialities, but collaboration between Shakespeare scholars and legal historians, although the latter are rare and often have not had much practical experience. Students of literature and drama must choose the questions, and legal historians must devil for them. Best of all, let the literary historians discover some more contemporary documents relating to Shakespeare's life, and then the lawyers will be pleased to interpret them.

One of the first persons to whom I mentioned my original project was Professor Charles Sisson, who kindly gave me some helpful advice for which, alas, it is too late to thank him. I am grateful to Professor T. J. B. Spencer, Director of the Shakespeare Institute, for expert advice on several matters, and to Dr T. P. Matheson, Fellow of the Shakespeare Institute, for kindly reading the proofs. Neither of them is in any way responsible for the result, and I only hope they will not feel embarrassed by being mentioned here. My thanks for help are also due to the Librarian of the Folger Library, Washington, D.C.; Mrs Frederick (*née* Payne) and Miss Hancox of the Birmingham Shakespeare Library; Mrs Bray of the Shakespeare Institute Library; and especially Miss Mary Blake and Mrs McDougall (*née* Hand), the resourceful and ever-patient Assistants in charge of the Harding Law Library at Birmingham University.

*Faculty of Law*                                                                    O.H.P.
*University of Birmingham*

ix

# I

## Records of Shakespeare's Life and Work

Official records of the life and work of William Shakespeare of Stratford-on-Avon are few, but not fewer than one would expect in the case of a man of Shakespeare's social position in the late sixteenth and early seventeenth centuries. Records which had been discovered down to 1930 are contained in Sir Edmund Chambers's *William Shakespeare: A Study of Facts and Problems*.[1] Chambers, a leading Shakespeare scholar, classifies the records as Ecclesiastical, Court, Tenurial, Municipal, National, Legal, Occupational and Administrative; he later used them as a basis for a projected biography of Shakespeare.[2] The collecting of sources was begun in the eighteenth century by Edmond Malone, the Irish lawyer and Shakespeare editor, but the search still goes on, the most successful discoverer in recent years being the American scholar, Leslie Hotson.

The register of Stratford-on-Avon parish church records that *Gulielmus filius Johannes Shakspere* was christened on 26 April 1564. The entry is an official transcript, probably by the vicar. The original may have got the genitive of *Johannes* right. If the inscription on Shakespeare's monument[3] (presumably the one mentioned in the First Folio of 1623) in Stratford parish church is correct in saying that he

---

[1] 2 vols., Oxford, 1930.

[2] E. K. Chambers, *Sources for a Biography of Shakespeare* (1946).

[3] The authenticity of the present monument, 'repaired' in 1749, is disputed by the anti-Stratfordian, Greenwood, and by Baconians such as Edward D. Johnson.

died in the fifty-third year of his age on 23 April 1616, he must have been born between 24 April 1563 and 23 April 1564.

We do not know which of his father's houses was his birthplace. Stratford-on-Avon magistrates in 1969 refused an application for a summons against the Shakespeare Birthplace Trust under the Trade Descriptions Act 1968. The Chairman of the Shakespeare Action Committee who made the application claimed that there was no evidence to show that the building in Henley Street was Shakespeare's birthplace. The Court found that the trustees were carrying out their obligations under the Birthplace Trust Act 1961, and were not carrying on a trade or business as defined by the Trade Descriptions Act.[4]

No record of Shakespeare's marriage has been found, but in the Bishop of Worcester's register there is an entry of a licence dated 27 November 1582, between William Shaxpere and Anne Whateley of Temple Grafton. This was a special licence enabling the marriage to be celebrated after only one reading of the banns, probably because Anne was pregnant. On the next day a bond was entered into by two Stratford farmers exempting the Bishop of Worcester and his officers from liability if by a marriage pre-contract or other lawful impediment William Shagspere was unable to marry Anne Hathwey of Stratford.[5] The name Hathwey in the bond is probably right and the name Whateley on the record of licences an error,[6] unless perhaps the two can be different versions of the same name: they are both still found with various spellings in Warwickshire at the present day.

[4] *The Times*, 2 October 1969.

[5] Sir Arthur Underhill, K.C., in *Shakespeare's England* (ed. Raleigh, Oxford, 1916), I, p. 408. Other lawyers who have written on Shakespeare's marriage are Charles Elton, K.C., *William Shakespeare, His Family and Friends* (1904) and Mr Justice D. H. Madden, *Shakespeare and His Fellows* (1916), pp. 176-81).

[6] Peter Alexander, *Shakespeare* (1964), pp. 30 et seq. Alexander suggests that Shakespeare and Anne may have already married by a *de praesenti* contract; cf. *Measure for Measure*.

The christenings of Shakespeare's three children are recorded in the register of Stratford parish church, that of Susanna about six months after Shakespeare's marriage. These are the only records of Shakespeare down to 1592, when he was twenty-eight years of age. The register of the scholars of Stratford-on-Avon Grammar School for that period has not been preserved. Hamnet (the name appears to be interchangeable with Hamlet), one of his younger twins, was buried at Stratford-on-Avon on 11 August 1596. The grant of arms to Shakespeare's father in the same year, manuscript drafts of which are in the College of Arms, entitled Shakespeare to call himself gentleman.

The burial of 'Will. Shakspere, gent.' is recorded in the register of Stratford parish church as having taken place on 25 April 1616. He is said to have been buried seventeen feet deep in the chancel, near the north wall. He had a right to interment in the church as part-owner of the tithes and therefore one of the lay rectors. His monument is on the north wall of the chancel.

There is evidence, much of it in unofficial documents, that Shakespeare was a successful actor-dramatist in London by 1592, writing for and acting with the Lord Chamberlain's Company (later the King's Men) from 1594. *Venus and Adonis*, *The Rape of Lucrece*, *The Phoenix and the Turtle* and the *Sonnets* were printed under Shakespeare's name between 1593 and 1609; the first two being printed by Richard Field, son of a Stratford neighbour. The identity of the person to whom the *Sonnets* were dedicated by their publisher, Thomas Thorpe, has always been hotly debated. A barrister named J. Pym Yeatman has suggested that Mr W. H. may be none other than 'William Hisself'.[7] Quartos of a number of the plays were published in his lifetime as being by William Shakespeare, the first being *Love's Labour's Lost* (1598), and he is first mentioned in the Stationers' Register as the author of *Much Ado about Nothing* (1600).

[7] J. Pym Yeatman, *The Gentle Shakspere: A Vindication* (4th ed.), p. 299.

More information is contained in Court accounts for plays
and revels, and in the diary or account book of Philip
Henslowe.[8] For James I's procession through the City of
London in 1604 four yards of red cloth were provided to
Shakespeare and each of the other King's Men to make
cloaks.

It is important to remember, in connection with the
questions both of publication and of Shakespeare's will
(which does not mention books or manuscripts), that there
was no author's copyright in the modern sense before the
Copyright Act, 1709.[9] In Shakespeare's time the printing
of books and the performance of stage plays were controlled
by royal charter or order of the Council under a licensing
system. Apart from the Universities of Oxford and Cambridge, printing was a monopoly of the Stationers' Company
of London. Copyright in a book lay with the printer or publisher, who registered it with the Stationers' Company of
which he was a freeman.[10] Publication was often decided on
to forestall pirating. A play was usually bought by a company of actors, whose property it became. Often they had
commissioned it, and they acted it, usually from manuscript
prompt copies, so long as it held the public favour. We do
not know whether an author received payment for subsequent performances. The Master of the Revels licensed or
censored plays for public performance. The Tonsons, who
purchased the copyright of *Paradise Lost* and in 1709 published Rowe's edition of Shakespeare, came to be regarded

[8] *Henslowe's Diary*, an account book for the years 1591-1609, was discovered
by Malone and printed by J. P. Collier in 1845. Henslowe built three theatres,
and had an interest in several companies of actors, including the Admiral's.

[9] cf. Sir George Greenwood, *The Shakespeare Problem Restated* (1908), chap. 10,
quoting Baron Parke in *Jefferys v. Boosey*, 4 H.L.C. 920, on the distinction between
the common law right to the copies which an author actually writes on his own
paper, and the exclusive right of multiplying copies of a work which the author
has published.

[10] See Holdsworth, *History of English Law*, VI, 361-8. 'Bookseller, stationer,
publisher were convertible terms in those days': Greenwood, op. cit., p. 263n.
And see W. W. Greg, *The Shakespeare First Folio* (1955), chap. 2.

as the proprietors of Shakespeare's plays, although as Lord Justice Mackinnon says we do not know that they had any assignment on which to rely.[11]

Shakespeare became a sharer in such a company of actors. He also became a property-sharer or 'housekeeper'. As an actor-sharer he was not only joint owner of plays, whether written by himself or others, but he would receive a share of the profit arising from the general charge for admission. As a property-sharer he was joint owner of the Globe (1599) and Blackfriars (1608) Theatres, as we learn from records of litigation in which the Heminges and Burbage were concerned,[12] and would receive part of the money paid for admission to the galleries.

From Pipe Rolls of 1598-9 and 1599-1600 we learn that Shakespeare owed what we should now call rates in Bishopsgate, and from depositions in the Court of Requests (1612) that he lodged for a time with the Mountjoys in Cripplegate. He does not appear to have owned a dwelling-house in London, but in 1613 he bought the Blackfriars Gatehouse from Henry Walker, citizen and minstrel of London, for £140, and mortgaged it the next day to the vendor to secure the balance (£60) of the purchase money.[13] The form of the conveyance to Shakespeare and three trustees (including John Heminge) had the effect – whatever the purpose may have been – of preventing Shakespeare's wife from acquiring a right of dower in this property, for Shakespeare would only become sole owner if he was the last survivor; meanwhile

---

[11] Sir Frank Mackinnon, 'Notes on the History of English Copyright', *Oxford Companion to English Literature* (2nd. ed., 1936), Appendix II.

[12] *Witter v. Heminges and Condell*, Court of Requests, 28 April 1619, Answer of Heminges and Condell; *Ostler v. Heminges*, Coram Rege Roll, 13 Jac. 1 (1615), Plea of Thomasina Ostler; *Keysar v. Burbadge and Others*, Court of Requests, 8 and 10 February 1610; Answer of Burbadge and Others to petition of Robert Benfield and Heliard Swanston to the Lord Chamberlain, August 1635. See C. W. Wallace, *The Newly Discovered Shakespeare Documents* (1905).

[13] The conveyance dated 10 March 1613 is in the Guildhall Library, London. The mortgage deed is in the British Museum. See further, L. Hotson, *Shakespeare's Sonnets Dated* (1949), Appendix A.

he could make another settlement. The conveyance and the mortgage both bear Shakespeare's signature.

Shakespeare was also acquiring landed property in Stratford-on-Avon. He bought New Place, the largest house in Stratford, in 1597.[14] The garden only remains to-day. The fact, which has long attracted attention, that two transactions were involved in this purchase was the subject of a special study by an Australian legal practitioner, Percy R. Watts, who was also for many years Reader in Conveyancing at Sydney University Law School and Conveyancing editor of the *Australian Law Journal*.[15] In Easter Term, 1597, Shakespeare purchased New Place from William Underhill[16] for £60 by means of a fine levied between the parties. In Michaelmas Term, 1602, the property was the subject of a second fine between Shakespeare and Hercules Underhill, the second son of William Underhill. The consideration here was also expressed to be £60. What was the need for the second fine, and why was it so long afterwards? Halliwell-Phillipps's theory was that some external flaw had been discovered in Shakespeare's title, and that the second fine was levied for the purpose of barring some outstanding interest not barred by the first. William Underhill died later in the same year as the first fine; his eldest son, Fulke, to whom he had devised all his lands, died childless while still a minor in the next year; it transpired that Fulke had poisoned his father; the Idlicote estate passed to his brother Hercules, who did not come of age until 1602. Mrs C. C. Stopes, who discovered that Fulke murdered William,[17] thought that this fact may have cast doubt on the title, and so Shakespeare secured his premises from future dangers by a new fine when Hercules came of age. This was accepted

[14] Foot of Fine, 4 May 1597.

[15] Percy R. Watts, 'Shakespeare's "Double" Purchase of New Place' (1947), 20 *Australian Law Journal*, pp. 330-36.

[16] Claimed as a collateral ancestor by Sir Arthur Underhill, K.C. in *Shakespeare's England*, I, p. 404. For this form of conveyance, see *post*, chap. 9.

[17] Mrs C. C. Stopes, *Shakespeare's Industry* (1916), pp. 260-61.

by a number of later commentators. Watts points out, however, that: (1) There could have been no forfeiture in the case of Fulke, as he was never prosecuted, let alone sentenced to death; (2) The incapacity of a criminal to enjoy the fruits of his crime depends on the fact of murder, not on trial or conviction, and the property goes to the person who under the will would have been entitled to it if the donee (Fulke) had died before the testator (William). In that case, the land would have gone to Hercules, the second son, as William's heir; (3) No equitable 'forfeiture' would have affected property that William had effectively conveyed to a third party in his lifetime. Shakespeare's purchase of New Place from William, therefore, would not have been put in jeopardy by the subsequent murder of William by a person for whose acts Shakespeare was not responsible. On the other hand, if the conveyance was in any respect defective, Shakespeare would have been concerned with the devolution of any outstanding estates; and if the defect was not discovered until after the death of William, the opportunity would not come until Hercules came of age in 1602. Now the parcels in the second fine include two orchards not mentioned in the first fine. This fact was noticed by previous commentators, but they did not attach importance to it as an obvious explanation of the second fine. It seems, then, that Shakespeare paid £60+£60 =£120, so that Hercules charged as much for the two orchards as his father had charged for the house, two barns and two gardens.

Shakespeare presumably succeeded to the two houses in Henley Street on his father's death in 1601. Next year he bought 127 acres of agricultural land at Welcombe on the outskirts of Stratford from William Combe, a lawyer of Middle Temple, and his nephew John.[18] He also had a copyhold cottage in Chapel Lane.[19] Then he bought some land

---

[18] Conveyance by William and John Combe to William Shakespeare, dated 1 May 1602.

[19] Entry in Court Roll of Rowington Manor, 28 September 1602.

in Shottery, and in 1605 acquired the leasehold of valuable tithes derived from Stratford and neighbouring hamlets.[20] He received a legacy of £5 in the will dated January 1613 of John Combe, who died in 1614.

It was as difficult in those days to go through life without being involved in civil litigation as it is now without appearing in a magistrates' court for a traffic offence. Shakespeare brought actions for debt in the Stratford Court of Record against Rogers, an apothecary, in 1604, and against Addenbrooke in 1609. He was also involved in litigation concerning his mother's estate at Wilmcote.

Halliwell-Phillipps, the Victorian biographer,[21] said there were almost certainly undiscovered notices of Shakespeare among the millions of papers in the Public Record Office, some of which might remain concealed for many generations. The present century has seen some important discoveries, notably those of C. W. Wallace, Professor of English Dramatic Literature at Nebraska, who not only found documents relating to several suits concerning Heminge, Condell and Burbage, which give information about the shares and Shakespeare's holdings in the Globe and Blackfriars theatres, but also discovered the Belott-Mountjoy papers.[22] These show that Shakespeare was back in London as a witness in the case of *Belott v. Mountjoy* in 1612. Belott, an apprentice, had married the daughter of his master, Mountjoy, eight years earlier. This was an action for the payment of dowry. Shakespeare, when lodging with the Mountjoys in Silver Street, near St Paul's, had on request helped to bring about this match, but by the time the action was fought he could not remember how much Mountjoy

[20] Abstract of assignment from Ralph Hubard to Shakespeare, 24 July 1605.

[21] J. O. Halliwell-Phillipps, *Outlines of the Life of Shakespeare* (1887), included all the documents then known. His book was largely superseded by Sir Sidney Lee's *Life of William Shakespeare* (1898, 6th ed., 1908), which included rather more than was known.

[22] C. W. Wallace, *Shakespeare and His London Associates as Revealed in Recently Discovered Documents* (1910).

had promised to provide. The deposition bears Shakespeare's signature.

Inspired by Halliwell-Phillipps's prophecy, Leslie Hotson[23] searched the rolls of the Queen's Bench, looked at petitions for sureties of the peace, and found the following entry for Michaelmas Term, 1596: that William Wayte craves sureties of the peace against William Shakespeare, Francis Langley and others. Langley had recently built the Swan Theatre, Bankside, where Shakespeare and his fellows were apparently playing. This suit was evidently in revenge for a petition three weeks earlier by Langley, seeking sureties of the peace against William Gardiner and the same William Wayte, his stepson. William Gardiner (Gardener or Gardyner) turns out to be a Justice of the Peace for Surrey, with jurisdiction over the Bankside district. Next year, Gardiner was given by the Privy Council the not unwelcome order to suppress the Bankside playhouses. The order was not completely carried out; but other records show that Gardiner brought three suits for slander against Langley in the same Michaelmas Term, 1596.

Shakespeare is often accused of being litigious and grasping. It must be remembered that his was a litigious age. Further, apart from parish registers, the records and official documents which exist for that period consist largely of Court records and conveyances. If we had a register of the members of the choir of Stratford-on-Avon parish church we ought not to conclude that Shakespeare's contemporaries spent most of their time singing in church.

Of all Shakespeare's source books, he gleaned most from Holinshed's *Chronicles*. Raphael Holinshed was employed by Thomas Burdett, of Bramcote, Warwickshire, who was Lord of the Manor of Packwood in the same county. Holinshed was for a long time Burdett's steward, and used to preside regularly over the Manor Court at Packwood. He was at Packwood at least as early as 1561, and his

[23] Leslie Hotson, *Shakespeare versus Shallow* (1931).

responsibilities there continued until he died in 1580, when Shakespeare was sixteen. Hotson[24] suggests that the young Shakespeare may therefore have known Holinshed at the time when the *Chronicles* were being compiled.

It is hardly within the competence of a lawyer to judge whether any of Shakespeare's works reveal autobiographical information, an exercise which in any case is specially hazardous with regard to statements put into the mouths of characters in a play. Legal opinion on the question whether the Sonnets reveal homosexual tendencies, however, may not be out of place. Sir Frederick Pollock,[25] the well-known jurist, in a letter to Justice O. W. Holmes, of the American Supreme Court, wrote: 'W. S. would surely not wish a scandal even "among his private friends" and must have been careful so to embroider the substratum of fact, whatever it was, that they could not make one.' In a similar vein E. S. P. Haynes,[26] a practising solicitor with literary tastes, confided to his notebook: 'to the legal mind it must necessarily occur that if Shakespeare was indulging in what was at the time a capital offence — sometimes punished at the stake — he would scarcely call attention to it in verse. Even literary vanity has its limits!'

The original of Shakespeare's will was removed a few years ago from the Principal Probate Registry to the Public Record Office. It was found in 1747 by the Rev. Joseph Green, of Stratford, in the Court of Probate, Doctors' Commons, where it had lain since the date of probate. It would have been proved in the Prerogative Court of Canterbury because the testator left personal property in more than one jurisdiction, that is, in London as well as Stratford-on-Avon. The will is dated 25 March 1616, about a month before the testator's death. It appears to be a corrected draft

[24] ibid., Appendix B.
[25] *The Pollock-Holmes Letters* (ed. Howe, Cambridge University Press, 1942), II, p. 103, letter dated 19 September 1922.
[26] E. S. P. Haynes, *More from a Lawyer's Notebook* (published anonymously, 1933), pp. 155-6.

rather than a fair copy. Each of the three pages bears his signature. Lord Campbell suggested that the will was probably composed by Shakespeare himself. 'It seems much too simple, terse, and condensed', he says,[27] 'to have been the composition of a Stratford attorney, who was to be paid by the number of lines which it contained.' 'But', he adds, 'a testator, without professional experience, could hardly have used language so appropriate as we find in this will, to express his meaning.' On the other hand an American lawyer, Franklyn Fiske Heard, thought there was no evidence whatever that Shakespeare's will was written (i.e. composed) by himself.[28] It is commonly assumed that the bequests to his wife and to Burbage, Heminge and Condell, being interlineations, were afterthoughts, but Charles Elton, K.C., an experienced real property lawyer, pointed out that this is not necessarily so.[29]

John Pym Yeatman, a barrister of Lincoln's Inn, at first thought that Shakespeare himself drafted the will with advice from Francis Collins, and that the will was in his handwriting. The writing deteriorates on each page, indicating that the testator was ill. Collins made some of the alterations, for example, inserting 'for better enabling of her [Susanna] to peform this my will' (which is bad English), and 'towards the performance thereof' (which is redundant). That, according to Yeatman, was almost the only instance where legal knowledge was at fault or legal terms were misapplied, and the mistake was not Shakespeare's.[30] Later Yeatman expressed the opinion that the will was probably not Shakespeare's, either in the sense that it represented his mind or that his hand wrote it. 'It is a terrible will', he says, referring to the 'wretched pittance'

[27] Lord Campbell, *Shakespeare's Legal Acquirements Considered* (1859), p. 103.

[28] F. F. Heard, *Shakespeare as a Lawyer* (1883), p. 101.

[29] C. I. Elton, K.C., *William Shakespeare: His Family and Friends* (1904), pp. 227-30.

[30] J. Pym Yeatman, *Is William Shakspere's Will Holographic?* (Darley Dale, 2nd. ed., 1901).

given to Judith;[31] 'it is the act of a man in a passion, who knew not what he did. It has cruelty and vindictiveness stamped upon it.' When the will was made on 25 January 1616 Shakespeare's mind was unhinged by Judith's misconduct. It was this, and not merrymaking with Ben Jonson and others, that caused his illness and death. In his agony on learning that his child had followed his own and her mother's example, Shakespeare probably (Yeatman suggests) had a fit of paralysis or possibly of apoplexy.

Tannenbaum,[32] an American physician who made a study of renaissance handwriting, came to the conclusion that the will was written by a clerk employed by Francis Collins. He points out that John Combe's will, drawn by Collins and written by his clerk, also contains several alterations and interlineations. The will was not a rough draft, though page 1 appears to have been rewritten. To one skilled in paleography Shakespeare's signatures indicate that he wrote a good, fluent, clear, simple, legible, and even somewhat artistic hand. The signature is that of a skilful penman, who could write his name neatly and with some degree of firmness. His handwriting appears indeed to be far neater and clearer than that of Heywood, Spenser, Raleigh and many of his other contemporaries.[33] The testator was a somewhat slow, deliberate, precise, unostentatious and clear-thinking writer. Tannenbaum, who as a physician was better qualified than Yeatman to deduce the state of the testator's health from his signatures, thought he might have been suffering from *angina pectoris*.[34]

[31] J. Pym Yeatman, *The Gentle Shakspere: A Vindication* (1896; 4th. ed., Birmingham, 1906), chap. 11.

[32] S. A. Tannenbaum, *Problems in Shakspere's Penmanship, including a Study of the Poet's Will* (1927). Tannenbaum was born in Hungary. He specialised in psychotherapy. Chapter 5 is strongly critical of Greenwood's opinions expressed in *The Shakespeare Signatures*, etc.

[33] Tannenbaum, op. cit., pp. 117, 130, 157-8.

[34] Tannenbaum, op. cit., pp. 74-5. Cf. R. R. Simpson, M.B., Ch.B., F.R.C.S., F.R.C.S.Ed., *Shakespeare and Medicine* (1959), pp. 56-7, suggests that Shakespeare may have died from one of the typhoid fevers. Stratford suffered from epidemics

That new discoveries in such a well cultivated field can still be made is shown by Hotson's[35] researches into the identity of Thomas Russell, Esquire, whom Shakespeare appointed to be one of the overseers of his will. He turns out to be the son of Sir Thomas Russell, and to have been educated at Queen's College, Oxford. Old forms of will often contained appointments of overseers as well as executors: 'Thou, Collatine, shall oversee this will.'[36]

More remarkable is a recent find among the papers of the Sackville family of Knole, deposited at the Kent Archives Office.[37] This is the Act Book recording the hearings in the Ecclesiastical Court held by the vicars of Stratford-on-Avon for the 'peculiar' jurisdiction of their parish, covering the period (incomplete) 1559-1606 and 1616. The peculiar jurisdiction was more or less exempt by charter from the jurisdiction of the Bishop of Worcester, and included the right to hold visitations and to grant marriage licences for two years out of every three. The vicar's authority to grant marriage licences appears to have been questioned, and quarrels broke out with the Bishop's Court. Mr Hanley thinks that Shakespeare's will was probably *drafted* in January 1616, in anticipation of Judith's marriage. It is commonly said that Shakespeare lacked confidence in Thomas Quiney, Judith's husband, because the couple were excommunicated by the Bishop of Worcester for failing to obtain a licence to marry during a prohibited season (10 February). But the vicar of Stratford claimed authority to issue marriage licences in that year, and Thomas Quiney probably obtained a licence from him. So Mr Hanley suggests that the excommunication (for non-appearance) was

---

after the flooding of the Avon, and 1616 was a bad year for this. The testator may have recognised the early symptoms when he made his will.

[35] Leslie Hotson, *I, William Shakespeare* (1937).

[36] *Rape of Lucrece*: quoted by W. L. Rushton, *Shakespeare a Lawyer* (1858), p. 45.

[37] H. A. Hanley, 'Shakespeare's Family in Stratford Records', *Times Lit. Supp.*, 21 May 1964.

the result of the dispute between the Bishop's Court and the Vicar's Court, for which Shakespeare would hardly hold his son-in-law responsible. Shakespeare's attitude was more probably due to Thomas Quiney's affair with Margaret Wheelan, who was buried with her illegitimate child at Stratford on 15 March 1616. An entry in the Act Book of the Vicar's Court dated 26 March 1616 shows that Thomas Quiney was presented for incontinence with Margaret Wheelan, which was admitted. The completion of the will may have been delayed when Shakespeare heard of Thomas Quiney's affair; the marriage with Judith may have been hurried because of pressure from the Wheelan family; and page 1 of the will must have been *rewritten* to take account of the fact that Judith's marriage had now taken place.

The most significant item in the will is the gift of 26s. 8d. apiece to Shakespeare's fellows, John Heminge, Richard Burbage and Henry Condell, to buy them rings. Heminge and Condell – after the deaths of Shakespeare and Burbage – collaborated in the publication of the First Folio, so that this gift connects William Shakespeare of Stratford-on-Avon with the actor-manager and dramatist.

Bequests were made to Judith Quiney, the newly-wed younger daughter, and others. New Place, the houses in Henley Street and other freeholds were settled on the elder daughter Susanna Hall, in tail male, for better enabling her to perform the will; and the residue of the personalty was given to Susanna and her husband, John Hall, who were appointed executors. Coke mentions a local custom by which the widow and the children of the deceased were each entitled to one-third of his personal property as their reasonable parts or portions, leaving one-third of which a testator was at liberty to dispose as he liked; but there is no evidence that this custom applied to Warwickshire.[38] This last gift, Mr Justice Madden explains,[39] made Susanna a

[38] S. O. Addy, 'Shakespeare's Will: The Stigma Removed', *Notes and Queries* 16 January 1926, pp. 39-42.

trustee of the property devised to her: an oral trust to maintain Shakespeare's widow would be binding if the property was accepted. 'The confidence placed in Hall and his wife', says Madden, 'was fully justified. Shakespeare's widow lived with them until her death in 1623.' A. Wigfall Green, Professor of Law at the University of Mississippi and a member of the District of Columbia Bar, after reviewing the law of inheritance of the early seventeenth century and discussing the various devises and bequests in Shakespeare's will, concluded[40] that there was only one important possible obscurity, that connected with the release which Judith was to give Susanna; and this is an obscurity merely because we do not understand the nature of a possible agreement existing among the members of the family. Incidentally he points out an error in line 7 of page 2 of the will, where the words 'at the date of this my will' should have been 'at my decease'.

John Hall left his books and manuscripts to Thomas Nash by his will in 1635. An action brought by Susanna for the recovery of moneys and papers belonging to her late husband John Hall, and possibly to her father, was discovered by Frank Marcham in reading among Chancery Proceedings in 1930.[41] Shakespeare's descendants in fact died out with his granddaughter, Elizabeth Hall (Lady Bernard), in 1670.

The attention of lawyers has naturally been drawn to the well-known fact that Shakespeare left nothing expressly to his wife except 'my second best bed with the furniture'. An article in the *Legal Observer* of 1841[42] accords to Charles Knight, author, editor and publisher, in his then recently

---

[39] D. H. Madden, *Shakespeare and His Fellows* (1916), pp. 185-91.

[40] A. Wigfall Green, 'Shakespeare's Will', (1932) 20 *Georgetown Law Journal*, pp. 273-92.

[41] Frank Marcham, *William Shakespeare and His Daughter Susannah* (1931). The cover is entitled, and the pages are headed, 'William Shakespeare and His Family'.

[42] 'Shakespeare's Will and His Wife's Dower', (1841) 21 *Legal Observer*, 166.

published *Pictorial Shakspere*,[43] the credit of being the first
to offer a satisfactory solution of this problem. Knight[44]
quotes Malone, who first dragged this 'offensive bequest'
into notice: 'His wife had not wholly escaped his memory;
he had forgot her, — he had recollected her, — but so recollected her, as more strongly to mark how little he esteemed
her; he had already (as it is vulgarly expressed) *cut her off*,
*not indeed with a shilling, but with an old bed*.'[45] Malone
added, 'what provision was made for her by settlement does
not appear.' Steevens, described as a conveyancer by profession, denied Malone's inferences, considered the bequest
'a mark of peculiar tenderness' and assumed that she was
provided for by settlement. Boswell, a third legal editor,
wrote: 'If we may suppose that some provision had been
made for her during her lifetime, the bequest of his second-
best bed was probably considered in those days neither as
uncommon or reproachful.' Knight later remarks,[46] citing
Coke,[47] that 'the best bed' was in all probability an heirloom;
it might have descended to Shakespeare himself as an heirloom, and as such it would be the property of his heirs. The
best bed was considered in some places to be among the
most important of those chattels that went to the heir by
custom of the house. Knight then reaches his triumphant
conclusion:[48]

> Shakspere knew the law of England better than his legal
> commentators. His estates, with the exception of a copy-
> hold tenement, expressly mentioned in his will, were

[43] *The Pictorial Edition of the Works of Shakspere*, ed. C. Knight (1st. ed.,
1839-42).

[44] *Pictorial Shakspere*, vol. 2 (1839), 'Postscript to Twelfth Night: Shakspere's
Will', pp. 187-93.

[45] Supplement to Johnson and Steevens, 1780, vol. 1, p. 667.

[46] *Pictorial Shakspere*, vol. 8 (1843), p. 530.

[47] Co. Litt. 18b: 'And note, that in some places chattels as heirloomes (as the
best bed, table, pot, pan, cart, and other dead chattels moveable) may go to the
heire . . . ; but the heire-loome is due by custome and not by the common law'.

[48] *Pictorial Shakspere*, vol. 2, p. 192.

*freehold.* HIS WIFE WAS ENTITLED TO DOWER. . . . She was provided for amply, *by the clear and undeniable operation of the English Law.*

Knight expressed great satisfaction at having been the first to point out the 'absolute certainty' that Shakespeare's wife was provided for. He tells us that other wills of the same period show how unusual it was to make any other provision for a wife than by dower,[49] and quotes the following lines which ought to have pointed earlier commentators to this solution:

> Now, fair Hippolyta, our nuptial hour
> Draws on apace; four happy days bring in
> Another moon; but, oh, methinks how slow
> This old moon wanes! she lingers my desires
> Like to a step-dame, or a *dowager*
> Long withering out a young man's revenue.
> *(A Midsummer Night's Dream,* I. I)

Lord Campbell[50], who tended to follow Malone, says Mrs Shakespeare was left 'without house or furniture (except the second best bed), or a kind word, or any other token of his love; and I sadly fear that between William Shakespeare and Ann Hathaway the course of true love never did run smooth.' And he quotes the advice probably given from experience:

> Then, let thy love be younger than thyself,
> Or thy affection cannot hold the bent.
> *(Twelfth Night,* II. 4)

On the other hand Halliwell-Phillipps in his *Life*[51] tells us that bedsteads were sometimes of elaborate workmanship,

[49] A widow was endowed with one-third of the husband's heritable lands for her life, if not barred; by custom in some counties she got one-half, and by custom in some boroughs she got the whole. She was also entitled to residence in the principal mansion house.

[50] *Shakespeare's Legal Aquirements Considered,* pp. 105-6.

[51] Halliwell-Phillipps, op. cit.

and gifts of them are often to be met with in ancient wills, the first-best bed no doubt being reserved for visitors. 'So far from being considered of trifling import', he says, 'beds were even sometimes solicited as portions of compensation for dower; and bequests of personal articles of the most insignificant description were never formerly held in any light but that of marks of affection'; and he recalls that in the year 1642 one John Shakespeare, of Budbrook, near Warwick, considered it a sufficient mark of respect to his father-in-law to leave him his best boots. Charles Elton[52] accepts Halliwell-Phillipps's theory that Shakespeare's wife was suffering from some chronic and fatal disease; he wished to relieve her of household anxieties and that she should live at New Place with her daughter and physician son-in-law. Madden[53] suggests that the second-best bed was the one Shakespeare and his wife had shared, and which she wanted. On the other hand another lawyer, Sir George Greenwood,[54] remained adamant in regarding this provision in the will as one more demonstration that Shakespeare was unworthy of being the author of the works ascribed to him. The interlineation suggested to Tannenbaum the possibility that Anne had been provided for on page 1 of the original draft, but that in the rewriting of that page her omission was not noticed; though he too regards the second-best bed as a compliment or token of affection.[55] More recently Mark Eccles has drawn attention to a will executed in 1573 in which William Palmer, of Leamington, Glos., left to his wife (together with other bequests) 'my second best fether-bed for hirselfe furnished'.[56] There was no excuse for Malone to attribute to Theobald the emendation, 'my *brown* best bed'.

We have no doubt that 'with the furniture' in this context

---

[52] Elton, op. cit., pp. 227-30.
[53] *Shakespeare and His Fellows*, pp. 190-91.
[54] Sir George Greenwood, *The Shakespeare Problem Restated* (1908); *Is There a Shakespeare Problem?* (1916), chap. 7.
[55] Tannenbaum, op. cit., p. 96.
[56] Mark Eccles, *Shakespeare in Warwickshire* (1961), pp. 164-5.

meant the furnishings of the bed, i.e. hangings, mattresses, pillows, blankets, linen, etc.[57] Indeed, Sir George Greenwood[58] was so overcome by righteous indignation against the testator that he was incapable of quoting the will accurately; in one book he interpolates a word so as to make it read: 'the second-best bed with the furniture *thereof*', and in another book he changes a word and reads: 'with *its* furniture'. The residual clause gave to the Halls the 'household stuffs', which would include the house furniture.

With regard to dower, Greenwood says[59] 'there can be little doubt that in the case of all his purchases of freeholds uses to bar dower had been inserted, as, indeed, was customary.' He has no evidence for his 'little doubt' in Shakespeare's case. Wears[60] also appears to think that Shakespeare barred his wife's dower in all his property, but he does not say how or when. It is true that dower attached only to land held by one person (solely), and it could be prevented in Shakespeare's day by adding as purchasers several friends (as trustees for him) in joint tenancy. When one died he could be replaced by another. Sir Sidney Lee[61] accepted the opinion of Charles Elton and Herbert Mackay, leading conveyancers in their day, that Shakespeare had barred dower so far as that could be done in relation to the Blackfriars Gatehouse, his latest purchase, in order to prevent his wife from acquiring it; but Sir Arthur Underhill,[62] whose opinion is of the highest authority, says it is clear to a conveyancer that that was necessary in order to enable Shakespeare to mortgage the property (as he did next day)

[57] J. Quincy Adams, *A Life of William Shakespeare* (London and Cambridge, Mass., 1923), p. 465; A. Wigfall Green, 'Shakespeare's Will', (1932) 20 *Georgetown Law Journal*, 273.

[58] *The Shakespeare Problem Restated*, p. 189; *Is There a Shakespeare Problem?* pp. 301-2.

[59] *The Shakespeare Problem Restated*, p. 188.

[60] T. M. Wears, 'Shakespeare's Will', (1942) 20 *Canadian Bar Review*, 53-5.

[61] Sir Sidney Lee, *Life of William Shakespeare* (1898), pp. 221-2, citing letter from Elton to Lee dated 9 December 1897.

[62] In *Shakespeare's England* (ed. Raleigh, Oxford, 1916), I, 405-6.

without the delay and expense of a fine. Mention of the widow's right of dower was omitted, according to Wigfall Green,[63] because there was no point in stating the existing law in the will. 'Shakespeare, we may be sure', he adds, 'intended his wife to live with the Halls, and he was positive that they would care for her.' Baconians may be reminded that Bacon, shortly before he died, added a codicil to his will: 'Whatsoever I have given, granted, confirmed, or appointed to my wife, I do now, for just and great causes, utterly revoke and make void, and leave her to her right only.'

Then objection is made that Shakespeare did not mention any books or manuscripts in his will. In fact this was one of Sir George Greenwood's main reasons for being an anti-Stratfordian.[64] There was, as we have seen, no author's copyright of which Shakespeare could dispose. Chambers[65] suggested that books and manuscripts might have appeared in the inventory, which is lost and may have perished in the Fire of London. Fripp[66] thought that books and manuscripts would be included in the residuary clause among the 'household stuff whatsoever' devised to Susanna and Dr John Hall. Wigfall Green,[67] after mentioning the suggestions that Shakespeare was probably ashamed of his library, particularly in comparison with that of Dr Hall, and also that perhaps he did not consider manuscripts in the light of property, deals with the opinion that the books and manuscripts passed under the residuary bequest to the Halls. He tells us that it was held by the Courts in the eighteenth and nineteenth centuries that a bequest of 'household stuff'

[63] A. Wigfall Green, op. cit., p. 285.

[64] *The Shakespeare Problem Restated*, pp. 190-97; *Is There a Shakespeare Problem?* chap. 7.

[65] E. K. Chambers, *William Shakespeare: A Study of Facts and Problems*, II, 178-9. 'A will', he points out, 'is a legal instrument for devising property and not a literary autobiography.'

[66] E. I. Fripp, *Shakespeare, Man and Artist* (1938), II, p. 823.

[67] Wigfall Green, op. cit., pp. 285 et seq.

included carpets, linen, china and similar articles, but not books; and that the library (intended not to be dismantled) passed with a devise of the *house*, but not with a bequest of household furniture to the same persons. It seems to follow that Shakespeare intended his library to go with the title to New Place, that is, to Susanna and her heirs male. Wigfall Green concludes that Shakespeare's will is a thoroughly formal instrument, showing adequate legal knowledge, and is neither a slovenly piece of work nor a mere draft. A fair copy was not necessary, even if there was time to engross it.

In any event, it was not an invariable custom for literary people to mention books in their will, as we can see in the case of Richard Hooker, author of *The Laws of Ecclesiastical Polity* (1593), and in that of Thomas Russell, the well-born Oxford graduate who was an overseer of Shakespeare's will. Bacon himself merely gave directions with regard to his published works and two manuscript volumes of his collected speeches and letters.

The First Folio of the plays, published posthumously under the name of William Shakespeare in 1623 (the year of Anne's death) with the acknowledged help of Heminge and Condell, in spite of the many editorial problems it raises, is acceptable to most lawyers as *prima facie* evidence of the authorship of a great part of most or all of the plays it contains, to which we may add the later acts of *Pericles*, which play is not included in the First Folio.[68] If the lines were in truth unblotted, wrote Augustine Birrell, all the Quartos as well as the new plays must have been printed from fair manuscript copies. From whom were these unblotted copies received? They may well have been in the theatre all the time.[69] Ben Jonson in his commendatory verses calls the author, William Shakespeare, 'Sweet Swan

[68] See W. W. Greg, *The Shakespeare First Folio* (Oxford, 1955).
[69] Rt. Hon. Augustine Birrell, K.C., 'Lawyers at Play' (1905), reprinted in *Collected Essays and Addresses*, vol. 3 (1922), pp. 235-6.

of Avon'. Leonard Digges, who also contributed a commendatory poem, was a stepson of Thomas Russell, the friend of Shakespeare, who lived in Stratford and was appointed overseer of Shakespeare's will and left him £5 in his own. Digges was barely fifteen when his mother married Russell, so he presumably moved to Stratford and came to know Shakespeare, and the verses show that he at least thought Shakespeare could and did write the plays. The verses by the minor poet Hugh Holland and by I. M.,[70] on the other hand, do not connect the playwright with the Stratford actor.

Other references to Shakespeare's family have been found in the Sackville manuscripts.[71] For example, an entry in the Act Book of the Vicar's Court shows that Susanna was presented for recusancy (failure to attend church) in 1606; water rents were due from Shaxpere in 1584; and an administration bond was entered into by John Shakespeare (William's father) in relation to the will of Henry Field in 1592. The main significance of this is that manuscripts may still be found relating to Shakespeare and his family. What we need, however, is more evidence linking the Stratford man with the plays and poems.

---

[70] John Milton's *Epitaph on the Admirable Dramatic Poet, William Shakespeare,* which was written in 1630 and appeared in the Second, Third and Fourth Shakespeare Folios, was published with the initials I. M. in an edition of Shakespeare's *Poems* in 1640. Milton is known to have written poetry at Cambridge when he was sixteen, but he was not yet fifteen when the First Folio was published.

[71] A. Hanley, 'Shakespeare's Family in Stratford Records'. loc. cit.

# 2

# *Shakespeare and the Inns of Court*

The Inns of Court in the reigns of Elizabeth I and James I filled the Christmas vacation with feasting and revelry, sometimes beginning as early as All Hallowe'en and continuing as late as Shrovetide. Masques and revels were devised and acted by young barristers and law students, and plays were performed in Hall by professional actors.[1] Devecmon,[2] an American lawyer, estimated that at least twenty per cent of Shakespeare's contemporary dramatists whose occupations are known were members of Inns of Court, including Beaumont (grandson of a Master of the Rolls and son of a Judge of the Common Pleas), John Ford (a nephew of Chief Justice Popham), Warner (thought to be translator of Plautus' 'Menaechmi'), Marston (son of a lecturer at the Middle Temple), Middleton and Lodge.

Gray's Inn included among its members three pseudo-Shakespeares — Bacon, Oxford and Rutland; a fourth, William Stanley, 6th Earl of Derby, had his name put down for Gray's Inn by his father in 1562, when he was in his infancy, but he entered Lincoln's Inn in 1594. Other Gray's Inn men were Southampton, to whom *Venus and Adonis* and *The Rape of Lucrece* were dedicated and who was present

---

[1] See e.g., A. Wigfall Green, *The Inns of Court and Early English Drama*, with a preface by Roscoe Pound (Yale University Press, 1931).

[2] W. C. Devecmon, *In Re Shakespeare's 'Legal Acquirements'* (New York, 1899), pp. 9-10.

when *The Comedy of Errors* was performed at the Inn in 1594; William Herbert, 3rd Earl of Pembroke, the lover of Mary Fitton (who may be the 'Dark Lady' of the Sonnets'), to whom the First Folio was dedicated and who has been identified with Mr W. H. of the Sonnets; and Sir Philip Sidney, an influence on Shakespeare's sonnet sequence and a probable source of sub-plots and character names.

Sir Francis Bacon himself, a Bencher of Gray's Inn from 1586 and Treasurer for eight years from 1608, was fond of masques, if decorously performed, and considered that plays had an educational value. Decorum was not always observed, and the Benchers on occasion felt constrained to bring the revels to an end. In January 1623, 'the gentlemen of Gray's Inn, to make an end to Christmas on Twelfth Night, in the dead time of the night, shot off all the chambers [small cannon] which they had borrowed from the Tower, being as many as filled four carts. The King awakened with this noise, started out of his bed, and cried 'Treason, Treason,' and that the city was in an uproar.'[3]

The Gray's Inn Christmastide revels of 1594-5 are described in a contemporary manuscript *Gesta Grayorum*, the records of Gray's Inn (1594), first published in 1688.[4] The revels centred on the mock court of a Lord of Misrule elected for the season from among the junior members ('The Griffins'), and called the Prince of Purpoole.[5] There was a special relationship, as it would now be called, between Gray's Inn and the Inner Temple. The Sports at the Second Entertainment on Holy Innocents Day (December 28) in 1594, a Grand Night, were intended for the Templarians, but the Hall was overcrowded and the Templarians left displeased. Although some semblance of order was now

[3] W. R. Douthwaite, *Gray's Inn, Its History & Associations* (1886), p. 238.

[4] ibid., pp. 227-30. Also *Gesta Grayorum*, ed. W. W. Greg (Malone Society, 1914).

[5] Gray's Inn originated in the Manor House of Purpoole, or Portpool, occupied from 1294 by Sir Reginald de Grey, Justiciar of the County Palatine of Chester. Portpoole Lane still leads off Gray's Inn Road towards Clerkenwell.

restored, it was not thought practicable to put on anything worthwhile. 'In regard whereof,' the record continues, 'it was thought good not to offer anything of Account, saving Dancing and Revelling with Gentlewomen; and after such Sports, a *Comedy of Errors* (like to *Plautus* his *Menechmus*) was played by the Players, so that night was begun and continued to the end, in nothing but Confusion and Errors; whereupon it was ever afterwards called *The Night of Errors*.' Next day the Gray's Inn men held a mock trial of a Sorcerer or Conjuror for causing the confusion and inconvenience. The last charge on which he was found guilty was that he had 'foisted a company of base and common Fellows, to make up our Disorders with a play of Errors and Confusions. . . .' Tradition has it that Francis Bacon was the Sorcerer.

It is now generally agreed that *The Comedy of Errors* was first produced on 28 December 1594.[6] On that date Shakespeare's company performed this play before the Queen at Greenwich, and it is usually assumed that the 'play of Errors' put on at Gray's Inn that evening was a repeat performance, with the same actors, among whom may well have been Shakespeare himself.[7] The tercentenary of this occasion was celebrated in Gray's Inn Hall in 1894 with a performance by the Elizabethan Stage Society. The learned editor of the special supplement to *Graya* issued to commemorate the performance of a Masque in Gray's Inn Hall in the presence of Queen Elizabeth II in November 1956, speculates with regard to the 1594 performance: 'It is an intriguing probability that "the Players" were the Lord Chamberlain's Company of professionals of which William Shakespeare was at this time a member, and whose patron was the Earl of Southampton, a member of Gray's

[6] Sidney Thomas, 'The Date of *The Comedy of Errors*' (1956) 7 *Shakespeare Quarterly*, p. 377. Douthwaite thought that the famous episode of 1594 took place on the first Grand Night, 20 December.

[7] Richard David, *Love's Labour's Lost* (4th. Arden ed., 1951), pp. xxx-xxxi.

Inn.'[8] H. F. Rubinstein,[9] in a note to a recent fanciful one-act play on the topic, accepts the tradition that Bacon himself was the 'sorcerer', and thinks it probable that he also composed the speeches with which the young lawyers concluded the Revels.

The Sixth Entertainment of that Gray's Inn season was on Twelfth Night (6 January) 1595. Preparations were being made for a journey by the Prince of Purpoole to assist the Emperor of Russia and Muscovy against the Tartars, when trumpeters announced the arrival of an Ambassador from the Emperor. This incident may have inspired the mock embassy of Muscovites, accompanied by blackamoors with music, in *Love's Labour's Lost*, v. 2, in which case the passage must have been added later to the original version.[10]

Gray's Inn also included Lord Strange, later 5th Earl of Derby, who had a company of players among whom was William Shakespeare himself. This company was transferred to another Gray's Inn man, Lord Hunsdon, the Lord Chamberlain, in the same year as the *Comedy of Errors* was performed there. *A Midsummer Night's Dream* is thought to have been produced for the wedding of Lord Strange's son, later 6th Earl of Derby. The Shakespeare Coat of Arms, issued in 1599, was prepared by two members of Gray's Inn, Sir William Dethicke, Garter King-of-Arms, and William Camden, Clarenceux King-of-Arms. And the great international lawyer, Alberico Gentile, an Italian refugee, joined that Inn in 1600, a fact that may perhaps explain the presence of references in *Henry V* and *Troilus and Cressida* to 'the law of nations', which Shakespeare did not find in Holinshed or his other main sources.

[8] '*Gesta Grayorum*: The Prince of Purpoole III', *Graya*, No. 44 Supplement, 1956, containing an account of *Gesta Grayorum*. The Prince of Purpoole II was created in 1617, perhaps to celebrate the appointment of Bacon as Lord Keeper.

[9] H. F. Rubinstein, *Night of Errors* (1964).

[10] Richard David, loc. cit.

An American writer who reprinted *Gesta Grayorum* some years ago[11] sought to show that Bacon had family associations with Warwickshire, and he conjectured that Shakespeare first met Bacon in that county before he went up to London. The same writer thinks that Bacon was first Shakespeare's patron and then his friend, from whom the dramatist would learn much about Gray's Inn, its members and their activities, and to whom he owed his advancement as an actor and the production of his plays at that Inn. It is further suggested that the statutes which the King seeks to impose on his fellow scholars in the opening scene of *Love's Labour's Lost* are a parody of the new statutes made by Elizabeth for Gray's Inn.

John Manningham, a young barrister of the Middle Temple, in a diary the manuscript of which is in the British Museum, happened to record an event in the new Hall of Middle Temple for 2 February 1602:

> At our feast [Candlemas] wee had a play called 'Twelue Night, or What You Will', much like the Commedy of Errores, or Menechmi in Plautus, but most like and neere to that in Italian called *Inganni*. A good practise in it to make the Steward beleeve his Lady widdowe was in love with him, by counterfeyting a letter as from his Lady in generall termes, telling him what shee liked best in him, and prescribing his gesture in smiling, his apparaile, etc., and then when he came to practise making him beleeue they tooke him to be mad.

This performance of *Twelfth Night* in Middle Temple is not claimed to be the first production. Queen Elizabeth the Queen Mother was present at the anniversary performance 350 years later on 1 February 1951. The play, according to Hotson,[12] was commissioned for and first performed at

[11] Basil Brown, *Law Sports at Gray's Inn* (1594) *including Shakespeare's connection with the Inns of Court, with a reprint of the Gesta Grayorum* (New York, 1921).
[12] Leslie Hotson, *The First Night of 'Twelfth Night'* (1954).

Elizabeth I's Court at Whitehall on 6 January (Twelfth Night) 1601, for the entertainment of Orsino, Duke of Bracciano, and the Muscovite ambassador.

*Troilus and Cressida* is thought likely to have been first acted before the Inns of Court. Hotson[13] goes so far as to say that extrinsic and intrinsic evidence combine to show that this play was written for the Middle Temple to act in 1598, though this is not universally accepted. He identifies it as the comedy *Love's Labour's Won* mentioned along with *Love's Labour's Lost* by Francis Meres in his *Palladis Tamia* (1598). 'Love's Labour's Won', according to Hotson, does not mean 'Love's Difficulty is Overcome' or 'Love's Task is Achieved', as has been thought by those who would identify it with *All's Well that Ends Well* or *The Taming of the Shrew*.[14] It means 'Love's Sorrow is Gained', and the only play to which this can be an alternative title is *Troilus and Cressida*. The extrinsic evidence includes the fact that most of the landed gentry from the neighbourhood of Stratford in Shakespeare's time were members of the Middle Temple.

On its Grand Days of revels the Middle Temple was the Kingdom of Love, and Hotson formerly concluded[15] that Shakespeare's linked plays *Love's Labour's Lost* and *Love's Labour's Won* by their titles, their tone, and their contents were pre-eminently suited for the witty entertainment of the Middle Temple. More recently, however, Hotson[16] has formed the opinion that *Love's Labour's Lost* was written to be performed at Gray's Inn at Christmas 1588. This play, he says, was certainly written for the entertainment of an Inn of Court ruled by a Prince named Love; but his new researches reveal, he believes, that the evidence must be

---

[13] Leslie Hotson, *Shakespeare's Sonnets Dated* (1949), pp. 37 et seq.

[14] *The Taming of the Shrew* is ruled out by the discovery in 1953 of a stationer's stocklist of 1603 mentioning both *Love's Labour's Won* and *Taming of a Shrew* (sic).

[15] *Shakespeare's Sonnets Dated*, p. 56.

[16] *Mr. W. H.* (1964), pp. 230 et seq.

transferred to the rival Gray's Inn, 'ancient Purpoole, under Prince True-Love, where it properly belongs, and where it fits like a glove to a hand.'

Among the publications in the quatercentenary year of 1964 was Leslie Hotson's *Mr. W. H.*, which propounds several very interesting and ingeniously argued theses concerning Shakespeare's relations with the Inns of Court. First, Hotson identifies Mr W. H. – the 'begetter' or inspirer to whom the first 126 Sonnets are addressed – with William Hatcliffe,[17] student of Gray's Inn. Coming from the old Leicestershire family of Hatcliffe manor, young William left Jesus College, Cambridge, like most gentlemen, without a degree. He was admitted to Gray's Inn in November 1586. A manuscript note in the British Museum long known to Shakespeare scholars, in the hand of Lord Burghley, Lord Treasurer, who was a member of Gray's Inn, lists as Prince or Lord of Purpoole, i.e., leader of the revels, at the presentation of a comedy in Gray's Inn Hall on 16 January 1588: 'Dominus de Purpoole: Hatclyff'. William Hatcliffe was chosen Prince of Purpoole in his second November at the Inn, for seven years. In the revels season of 1587-8 he was nineteen and Shakespeare twenty-three years of age. Hotson believes that Hatcliffe was the 'fair youth' to whom a number of the Sonnets are addressed. He came of age in September 1589, the date when Sonnet 104 ('To me, fair friend, you never can be old') was written. As well as being a Will, he was a sovereign, king or prince, over whom a canopy would be borne (cf. Sonnet 125: 'Were't aught to me I bore the canopy'). The first seventeen sonnets urge the young man to marry, because he was a 'King' and issue was necessary to secure the succession. William Hatcliffe in fact married in 1595, at the age of 27, Dorothy Kay, daughter of the late John Kay of Hackney,[18]

---

[17] Commonly pronounced 'Hatliff', and variously spelt.
[18] Quite close to Clerkenwell, *infra*.

Esquire, a Clerk of the Green Cloth. Professor G. Wilson Knight[19] has also suggested that if Mr W. H. should eventually turn out to be a law student at the Inns of Court, we might suppose him to be in some measure responsible for Shakespeare's love of legal metaphor.

Hotson further identifies William Hatcliffe as the subject of Nicholas Hilliard's celebrated miniature portrait of 'A Young Man leaning against a Tree' in the Victoria and Albert Museum. The Hatcliffe's heraldic emblem, the primrose or 'True Love', is depicted; and the portrait – an *impresa* with its motto from Lucan: *Dat poenas laudata fides* – is the work of 'this Time's pencil', an expression in Sonnet 16 suggesting that a portrait of the young man has been made. How satisfying it would be if we had stronger evidence for relating some of Shakespeare's Sonnets to one of the gems of English pictorial art.

In a review of Hotson's book in *Graya*, Francis Cowper,[20] a barrister of Gray's Inn and literary editor of the magazine, expresses the opinion that: 'The reasoning by which Dr Hotson supports his identification is both cogent and copious. . . . By the very nature of the case it falls short of being conclusive, but the inferences are exceedingly strong and leave fewer difficulties in the mind than any theory hitherto put forward.'

The identification of Mr W. H. with Hatcliffe does not appear to have won the general assent of Shakespeare scholars. Importance must attach to the date or dates when the Sonnets were written. Hotson thinks this was about the year 1588, and those who hold that the zenith of a lyric poet's working life is about the age of twenty-five would expect most of the Sonnets to have been written by 1589. We know from Meres (*Palladis Tamia*) that some of Shakespeare's 'sugred Sonnets' were circulating among his private

---

[19] G. Wilson Knight, *The Mutual Flame* (1955), p. 9.
[20] 'The Prince and the Poet', *Graya*, Mich. Term, 1964, p. 111. See also Francis Cowper, *A Prospect of Gray's Inn* (1951), chap. 3.

friends by 1598. Lord Simon of Glaisdale[21] is unconvinced by Hotson's arguments, for in a number of Sonnets the poet describes himself as being no longer young. His Lordship thinks that one of Essex's musicians called William Hewes (or Howes) is more likely than Samuel Butler's naval cook;[22] but he also draws attention to a William Hughes who entered Gray's Inn on 7 November 1606, and whose claim does not seem to have been investigated so far, though this seems to be too late a date to begin inspiring the earlier Sonnets.

The identity of Mr W. H. remains a mystery. The internal evidence seems to favour Malone's suggestion of William Hews (Hughes), and as Samuel Butler pointed out, it does not indicate that the addressee of the Sonnets was the poet's patron, or that he was of high birth or wealthy. A privately printed pamphlet, recently reviewed in *Graya*,[23] suggests the possibility that Shakespeare was admitted to Gray's Inn under the name of William Rich in 1579 (when he would be fifteen), through the patronage of the second Lord Rich. The author supports this suggestion with quotations of the punning on the word 'rich' in the Sonnets, and with clues drawn from contemporary literature.

Nearly forty years ago G. B. Harrison[24] very tentatively identified the 'Dark Lady' of the Sonnets as Lucy Parker (*née* Morgan) or 'Lucy Negro, Abbess de Clerkenwell'. Lucy was formerly one of Queen Elizabeth's gentlewomen from 1579 to 1582, but she later became a notorious courtesan and brothel-keeper. Her bawdy-house was in St John's Street, Clerkenwell, very near to Gray's Inn. *Gesta Grayorum* in the chronicle of Henry Prince of Purpoole's

---

[21] Sir Jocelyn Simon, Q.C., 'Shakespeare's Legal and Political Background', (1968) 84 *Law Quarterly Review*, 33, at pp. 37-40.

[22] Samuel Butler, *Shakespeare's Sonnets Considered* (1899).

[23] F. J. M. Marrian, '*Shakespeare at Gray's Inn – A Tentative Theory*', reviewed in *Graya*, No. 65, Hilary Term, 1967.

[24] G. B. Harrison, *Shakespeare under Elizabeth* (1933), p. 310. See also Harrison's Penguin edition of *The Sonnets* (1938), p. 122, note to Sonnet 127, the first of the 'Dark Lady' Sonnets: 'In the old age black was not counted fair.'

reign, 1594-5, recounts that among those brought in to pay mock homage to the Prince of Purpoole in the revels:

> Lucy *Negro*, Abbess *de Clerkenwell*, holdeth the Nunnery of *Clerkenwell*, with the Lands and Priviledges thereunto belonging, of the Prince of *Purpoole* by Night-Service in *Cauda*, and [was required] to find a choir of nuns, with burning Lamps, to chaunt *Placebo* to the Gentlemen of the Prince's Privy-Chamber, on the Day of His Excellency's Coronation.

Lucy was committed to the Bridewell in 1600, and was probably dead before the Sonnets were published in 1609.

The scene in *1 Henry VI*, II. 4 is 'London. The Temple Garden'. A quarrel between Yorkists and Lancastrians having arisen out of an argument in Hall, Suffolk says:

> Within the Temple hall we were too loud;
> The garden here is more convenient.

It is going rather far to claim with a historian of the Middle Temple that this reveals an intimate knowledge of the system of Mootings;[25] but the end of the scene clearly shows knowledge of the custom of dining in messes of four, when Plantagenet says to his followers: 'Come, let us four to dinner'. In another early play Berowne confesses that 'you three fools lacked me fool to make up the mess' (*Love's Labour's Lost*, IV. 3). There are said to have been during the Tudor period in term time at least one thousand students at the Inns of Chancery, and some eight hundred to a thousand at the four Inns of Court. At dinner the rule, except on mooting nights, was for the puisne at every mess to put a short case which the rest were bidden to argue thoroughly, and not to depart under penalty of twelve pence. 'Thus they learned in Shakespeare's phrase', says Richard O'Sullivan Q.C., 'to practise rhetoric in their common

25 George Godwin, *The Middle Temple* (1954), p. 65.

talk'.[26] Cade tells his men to pull down all the Inns of Court, for they came under his anathema along with grammar schools and other signs of education as well as administration of the law (*2 Henry VI*, IV. 7).

One met at the Inns of Court and fought behind them. So Prince Hal tells Falstaff to meet him next day in the Temple Hall at two o'clock in the afternoon (*1 Henry IV*, III. 3); and Justice Shallow boasts that in his student days he had fought with one Sampson Stockfish, a fruiterer, behind Gray's Inn (*2 Henry IV*, III. 2).

Lawyers in Shakespeare's time patronised the stage and attended regularly at the theatre. 'From time whereof the memory of man runneth not to the contrary', a nineteenth-century Irish lawyer has said,[27] 'the English stage and the English Bar have been close friends. The young Templar is usually a man about town, proud of his acquaintance with the greater and lesser lights of the stage, and not wholly ignorant of the mysteries of the green room.' Shakespeare's audience would include young Templars who knew something of Italian as well as classical literature. We are invited by G. M. Young[28] to imagine them relaxing their brains at the play between a morning over Littleton's *Tenures* and their evening moot, or buying a Quarto to read under cover of *Coke upon Littleton*. Here we have a public which is disputatious, which can take a point, dissect a character and treasure a phrase – a society where the terms of the law were current coin.

The somewhat idealistic account of life at the Inns of Court as a centre of training for gentlemen given by Fortescue in *De Laudibus legum Angliae* is often quoted in this context; but Fortescue's description, dating from about 1470, would apply to a period more than a century before

[26] *The Spirit of the Common Law*, pp. 45-6.
[27] 'Shakespeare's Lawyers (1885), *Irish Law Times*, p. 422.
[28] G. M. Young, 'Shakespeare and the Termers', *Proceedings of the British Academy*, vol. 33 (1947), p. 81, 88-92.

Shakespeare's working life. The fact that many eminent persons were admitted to the Inns in Shakespeare's day does not necessarily mean that they continued to study. There was undoubtedly a decline in the educational system of the Inns of Court, both liberal and legal, after Fortescue's time. Sir William Holdsworth inferred, from a comparison of two sets of Judges' Orders, that this decline began in the latter half of the sixteenth century;[29] but Professor Kenneth Charlton[30] finds it already beginning in the fifteenth century and well advanced by the time of Henry VIII. It was due to the bad behaviour of the students, idleness in their studies and neglect of mooting. Senior members also often failed to fulfil their teaching and supervising duties, feeling the counter-attraction of practice. In the sixteenth century, too, students began to read printed books rather than listen to lectures. They learned from Abridgments, Reports and manuals rather than attendance at an Inn.

It is convenient to add a note here on the popular interest in the law in Shakespeare's day. Most of Shakespeare's legal allusions are drawn from the history of the Plantagenet and Tudor periods, the procedure of the courts, the jargon of real property law, or certain generally-known aspects of contemporary criminal or constitutional law. He had many ways of acquiring some knowledge of these subjects. Hall's and Holinshed's *Chronicles* and other sources gave much information about crime and constitutional problems. His father indulged in property deals and litigation, as did Shakespeare himself on a smaller scale.

The legalism of sixteenth-century England had many causes and found many outlets. There were plenty of oppor-

[29] W. S. Holdsworth, 'The Disappearance of the Educational System of the Inns of Court', (1921) *University of Pennsylvania Law Review*, pp. 201-22.

[30] Kenneth Charlton, 'Liberal Education and the Inns of Court in the Sixteenth Century', (1960) 9 *British Journal of Educational Studies*, p. 25.

tunities for taking part in jury trial; the method of conveying property known as the fine was a fictitious lawsuit; the administration of estates was largely a matter of keeping, or attending at, the manor court; justices in Quarter Sessions administered such important parts of local government as highways and bridges, tolls and markets, statutes of labourers and the poor law; ecclesiastical courts were concerned with matters of faith and morals.[31] At a time when there were few places of recreation in town, people found attending the courts and watching judicial procedure a dramatic and diverting pastime. They derived amusement from the technicalities of property law suits, and were impressed by political trials and public executions. In Elizabethan times law was not, as now, remote from the experience of even educated people. The plays of Shakespeare abound with precise legal allusions which Professor Ryder, an authority on the land law, says he would not have made if he had not expected them to be understood.[32]

The Stratford-on-Avon Court of Record by royal charter of 1553 had jurisdiction over all personal actions up to £30 arising within the Borough, the records of which are still extant. The Court sat every fortnight. Besides the Town Clerk there belonged to it six Attorneys, some of whom must have practised at Westminster and had extensive conveyancing business. William's father, John Shakespeare, made frequent appearances there. Stratford also had a Bench of Justices, a Court Leet, a Tithingman and Constables. John Shakespeare was appointed Constable in 1558.[33] Warwick was an assize town. Chief Justice Coke was at Warwickshire Assizes in Lent 1616, and heard a petition against the enclosure of open fields at Welcombe, in which Shakespeare

[31] E. W. Ives, 'The Law and the Lawyers', in 'Shakespeare in His Own Age', (1964) 17 *Shakespeare Survey*, p. 73.

[32] Professor E. C. Ryder, *Law and the Universities* (Inaugural Lecture at King's College, Newcastle-upon-Tyne, 1955), pp. 10-11.

[33] *Minutes and Accounts of the Corporation of Stratford-on-Avon, vol. I, 1553-1566,* ed. E. I. Fripp (Dugdale Society, vol. I), pp. xx-xxiv, xxxix-xli.

as tithe-owner was probably concerned, though he died before judgment was given.

Nearby Henley-in-Arden had a Court Leet and a Court Baron, whose records are extant from 1592.[34] In *Love's Labour's Lost*, v. 2, Rosaline says: 'Better wits have worn plain Statute Caps.' The reference would surely not be lost on the inhabitants of Henley-in-Arden who in 1596, between the writing and the publication of that play, were prosecuted in the Court Leet for breach of the statute — passed to help the woollen industry — which required the wearing of woollen caps on Sundays and Holy Days. In the record of the Court Baron for 23 November 1616 we find the alienation of a tenement with garden and orchard involving Francis Collins, the Town Clerk of Stratford who drafted and witnessed Shakespeare's will. Most remarkable is the inquest held at Stratford on 11 February 1580, when Shakespeare was in his sixteenth year, on Katherine Hamlett, spinster, who was drowned while drawing water in a pail from the Avon at Tiddington, a village adjoining Stratford. She had slipped and fallen into the river. The verdict, no doubt after some argument on the possibility of suicide, was that the death was accidental.[35] Curiously enough, one William Shakespeare of Warwick had been drowned in the Avon in July 1579. The verdict of the coroner's jury was that he was walking to the river to bathe himself when he accidentally fell into a deeper part.[36]

Law for the Elizabethans, then, took the place of politics and sport as a main interest. 'Star Chamber and Chancery, the Courts and the Inns', says G. M. Young,[37] 'the stories that came back from assizes, and the evidence of rustics taken on commission, furnished a mirror in which the whole of English life from high to low could be observed.'

[34] William Cooper, *Henley-in-Arden* (1946), p. 25.
[35] *Minutes and Accounts of the Corporation of Stratford-on-Avon, vol. III, 1577-1586*, ed. E. I. Fripp (Dugdale Society, vol. V), pp. 50-1; Fripp, *Shakespeare Studies, Biographical and Literary* (1930), § 18.
[36] *Minutes and Accounts*, pp. 129-30.   [37] G. M. Young, op. cit., p. 95.

# 3

## *Legal Terms, Allusions and Plots*

Hundreds of legal terms, expressions and allusions are contained in the works of Shakespeare. These have been the subject of identification, explanation and criticism, both for the sake of elucidating their meaning and significance within the context and for the purpose of speculating on the legal qualifications of the poet and dramatist. Examples of different kinds will be found in various parts of this book.

In the first place, there will always be differences of opinion as to what is a legal allusion, and there will never be agreement on how many there are in Shakespeare. To take a somewhat trivial example, is there a legal allusion in the following passage from *Much Ado About Nothing*, III. 2?

*Benedict.* I have the toothache.
*Don Pedro.* Draw it.
*Benedict.* Hang it.
*Claudio.* You may hang it first, and draw it afterwards.

Similar is the advice given by Escalus to Froth: 'I would not have you acquainted with tapsters; they will draw you, Master Froth, and you will hang them' (*Measure for Measure*, II. 1). The macabre spectacle of an execution for treason may even support an image of the pains of love:

*Bastard.* Drawn in the flattering table of her eye!
    Hang'd in the frowning wrinkle of her brow!
    And quarter'd in her heart! he doth espy
    Himself love's traitor.

(King John, II. 1)

The eloquent Richard II, when fortune turns against him, naturally thinks of wills:

> Let's talk of graves. . . .
> Let's choose executors and talk of wills:
> And yet not so — for what can we bequeath
> Save our deposed bodies to the ground?
>
> *(Richard II*, iii. 2)

And the eloquent Hamlet uses legal expressions in moments of crisis. While contemplating suicide he names 'the law's delay' as one of the evils of human life (*Hamlet*, iii. 1), and in the churchyard scene the examination of a skull suggests a lawyer (v. 1).

Among the poems, Churton Collins,[1] who had graduated at Oxford in Law and Modern History, noted eleven legal allusions in *The Rape of Lucrece*, for example:

> The deep vexation of his inward soul
> Hath serv'd a dumb arrest upon his tongue.
>
> (St. 255)

These allusions are not very technical, and 'colour' in Stanza 39 was not in Shakespeare's time a specifically legal expression. Churton Collins also quoted three legal allusions from *Venus and Adonis*, namely:

> But when the heart's attorney once is mute,
> The client breaks, as desperate in his suit.
>
> (St. 56)

> Which purchase of them make, for fear of slips
> Set they seal-manual on my wax-red lips.
>
> (St. 86)

> Say for non-payment that the debt be double.
>
> (St. 87)

---

[1] J. Churton Collins, *Studies in Shakespeare* (1904), p. 228. The other stanzas referred to are nos. 68, 69, 86, 114, 132, 133, 135, 147 and 173. Lord Campbell gives three quotations from *Venus and Adonis*, four from *Rape of Lucrece* and twelve from the Sonnets: *Shakespeare's Legal Acquirements Considered* (1859), pp. 99 et seq.

And Stanza 21 of *A Lover's Complaint* (if that was written by Shakespeare) contains the lines:

> My woeful self, that did in freedom stand
> And was my own fee-simple.

A fee simple is the largest estate (i.e. the longest-lasting interest, the nearest possible to ownership) in land in English law, lasting so long as there are heirs to succeed.

Out of 154 Sonnets about twenty certainly, and probably more, employ legal figures of speech. Sonnets 4, 46, 87 and 134[2] are wholly constructed of legal imagery. Sonnets 46 ('Mine eye and heart are at a mortal war') and 134 ('So now I have confess'd that he is thine') are discussed later. W. H. Auden has said that in Sonnet 87 ('Farewell! thou art too dear for my possessing') the character of an emotional relationship is expressed in terms of a legal contract.[3] Illustrations are difficult to choose because some of the passages from which they are selected are too well known for repetition here, while others are too complex to be taken out of their context:

> Unthrifty loveliness, why dost thou spend
> Upon thyself thy beauty's legacy?
> Nature's bequest gives nothing. . . .
> > Thy unused beauty must be tomb'd with thee,
> > Which, used, lives th' executor to be.
>
> > > (Sonnet 4)

> Then, gentle cheater, urge not my amiss,
> Lest guilty of my faults thy sweet self prove:
> For, thou betraying me, I do betray
> My nobler part to my gross body's treason.
>
> > > (Sonnet 151)

Legal terms and expressions naturally abound in the plays dealing with problems of law and government, crime

---

[2] The Sonnet numbers given here are those of the first printed edition of 1609.
[3] *The Listener*, 2 July 1964.

and justice, and in those containing trial scenes. Here, whatever the legal system to which they are supposed to be related, they would tend to be used in their straight sense. When the Officer in *The Comedy of Errors*, IV. 4, says:

> He is my prisoner: if I let him go,
> The debt he owes will be requir'd of me

we have a clear reference to the (English) law of Shakespeare's day that a gaoler was personally responsible for the debt if he allowed the prisoner to escape. Arrest of the defendant in civil (as well as criminal) cases was common form in Elizabethan times. Hamlet, when he knows himself to have been fatally poisoned, says:

> This fell sergeant, death,
> Is strict in his arrest.
>
> (v. 2)

This passage is compared by Malone with that in Sonnet 74:

> When that fell arrest
> Without all bail shall carry me away.

'Fell sergeant, death' appears to have been a stock phrase in Shakespeare's time. 'Bond' and 'seal' figure prominently, as will be seen among the following examples:

*Macbeth.*   But yet I'll make assurance double sure,
And take a bond of fate.
> (*Macbeth*, IV. 1)

*Posthumus.*        Take this life
And cancel these cold bonds.
> (*Cymbeline*, v. 4)

*Romeo.*        Seal with a righteous kiss
A dateless bargain to engrossing death.
> (*Romeo and Juliet*, v. 3)

*Patroclus.* Omission to do what is necessary
Seals a commission to a blank of danger.[4]
(*Troilus and Cressida*, III. 3)

*Gaunt.* This land of such dear souls, this dear,
dear land . . .
Is now leas'd out, — I die pronouncing it, —
Like to a tenement, or pelting farm:
. . . is now bound in with shame,
With inky blots, and rotten parchment
bonds.
(*Richard II*, II. 1)

*Iago.* who has a breast so pure
But some uncleanly apprehensions
Keep leets and law days, and in session sit
With meditations lawful?
(*Othello*, III. 3)

*Rosalind.* Be it known unto all men by these presents.
(*As You Like It*, I. 2)

We have terms of property and procedure such as:

*Olivia.* Let thy fair wisdom, not thy passion, sway
In this uncivil and unjust extent
Against thy peace.
(*Twelfth Night*, IV. 1)

This refers to the writ of extent (*Extendi facias*)[5].

*Mrs Page.* If the devil have him [Falstaff] not in fee
simple, with fine and recovery, he will never,
I think, in the way of waste, attempt us
again. (*The Merry Wives of Windsor*, IV. 2)

---

[4] There is probably also a play upon the words 'omission' and 'commission'.
[5] See *post* chap. 9.

*Benvolio.*      An I were so apt to quarrel as thou art, any man should buy the fee simple of my life for an hour and a quarter. (*Romeo and Juliet,* III. 1)

*Parolles.*      I beseech you, let me answer to the particular of the inter'gatories: demand them singly. (*All's Well That Ends Well,* IV. 3)

Interrogatories (the accent nowadays is on the third syllable) are preliminary questions asked by one party of the other in a civil action; formerly, as here, they were questions put to a person suspected of, or charged with, certain offences.

When Pandarus, on seeing Troilus and Cressida kiss, says 'How now! a kiss in fee-farm?' (*Troilus and Cressida,* III. 2), he asks whether there is to be no fealty or other obligation on the part of Cressida. Petruchio paraphrases, or caricatures, the common law principle that husband and wife were one person, and the husband was that one:

> I will be master of what is mine own;
> She is my goods, my chattels; she is my house,
> My household stuff, my field, my barn,
> My horse, my ox, my ass, my anything.
> (*The Taming of the Shrew,* III. 2)

A great many of Shakespeare's legal expressions, of course, are figures of speech, metaphors and images, and – it must be admitted – not a few are puns. Among legal figures of speech, Shakespeare is specially fond of 'leasehold' (particularly in the Sonnets), 'fee simple' and 'pressing to death'. A number of them – like 'nonsuit', 'lawful prize' and 'vassal' – were common usage among Elizabethan writers. Words like 'guilty', 'warrant', 'witness' and 'acquit' were also common in Shakespeare's day, and their use was not confined to lawyers. They may have a general meaning as well as a special legal meaning. Similarly the use of some words, which is now technical only, may have been ordinary as well as technical in Shakespeare's day. 'Determine', for example, in the sense of 'put an end to', now only used by lawyers, was common in the time of Shakespeare. Thus we have the legal sense in:

> So should that beauty which you hold in lease,
> Find no determination.
>
> (Sonnet 13)

and the ordinary use in:

> That he and Caesar might
> Determine this great war in single fight!
>
> (*Antony and Cleopatra*, IV. 4)

Among the few legal maxims we have: 'The law hath not been dead, though it hath slept' (*Measure for Measure*, II. 2), probably an echo of one of the many Latin maxims attributed to Coke[6]. Phoebe's 'Omittance is no quittance' (*As You Like It*, III. 5) is a proverb rather than a maxim, and is found in Heywood's *Proverbs* (1546).[7] When Marcus says '*Suum cuique* is our Roman justice' (*Titus Andronicus*, I. 1) he refers to Ulpian's definition of natural justice put at the beginning of Justinian's *Institutes: 'Justitia est constans et perpetua voluntas ius suum cuique tribuere'*; and Hector alludes to this in 'Nature craves All dues be render'd to their owners' (*Troilus and Cressida*, II. 2).

Lord Simon of Glaisdale, when Solicitor-General, began a study of English idioms derived from the law[8] in which he makes nine references to Shakespeare. In addition to 'lease of life' (of which Sonnet 146 contains an example) and 'pound of flesh' (which is derived from *The Merchant of*

---

[6] Coke's report of *Mary Portington's Case* (10 Co. Rep. 42-3) quotes the maxim *dormit aliquando lex, moritur nunquam*, citing as authority Coke's Second Institute: *Dormiunt aliquando leges, moriuntur nunquam* (2 Co. Inst. 161).

[7] Donald F. Bond, 'English Legal Proverbs', (1963) *Publications of Modern Language Assocation of America*, 921.

[8] Sir Jocelyn Simon, Q.C., 'English Idioms from the Law', (1960) 76 *Law Quarterly Review*, 283, 429; (1962) 78 *Law Quarterly Review*, 245.

*Venice*), the most noteworthy idioms found in Shakespeare include:

SCALES OF JUSTICE

> And poise the cause in justice equal scales,
> Whose beam stands sure.
>
> *(2 Henry VI, II. 1)*

PILLAR OF THE LAW

> The Law,
>
> Whereof you are a well-deserving pillar.
>
> *(The Merchant of Venice, IV. 1)*

PIN'S FEE

> I do not set my life at a pin's fee.
>
> *(Hamlet, I. 4)*

QUIETUS[9]

> For who would bear the whips and scorns of time. . . .
> When he himself might his quietus make
> With a bare bodkin?
>
> *(Hamlet, III. 1)*

To which we may add Sonnet 126: Nature's 'audit (though delay'd) answer'd must be, And her quietus is to render thee.'

A humorous confusion of legal terms appears in *Measure for Measure*, II. 1:

*Elbow.* Prove this, thou wicked Hannibal, or I'll have mine action of battery on thee.

*Escalus.* If he took you a box o' th' ear, you might have your action for slander too.

With regard to puns, Sister Miriam Joseph[10] explains that

to play upon the various meanings of a word represented an intellectual exercise, a witty analysis commended and

---

[9] See *post*, chap. 9.

[10] Sister Miriam Joseph, *Shakespeare and the Arts of Language* (1947).

relished by Aristotle, practised by Plato, and by the great dramatists of Greece, esteemed and used by Cicero, employed by medieval and Renaissance preachers in their sermons, regarded as rhetorical ornament by the Elizabethans, but frequently despised as false or degenerate wit from the eighteenth century to the present day.

Costard's triple pun is a joke at the expense of legal terminology:

> In manner and form following, sir; all those three: I was seen with her in the manor-house, sitting with her upon the form, and taken following her into the park; which, put together, is, in manner and form following[11] (*Love's Labour's Lost*, I. I.)

In its context Maria's pun is not bad:

> My lips are no common, though several they be.[12]
> (*Love's Labour's Lost*, II. 1)

Adriana plays on the terms 'bond' and 'recovery':[13]
> Let us come in, that we may bind him fast,
> And bear him home for his recovery.
> (*The Comedy of Errors*, V. 1)

and Hamlet to his mother on the legal pleading expression, 'confession and avoidance':

> Confess yourself to Heaven;
> Repent what's past; avoid what is to come.
> (*Hamlet*, III. 4)

A metaphor may contain a pun:

> *Prince*. Percy is but my factor, good my Lord,
> To engross up glorious deeds on my behalf.
> (*1 Henry IV*, III. 2)

---

[11] For 'taken with the mainour' see *post*, chap. 9.
[12] cf. *post*, chap. 9.
[13] For 'recovery', see *post*, chap. 9.

W. H. Auden has said somewhere that good writers enjoy weak puns. Here is a pretty weak one from 2 *Henry IV*, I. 2. Falstaff has impudently asked Chief Justice Gascoigne for the loan of a thousand pounds: at that time coins had the sign of the cross impressed on them, and the Chief Justice replies: 'Not a penny, not a penny: you are too impatient to bear crosses.'

One can go further than terms and allusions and can show that Shakespeare's attitude towards law influenced his choice of subjects and construction of plots. The dramatist's predilection for plays with a legal basis has been commented on by Louis Marder,[14] who set out to show that Shakespeare's legal language is not merely figurative but is integral and important in the dramatic action, and that he relied on legality or quasi-legality for audience rapport. Not only is the action of a play often advanced by legal means, for example, the legal process of arrest or appeal, but when seeking a subject for a play Shakespeare preferred one in which the initial action had some legal foundation. The legal basis may have been contained in the sources, but the choice was his. 'Histories, comedies, tragedies, romances, even the poems have legalistic foundations,' says Marder,[15] 'and when subsidiary actions or plots are introduced, Shakespeare gives them also a legal basis.' Examples are *Cymbeline*, *Troilus and Cressida*, *1, 2 and 3 Henry VI* (primogeniture), *Richard III*, *Henry V*, *The Comedy of Errors* (Ephesian law against Syracusans), *Love's Labour's Lost* (Ferdinand's decree), *A Midsummer Night's Dream* (Athenian law of marriage), *The Merchant of Venice*, *All's Well That Ends Well* (wardship), *Measure for Measure*, *Much Ado* (Dogberry and Verges), *Pericles* (Antiochus's decree), *Romeo and Juliet* (breaches of the peace between the rival families), *Othello* ('the bloody book of the law'), *Coriolanus* (the 'piercing

---

[14] Louis Marder, 'Law in Shakespeare', *Renaissance Papers* (University of South Carolina Press, 1954), p. 40.
[15] Marder, op. cit., p. 42.

statutes' against the poor), *Timon of Athens* (Timon's debts), and *The Rape of Lucrece* (Tarquin's breaches of the law). To these we may add the discussion in *The Winter's Tale* on the question whether a child (Perdita) born to a mother (Hermione) in prison is also a prisoner or is by nature born free. Shakespeare gives his plays a semblance of reality, Marder continues,[16] by providing them with a legal foundation such as 'the drama of arrest, the tenseness of the trial scene, the legality or illegality of punishment, the suspense of the appeal, the correctness of the document, the validity of the seal.'

Revenge, described by Bacon as a kind of wild justice, is an instinctive way of taking the law into one's own hands. The theme of revenge that we find in *Hamlet*, *Othello*, *The Merchant of Venice* and *Titus Andronicus* was in the fashion of Elizabethan drama, and Shakespeare had exemplars in Kyd's *Spanish Tragedy* (with ghost) and Marlowe's *Jew of Malta*.[17]

[16] Marder, op. cit., p. 43.

[17] Elizabeth Mary Brennan, *The Theme of Revenge in Elizabethan Life and Drama 1580-1605* (unpublished thesis, Belfast University, 1955). Miss Brennan does not seem to include *The Merchant of Venice*.

# 4

## Problems of Law, Justice and Government

There has recently been a revival of interest in Shakespeare's historical plays. Productions even of the *Henry VI* trilogy, condensed into two plays, have captured the public imagination. Shakespeare's treatment of the Wars of the Roses, it is thought, may have some message for our own troublesome times. Those who are interested in drama rather than language are concerned with the general problems of law, justice and government in Shakespeare's plays. Literary historians have therefore done a great deal of work on the sources and background of the historical and classical plays.[1] L. C. Knights prefers to think of the English history plays as 'political' plays, since they are concerned with the nature and transfer of power.

For the English historical plays Shakespeare derived his philosophy of history and sense of moral drama from Hall's *Chronicle* (1548) of 'The Union of the two noble and illustrious Families of Lancaster and York.' This covers the period from Henry IV to Henry VIII, nearly half the book consisting of 'the triumphant reign of Henry VIII'. 'Hall's ideas', writes Tillyard,[2] 'became a part of his [Shakespeare's] mind' — notably, that history teaches lessons for the future. More detailed narrative was derived from Holinshed's

---

[1] Recent studies include Clifford Leech, *The Chronicles*; L. C. Knights, *The Histories*; and T. J. B. Spencer, *The Roman Plays*; reprinted in *Shakespeare, The Writer and His Work*, ed. Bonamy Dobrée (1964). And see Philip Styles, 'The Commonwealth' in *Shakespeare in his own Age*, (1964) 17 *Shakespeare Survey*, 103.

[2] E. M. W. Tillyard, *Shakespeare's History Plays* (1944).

*Chronicle*, the second edition of 1587 being used. It is written in a simpler style than Hall, but has a wider range, including Scottish and Irish history. Holinshed's language was followed most closely in *Henry VIII*. Some confusion may be felt by the fact that the three parts of *Henry VI* and *Richard III* (the 'first tetralogy'), though chronologically later, were written before *Richard II*, the two parts of *Henry IV* and *Henry V* (the 'second tetralogy'). *King John*, chronologically the earliest, whose chief source is thought to be *The Troublesome Raigne of John, King of England*, was written about the same time as *Richard II*, though *Henry VIII* was appropriately written last. Other sources included Froissart's *Chronicle* (translated by Lord Berners) for *Richard II*, and Sir Thomas More's *History of Richard III* which was incorporated into later Chronicles.

Morality plays, which exercised a pervasive influence on Shakespeare's plays, provided no ideas about the philosophy of history. They may have influenced the structure of *Henry IV*, for example, though Falstaff is much more than a lord of misrule. But Shakespeare's hero is England rather than any individual. Something may have been owed by the dramatist to Chronicle plays, though less than is sometimes thought. Probably the only idea that came from Chronicle plays was jingoism. They would be concerned mainly with the simple facts of history, and intended for unsophisticated audiences.

Many other sources must have influenced Shakespeare indirectly rather than directly, such as the writings of the fifteenth-century Chief Justice Fortescue; Sir Thomas Smith, lawyer and Secretary of State, whose *Republic of England* was published in 1583; the 'judicious' Richard Hooker, Master of the Temple from 1585 to 1591, whose *Ecclesiastical Polity* (1593) contains the classic English exposition of the sixteenth-century conception of the authority of law; and also a mass of material that formed part of what has been called the collective consciousness of the age. In addition we may be sure that Shakespeare was familiar with the Bible in translation, notably *Romans*, chap. 13:

> Let every soul be subject unto the higher powers. For there is no power but of God: the powers that be are ordained of God. Whosoever therefore resisteth the power, resisteth the ordinance of God: and they that resist shall receive to themselves damnation.

He would also often have heard the Homilies appointed to be read in churches throughout the country, notably *An Exhortation Concerning Good Order and Obedience to Rulers and Magistrates* (1547):

> So that in all things is to be lauded and praised the goodly order of God: without which no house, no city, no commonwealth can continue and endure. . . . Take away kings, princes, rulers, magistrates, judges, and such estates of God's order, . . . and there must needs follow all mischief and utter destruction both of souls, bodies, goods and commonwealths;

and the *Homily Against Disobedience and Wilful Rebellion* (1570) which year by year impressed upon congregations the doctrine that rebellion is a horrible and inexpressible sin.

The most comprehensive survey made by a lawyer of the constitutional background to Shakespeare's plays is Professor Keeton's *Shakespeare's Legal and Political Background*.[3] The main constitutional problem in the English historical plays before *Henry VIII*, as Keeton sees it, is the title to the throne. Shakespeare's conception is dynastic: the Crown descends in the manner of real property by primogeniture.[3a] Thus John is a usurper, and has to assert that

[3] G. W. Keeton, *Shakespeare's Legal and Political Background* (1967), Part II.

[3a] In the succession to the thrones of Denmark and Norway in *Hamlet*, however, Hamlet and Fortinbras have been postponed to their uncles, presumably in accordance with Scandinavian customary law favouring election.

Arthur is illegitimate. Henry IV also is regarded as a usurper. The modern notion is that the people's approval is also necessary. The three parts of *Henry VI* depict the Wars of the Roses as an essentially dynastic struggle. In *2 Henry IV*, ii. 2, the Duke of York (Richard Plantagenet) seeks to prove his title to his supporters, as it was not sufficient to demonstrate the flaws in the title of Henry VI, who was in possession. It appears from the opening of *3 Henry VI* that Shakespeare himself favoured the Yorkist claim by hereditary right. The dramatist ignores the support of the merchants and the City of London, and minimises the part played by Parliament in 1455. The Lancastrian claim rested to some extent on a Parliamentary title, which is reflected in the treatise of the Lancastrian lawyer, Fortescue, *De Laudibus Legum Angliae*. Edward IV was therefore rightful King, and Richard III (who is supposed to have murdered the two princes in the Tower) is a usurper. Henry VII, according to Shakespeare, has every good reason to take Richard's place, and thus the House of Tudor is firmly established.

*Henry V* gives us Shakespeare's idea of the well-ordered State in the Archbishop's speech in Act I, Scene 2 on order and degree, with the analogy of the beehive ('The singing masons building roofs of gold'); which is paralleled by the speech of Ulysses in *Troilus and Cressida*, i. 3, and Menenius's allegory of the body and its members in *Coriolanus* i. 1. 'The view of kingship which appears in Shakespeare's plays,' Keeton writes,[4] 'and which is ultimately derived from the conception of a harmonious commonwealth in which the position of the ruler is unchallengeable, and his office is a sacred trust, involves a clearly defined attitude towards usurpers.' He points out that *As You Like It* begins with the overthrow of the Duke and ends with his restoration; at the end of *The Tempest* the exiled Duke is restored; in *Macbeth* King Duncan is murdered by Macbeth, and in *Hamlet* the

4 *Shakespeare's Legal and Political Background*, pp. 268-9.

king has been murdered by Claudius; Caesar is assassinated in the first part of *Julius Caesar*, but the play ends with the supremacy of Octavius. So John, Henry IV, Edward IV and Richard III all suffer for their usurpation.

It is often asked why Shakespeare did not mention Magna Carta in *King John*. Although it was not mentioned in the old play *The Troublesome Raigne of John*, it was much relied upon in *Bate's Case* (1606).[5] Sir Frederick Pollock[6] thought that the omission of Magna Carta (which was not yet a popular rallying cry anyway) was probably a deliberate touch of dramatic fitness; for John was becoming an English champion against foreign encroachment, and it would have spoilt that effect to bring in his constitutional differences with the barons. The distinguished jurist, Max Radin[7], has shown that after the end of the thirteenth century it was the Charter of 9 Henry III, rather than that of John, which remained in people's minds. In the Elizabethan period the conflict between the royal power and the rights of the subject was symbolised by Richard II rather than John. For Shakespeare, John is weak rather than wicked, and he was England's champion against France and the Pope. We may add that even if all this were not so, and Magna Carta were relevant to the theme of the play, it might have been dangerous to show a sovereign bowing to the superior force of his barons.

The theory of kingship is worked out most fully in *Richard II*, *Henry IV* and *Henry V*. Maitland's reading in Plowden's Reports familiarised us with the sixteenth-century idea – not mentioned in the Year Books – of the King's 'two bodies', the one natural and the other non-natural, though of the latter Plowden could say little but

[5] Sir Frederick Pollock, K.C., *Outside the Law* (1927), p. 99, 'War and Diplomacy in Shakespeare.'

[6] *Case of Impositions*, 2 St. Tr. 371.

[7] Max Radin, 'The Myth of Magna Carta', (1947) 60 *Harvard Law Review*, 1060, at pp. 1085 et seq.

that it is 'politic', whatever 'politic' may mean.[8] Edward VI, while under age, had made a lease of certain land in the Duchy of Lancaster, which the Lancastrian kings owned as private property. In the *Case of the Duchy of Lancaster* (1561)[9] Plowden reports the Crown lawyers as saying that

> the King has in him two Bodies, viz. a Body natural, and a Body politic. His Body natural . . . is a Body mortal, subject to all Infirmities that come by Nature or Accident. . . . But his Body politic is a Body that cannot be seen or handled, consisting of Policy and Government, and constituted for the Direction of the People, and the Management of the public weal, and . . . what the King does in his Body politic, cannot be invalidated or frustrated by any Disability in his natural Body.

And in *Willion v. Berkley* (1559)[10] Plowden reports the argument that when the Body politic of the King is joined to the Body natural, the capacity and effects of the Body natural are altered and partake of the effects of the Body politic. Maitland went on to cite *Hales v. Petit*[11] without mentioning *Hamlet*, but a medieval historian, Ernst Kantorowicz, inspired by a conversation with Max Radin, has devoted to Shakespeare's *Richard II* a chapter in a book on 'medieval political theology' entitled *The King's Two Bodies*.[12] The body politic was also called a 'mystical body', and Kantorowicz shows that English jurists not only developed a 'theology of Kingship' but worked out a 'Royal Christology', which, as Maitland had remarked, might be set beside the doctrine of the Trinity contained in the Athanasian Creed. Shakespeare made the metaphor not only the symbol, but the very substance and essence of the play:

[8] F. W. Maitland, 'The Crown as Corporation', *Selected Essays* (1936), pp. 108-10; reprinted from (1901) 17 *Law Quarterly Review*, 131.

[9] Plowden 212.

[10] Plowden 223.

[11] Plowden 261.

[12] E. H. Kantorowicz, *The King's Two Bodies* (Princeton U.P., 1957), chap. 2.

'*The Tragedy of King Richard II* is the tragedy of the King's Two Bodies.'[13] The King, as Henry V is made to say, was 'twin-born with greatness' (*Henry V*, IV. 1). Richard discards one by one the symbols of his kingship, though not his private griefs, in a scene reminiscent of the unpoping of Pope Celestine V in 1294. 'What subject can give sentence on his King?' is the rhetorical question asked by the Bishop of Carlisle (*Richard II*, IV. 1), and again put by Charles I in Westminster Hall. The play was not freely performed before the end of the seventeenth century: the violent separation of the King's two bodies was too close to the martyrdom of Charles I. The doctrine of Divine Right, to be developed by James I, was earlier propounded by John and Richard II.

Joseph Kohler, the distinguished German jurist, was also interested in *Richard II*, which he translated and to which he applied the Hegelian philosophy of world history. Kohler calls this play the supreme song of kingship and one of the grandest hymns of royal dignity.[14] The personality of Richard is attractive even after his fall. He never forgets his position as ruler, but accepts his bad fortune as the will of God. The king is said to be godlike and to be appointed by God. On the other hand he loses himself in licence and creates intolerable conditions, as described by John of Gaunt in Act II, Scene 1, and by the Gardener's mate in Act III, Scene 4:

> . . . our sea-walled garden, the whole land,
> Is full of weeds, her finest flowers chok'd up,
> Her fruit trees all unprun'd, her hedges ruin'd,
> Her knots disordered, and her wholesome herbs
> Swarming with caterpillars.

Richard gibed at law and justice, and thus destroyed the basis on which the kingship rests. After he is completely

[13] Kantorowicz, op. cit., p. 26.

[14] Josef Kohler, 'Die Staatsidee Shakespeares in "Richard II"', (1917) 53 *Shakespeare Jahrbuch*, pp. 1-12.

betrayed and forsaken he must allow judgment to be given against him in Westminster Hall. Two incompatible principles – the divinity of kings and the right of subjects to sit in judgment over the king – oppose each other: there is no juristic solution; the conflict can only end in the destruction of one or the other. In former times the Papacy could act as divine judge; but this power fails now, and it is force that is victorious, though it is sanctified by vengeance. Vengeance is formally unjustified, but it is legitimised in fact by the justice of history. What Shakespeare says in *Richard II* about the importance of kingship is like a poetic version of the chapter in Bodin on *majestas* (the King is *legibus solutus*, but under divine and natural law). It was established principle that a tyrant must not be killed by an individual, but the whole people only must sit in judgment on him. It is such a court that deposed Richard II and later condemned Charles I to death. Tyranny naturally arouses opposition to itself, though this is not subject to the sanction of legal rules, but to the sanction of history to which we are all subject. It is more a matter of intuition than dialectical discussion, Kohler concludes, whether a poet has listened to the voice of world history. This idea comes out very clearly in *Richard II*, as in all Shakespeare's kingly dramas.

Henry V's speech before Agincourt is an exposition of the orthodox theory of kingship (*Henry V*, IV. 1). Although his inherited title is imperfect, Henry V is the ideal ruler. 'He will only make war in a just cause', says Keeton,[15] 'and when he does it is strictly in accordance with the laws of war.' The royal hero – whose father, Henry IV, had recommended war with France as a means of keeping his barons in order – must be satisfied that his claim to the French throne is lawful and his cause just. He is, therefore, convinced (as the French are not) by the lengthy argument put forward by the Archbishop of Canterbury at the beginning of the play (*Henry V*, I. 2). This involves some juggling with

---

[15] Keeton, *Shakespeare's Legal and Political Background*, p. 282.

the complicated pedigree of Edward III; a repudiation of the Salic law on which the French King was said to base his claim, although that law actually concerned the succession to private property; and the assumption that if Edward III had a good title to the throne of France then Henry V must too. Any audience that tries to follow the Archbishop's exposition (taken from the *Chronicles*) for fifty lines or so must smile when His Grace calls it 'as clear as is the summer sun'.

Shakespeare's attitude towards Jack Cade's followers in *2 Henry VI* is similar to that towards the rabble in *Julius Caesar* and *Coriolanus*. In this Cade, too, there is an element of Wat Tyler, who is not mentioned in *Richard II*. The account of Cade's rebellion was described by John E. Hannigan, Professor of Law at Boston University, as a great satire on communism and bolshevism.[16]

Shakespeare's Richard III is seen by Keeton as a Machiavellian hero. Sir Thomas More's *History of Richard III* was used by Hall and Holinshed, and therefore indirectly by Shakespeare; and so More as historian provides another link between lawyers and the playwright. Although Richard himself could not have heard of *The Prince*, Shakespeare makes him, when still Duke of Gloucester, say that he could 'set the murderous Machiavel to school' (*3 Henry VI*, III. 2). The establishment of the Tudors settled the succession to the throne, and all the principal characters in *Henry VIII* acknowledge the supremacy of the law. Cranmer's final speech prophesies the reign of peace and plenty under Elizabeth and, by implication, James I.

At the time of the tercentenary of Shakespeare's death in the middle of the First World War, Sir Frederick Pollock delivered an address on 'War and Diplomacy in Shakespeare', in which he showed that, although a new diplomacy and new arts of war were developing in Shakespeare's

[16] John E. Hannigan, 'Shakespeare and the Young Lawyer', (1926) *Boston University Law Review*, 168.

youth, the playwright did not deal with these. The treatment of public affairs is wholly subordinate to stage effect. Thus Shakespeare's Henry V, a military hero, is most human when he talks with his soldiers as a plain gentleman. They reason about the King's responsibility in a thoroughly medieval fashion, the point being, not whether a King who goes to war should reproach himself with what we now regard as the horrors of war, but the risk that men slain in battle may die in mortal sin.

The political philosophy underlying the classical plays is similar to that of the English historical plays, and Shakespeare's attitude to the mob is the same. He clearly relied much on North's translation from Amyot's French translation of Plutarch's *Lives of the Noble Grecians and Romans* (1579) for *Julius Caesar*, *Antony and Cleopatra* and *Coriolanus*. Incidentally, North was a member of Gray's Inn. The main sources of the satirical *Troilus and Cressida* were Chaucer (from Boccaccio), Caxton, and Chapman's *Iliad* (1598).

In the classical plays Shakespeare deals further with the problems of kingship and the nature of the State, but the conclusion of one expert[17] is: 'There is little evidence of originality in the concepts of the state which appear in his plays. The theory of political organisation is consistently that accepted by the conservative and orthodox thinkers of his day.' As Lord Simon of Glaisdale has said,[18] conservatism can claim Shakespeare as one of its spiritual ancestors. We find it difficult not to identify Ulysses' impassioned speech on order with the dramatist's own convictions:

> Take but degree away, untune that string,
> And, hark, what discord follows!
>
> (*Troilus and Cressida*, I. 3)

[17] J. E. Phillips, Jr., *The State in Shakespeare's Greek and Roman Plays* (Columbia U.P., 1940), p. 208.

[18] Sir Jocelyn Simon, Q.C., 'Shakespeare's Legal and Political Background', (1968) 84 Law Quarterly Review, 33, at p. 45.

Shakespeare fears and hates disruption of the social order, says Caroline Spurgeon,[19] for the frame of human society — the laws that bind man to man — seems to him to have a mystical significance, to be one with a higher law and to partake of the same nature as the mysterious agency by which the order of the universe is determined. The ideal of the Commonwealth shared by Shakespeare with his contemporaries was not so much a political ideal as 'an ideal of justice, of duty, of unity rather than freedom to differ, of the manifestation of the will of God.'[20]

*Measure for Measure* is concerned with the question of justice in relation to the individual. The main source of the play was Whetstone's *Promos and Cassandra* (1578), though Shakespeare considerably altered the story. The preliminary question relevant here is the relationship between Claudio and Juliet. They are betrothed; Claudio has seduced Juliet; their formal marriage had not been celebrated because there was a dispute about dower. According to the Church they are not married, but in civil law they are as good as married in that neither was free to marry anyone else. Claudio's offence against the statute forbidding fornication, therefore, could hardly be less serious. The moral problem that concerns the audience through much of the play is Isabella's refusal to save her brother by means of her own dishonour. Isabella in her plea to Angelo echoes Portia's speech on mercy:

> No ceremony that to great ones longs,
> Not the King's crown nor the deputed sword,
> The marshall's truncheon nor the judge's robe,
> Becomes them with one half so good a grace
> As mercy does.
>
> (*Measure for Measure*, II. 2)

[19] Caroline Spurgeon, *Shakespeare's Imagery and What It Tells Us* (1935), pp. 75-6.
[20] Styles, op. cit., p. 119.

Finally, the sentences decreed by the Duke when he eventually resumes his authority offer themselves for the spectators' judgment, especially the breath-taking pardon of his false deputy, Angelo.

The name of the play, of course, comes from a not very poetical passage in the Duke's speech in Act V, Scene 1:

> The very mercy of the law cries out . . .
> 'An Angelo for Claudio, death for death!'
> Haste still pays haste, and leisure answers leisure,
> Like doth quit like, and Measure still for Measure.

This surely does not (as is sometimes supposed) refer to the Old Testament *lex talionis* between litigants, but to the judgment passed in the New Testament on judges: 'Judge not, that ye be not judged. For with what judgment ye judge, ye shall be judged: and with what measure ye mete, it shall be measured to you again' (*Matthew, vii*, 1). According to Walter Pater[21] it is poetical justice (an expression apparently coined by Rymer), the true justice of which Angelo knows nothing because it lies mostly beyond the limits of any acknowledged law. Some of our perplexity may be due to the fact that the play changes its nature, as well as its literary style, half-way through.[22]

Josef Kohler[23] used *Measure for Measure* as a text for a disquisition on pardon or forgiveness as a religious doctrine, as a royal prerogative, and as a principle of natural law. The verdict against Claudio was wrong, in Kohler's view, because the law prescribing the death penalty for fornication should have been regarded as repealed by desuetude. Angelo ought therefore to have exercised the prerogative of mercy. Even if the verdict was technically right, Angelo ought to have

---

[21] Walter Pater, *Appreciations* (1889), chap. 'Measure for Measure'.

[22] E. M. W. Tillyard, *Shakespeare's Problem Plays* (Penguin ed., 1965), p. 123.

[23] Josef Kohler, *Shakespeare vor dem Forum der Jurisprudenz* (2nd. ed., Berlin, 1919), Bk. II.

pardoned Claudio because of the extenuating circumstances. The pardoning of Angelo by the Duke, on the other hand, was considered by Kohler to be one of Shakespeare's few mistakes as an exponent of juridical principles.

A more recent German jurist, Gustav Radbruch,[24] who was Professor of Law at Heidelberg and Minister of Justice under the Weimar Republic, in discussing Law in the Arts (or the Law as an Artistic subject) wrote that the appeal of the law to the artist lies in the variety of its inherent antitheses – the opposition of Is and Ought, of positive and natural law, legitimate and revolutionary law, freedom and order, justice and equity, law and mercy. Dramatists have been especially attracted to the law, from Sophocles' *Antigone* down to Shakespeare's *Merchant of Venice* and *Measure for Measure*. Discussing the psychology of the man of law, Radbruch says that justice without love hardens into self-righteousness, against which the suppressed desires sooner or later take a terrible revenge. Angelo presents such an image of the zealot for law who slides into self-righteousness and injustice.

Professor Keeton stresses the dichotomy between justice and mercy. The Duke at the end of the play throws off his disguise, and is determined to make all punishments, as far as possible, proportionate to their crimes. In the Duke and Angelo we have two contrasted conceptions of criminal justice.[25] Not everyone would agree with Keeton, however, when he says that, in bringing about the marriage of Angelo and Mariana, the Duke is fulfilling one of the objects of modern criminal law by redressing the harm done.[26] A modern audience has little faith in forced marriages.

The quatercentenary year of Shakespeare's birth was marked in Peru by the publication of a survey of the various

[24] Gustav Radbruch, *Rechtsphilosophie* (3rd. ed., Leipzig, 1932), §§ 13 and 14.
[25] *Shakespeare's Legal and Political Background*, pp. 381-2.
[26] ibid., p. 392.

aspects of justice in Shakespeare's works.[27] In the plays Shakespeare gives us a theatrical interpretation of justice, the image of the just ruler. He must accept his responsibility, even though this involves abandoning the friendship of Falstaff or the love of Cleopatra; he must be neither traitor nor cruel like King John or Richard III; he must not abuse his power to satisfy his own appetites or lust like Angelo; he must not be a usurper like Henry IV, Macbeth or Claudius; he must not be irascible like Lear, or too suspicious like Leontes; he must not allow himself to be deceived by bad counsellors like Othello; he must not put personal pride before patriotism like Coriolanus; he must not let himself be carried away by self-pity like Richard II or be guided by abstract ideals without considering their effects like Brutus; nor even like Henry VI should he allow his sanctity to reach the limits of ineptitude. Worse than injustice is arbitrariness, the negation of law, as Portia teaches us and as we learn from Angelo. Finally, Shakespeare conceives of justice as the hope of men, and as the affirmation of Hamlet's words that there are more things in heaven and earth than were dreamt of in Horatio's philosophy.

[27] Roberto MacLean U., 'La Justicia en las obras de Shakespeare', *Letras* No. 36 (1964) (Universidad Nacional Mayor de San Marcos de Lima, Peru), pp. 48-57.

# 5

## Descriptions of Lawyers and Officers of the Law

There are no complimentary references to lawyers (other than the real Chief Justice Gascoigne) in any of the plays, except perhaps Tranio's oft quoted advice to the pair of rival swains:

> And do as adversaries do in law, —
> Strive mightily, but eat and drink as friends.
>
> *(The Taming of the Shrew*, 1. 2)

The adversaries here are counsel, not the parties themselves. 'This might, however, be considered an *obiter dictum*', says Herrington,[1] 'and not very complimentary at its best, when taken with the context.' When it is said of Autolycus that he has 'points more than all the lawyers in Bohemia can learnedly handle' (*The Winter's Tale*, IV. 3), this refers to the lawyer's duty to know all the law and facts relating to his client's case. Did Shakespeare distrust the sound of a lawyer's voice? Bassanio, in his speech on ornament in the casket scene, asks mildly:

> In law, what plea so tainted and corrupt,
> But, being season'd with a gracious voice,
> Obscures the show of evil?
>
> *(The Merchant of Venice*, III. 2)

---

[1] W. S. Herrington, 'The Legal Lore of Shakespeare', (1925) 3 *Canadian Bar Review*, 537.

but the misanthropic Timon rants:

> Crack the lawyer's voice,
> That he may never more false title plead,
> Nor sound his quillets shrilly.
>
> *(Timon of Athens*, IV. 3)

And when Kent says, 'This is nothing, fool', the Fool retorts, 'Then 'tis like the breath of an unfee'd lawyer, – you gave me nothing for't' (*King Lear*, I. 4). A correspondent in the *Law Society's Gazette*[2] thinks that Shakespeare's view of the law is reflected in Falstaff's expression 'the rusty curb of old father antick, the law' (*1 Henry IV*, I. 2), and Mercutio's description of Queen Mab's nocturnal gallop 'o'er lawyers' fingers who straight dream on fees' (*Romeo and Juliet*, I. 4). An understandable printer's error may have been corrected by Steevens when he suggested the emendation in *The Two Gentlemen of Verona* from 'the society of awful men' to 'the society of lawful men'. Falstaff counts time by the four terms of the legal year (*2 Henry IV*, v. 1) as was commonly done in the sixteenth century. And with whom does Time stand still? asks Orlando. 'With lawyers in the vacation', Rosalind replies: 'for they sleep between term and term and then they perceive not how time moves' (*As You Like It*, III. 2).

On the other hand, Shakespeare's general attitude towards the importance of law and order by no means suggests that he sympathised with Dick the Butcher's proposal, approved by Jack Cade, to kill all the lawyers (*2 Henry VI*, IV. 2). The idea comes from Holinshed, iii, 437, where we read that John Ball exhorted the people assembled at Blackheath that 'they might destroy first the great lords of the realm, and after the judges and lawyers, questmongers, and all other when they undertook to be against the commons.' One of those executed in Cheapside was the first Lord Saye and Sele, Lord Treasurer, whose country seat was Broughton

---

[2] Letter from D. P. Assersohn in (1964) 61 *Law Society's Gazette*, 208.

Castle, not far from Stratford-on-Avon. The dramatist himself was more likely to adopt Angelo's warning: 'We must not make a scarecrow of the law' (*Measure for Measure*, II. I).

Magistrates and constables fare no better. Menenius says to Brutus and Sicinius that, if they could see into themselves: 'Why, then, you should discover a brace of unmeriting, proud, violent, testy magistrates — alias fools — as any in Rome' (*Coriolanus*, II. I). Jaques's supposed burlesque of the medieval dance of the Seven Ages of Man includes the passage:

> And then the justice,
> In fair round belly with good capon lin'd,
> With eyes severe, and beard of formal cut,
> Full of wise saws and modern instances.
>
> (*As You Like It*, II. 7)

Corrupt county magistrates in Shakespeare's day were known as 'capon justices'. Lear, fantastically dressed with flowers, observes: 'see how yond justice rails upon yond simple thief . . . change places; and, handy-dandy, which is the justice, which is the thief?' And later:

> Robes and furr'd gowns hide all. Plate sin with gold,
> And the strong lance of justice hurtless breaks.
>
> (*King Lear*, IV. 6)

Maitland in his essay 'The Shallows and Silences of Real Life'[3] borrows nothing except the title from Shakespeare, but in contrasting 'lawyer's law' with 'justices' justice' he probably expresses an opinion that was as commonly held in Elizabethan times as it is today. 'Englishmen have trusted the law', he says: 'it were hardly too much to say that they have loved the law; but they have not loved and do not love lawyers.'[4] At the end of a lecture on the

---

[3] F. W. Maitland, *Collected Papers* (3 vols., Cambridge University Press, 1911), I, 466.

[4] idem.

general characteristics of English law in the Tudor period, Maitland[5] reminded his undergraduates: 'there is one book for the vacation in which some profitable things may be found about Elizabethan justices and Elizabethan constables – if you cannot yet enjoy Lambard's *Eirenarcha*,[6] you can at least enjoy Shallow and Silence, Dogberry and Verges.'

Robert Shallow is an esquire, justice of the peace for the county of Gloster, Commissioner of Musters, and formerly a fellow member with Falstaff of Clement's Inn, an Inn of Chancery preparatory to joining the Inner Temple. He appears in several scenes in *2 Henry IV* and *The Merry Wives* as a pathetic old braggart. Shallow threatens to make a Star Chamber matter of Falstaff's conduct in beating his men, killing his deer and breaking open his lodge (*The Merry Wives*, I. I). His cousin Slender gives him moral support by recounting his offices:

> *Slender.* In the county of Gloster, justice of the peace, and *coram.*
> *Shallow.* Ay, cousin Slender, and *custalorum.*
> *Slender.* Ay, and *Ratolorum* too.

Lawyers will not need a translation of this, though they may differ about '*coram*'. It has been suggested that Slender thinks the formula '*jurat coram me*' on an attestation to be part of the justices' title, but it is much more likely, as Sir Carleton Allen[7] says, that the reference is to Shallow's being a justice of the *quorum*. Shallow continues: 'The Council shall hear it; it is a riot', only to be corrected by Sir Hugh Evans, a Welsh parson: 'It is not meet the Council hear a riot; there is no fear of Got, in a riot: the Council, look

---

[5] Maitland, *Constitutional History of England* (Cambridge University Press, 1908), p. 236.

[6] William Lambard, *Eirenarcha, or the Office of the Justices of the Peace*, first published in 1581, was largely derived from a reading by Marowe at the Inner Temple in the reign of Henry VII. To it was added *The duties of Constables, Borsholders, Tythingmen, and such other low and lay Ministers.*

[7] Sir Carleton Kemp Allen, Q.C., *The Queen's Peace* (1953), p. 145.

you, shall desire to hear the fear of Got, and not to hear a riot.'

The question whether Justice Shallow was intended to be a caricature of Sir Thomas Lucy of Charlecote, near Stratford-on-Avon – whose deer the young Shakespeare is supposed to have poached – was left open by Mr Justice Barton,[8] who was content to point out the strong connection between the Lucy family and the Inns of Court in the sixteenth century. Madden,[9] Attorney-General for Ireland and later a judge, did not think that the Gloster Justice of *2 Henry IV* and *The Merry Wives of Windsor* was intended to be the self-important Puritan, Lucy of Charlecote. He saw a change in Shallow between the two plays. 'The old Gloucestershire Justice is fussy', he writes,[10] 'important in his way, and self-complacent; but deferential rather than self-asserting. Shallow, the *custos rotulorum*, is decidedly pompous. He dwells on his dignities, and poses as a personage.' It may be that the changed Shallow was inserted in the revised version of *The Merry Wives*. The dramatist perhaps had some resentment against Lucy, but the least probable of all theories is that the portrayal was intended to avenge an old quarrel about deer stealing. 'It is more probable', Madden concludes,[11] 'that the deer-stealing legend had its origin in the first scene of the rewritten *The Merry Wives*.' Keeton[12] raises several objections to the Lucy theory: (i) Shakespeare could have made his caricature in *1 Henry VI* (Sir William Lucy); (ii) London would not understand what Stratford would; (iii) the personal particulars do not tally, apart from the fact that Lucy was a knight and Shallow merely an esquire; and (iv) 'luce' and 'louse' is an obvious and common pun.

[8] Sir Dunbar Plunket Barton, *Links between Shakespeare and the Law* (1929) pp. 37-43.
[9] D. H. Madden, *The Diary of Master William Silence* (1897), chap. 8.
[10] ibid., p. 116.
[11] ibid., p. 115.
[12] *Shakespeare's Legal and Political Background*, pp. 99-100.

The researches of Leslie Hotson[13] suggest that in portraying Justice Shallow, Shakespeare was getting his own back on William Gardiner, the Surrey justice who attempted to suppress the Bankside playhouses in 1596. Gardiner's first wife was a Luce or Lucy, widow of Edmund Wayte; and her arms – the three white luces – were impaled on his. Abraham Slender would then represent Gardiner's stepson, William Wayte, who was involved in judicial proceedings with Shakespeare in the same year. The representation of Gardiner and Wayte by Shallow and Slender was accepted by D. B. Somervell, K.C.[14] Justice Silence upholds his name in the wonderful scene he shares with Shallow and Falstaff (*2 Henry IV*, III. 2), but in a later scene in that play, emboldened by sack, he sings tippling songs.

The chief upholders of law and order in *Much Ado About Nothing* are Dogberry and Verges. In the list of characters they are described merely as 'two foolish Officers'. In the text, Dogberry is 'a constable' and Verges 'a headborough'. Keeton[15] thinks they are borough or city justices of Messina, that Dogberry is high constable of the hundred and that the court over which he presides is the Court Leet. Lord Campbell[16] suspected that Shakespeare was slyly aiming not only at justices of the peace but also at chairmen of quarter sessions or even judges of assize. Dogberry in telling the Watch to 'keep your fellows' counsels and your own' used the very words of the oath administered to the grand jury by the judges' marshall. It was never the law or custom in England, says Lord Campbell, to give a charge to constables or the Watch; but he must have overlooked Malone's note that to 'charge' his fellows seems to have been a regular part of the duty of the Constable of the Watch.[17] Yet the

---

[13] Leslie Hotson, *Shakespeare versus Shallow* (1931), *ante*, p. 9.
[14] D. B. Somervell, K.C., 'Shakespeare and the Law', *Stratford-on-Avon Herald*, 15 April 1932.
[15] *Shakespeare's Legal and Political Background*, p. 104.
[16] *Shakespeare's Legal Acquirements* (1859), p. 145.
[17] *Much Ado About Nothing*, New Variorum edition (ed. Furness, 1899), p. 161.

words of the charge here are similar to those of the charge to the now obsolete grand jury. J. W. Draper[18] also replies that the archives of the quarter sessions do not seem to support Lord Campbell. Professor Draper is probably right in thinking that Dogberry and Verges are both meant to be petty constables of the borough. Dogberry is too ignorant, and Verges too old, to command respect. It has been suggested that Dogberry was probably brought up in a foundling hospital for he exclaims 'God save the foundation', but this appears to have been a stock phrase. It is evident that he had memorised phrases from elegant conversation manuals.

It was the constables' night duty to set and keep the Watch; but Dogberry wants to go to bed, so he appoints George (or Francis)[19] Seacoal his deputy, and invests him with the lanthorn as the sign of his office of chief or 'constable' of the Watch. The Watch and the constables at their head were proverbial among Shakespeare's contemporaries for their blundering simplicity, and were invariably portrayed with the 'mistaking of words'. The unnamed Sexton (Sacristan) and Town Clerk is the only intelligent member of the company. He takes over the examination of the prisoners, which by English law should have been conducted before two justices, decides that they shall be brought before the Governor and is fortunately able to explain the prisoners' examination to the Governor. In spite of their deranged vocabulary and ambivalent attitude towards their duties, the officers of the law have stumbled across the right malefactors, and by their means the formal part of the plot is brought to a satisfactory conclusion.

Dogberry, a member of the lower bourgeois class, is a satire on constables and all minor officialdom. Elbow is a 'simple' constable of Vienna, who leans upon justice. He has

[18] J. W. Draper, 'Dogberry's Due Process of Law', *Journal of English and Germanic Philology*, vol. 42, p. 563 (University of Illinois, Urbana, Ill., 1943), citing Webb, *English Local Government*, I, 469.

[19] George and Francis are not necessarily the same person. Francis could be the Sexton and Town Clerk.

been in the Duke's service for seven and a half years, allowing himself to be chosen annually by the men in his ward 'for some piece of money'. Elbow also has the habit of using words in a sense opposite to their proper meaning (*Measure for Measure*, II. 1). Dull, a constable in the Kingdom of Navarre, describes himself as 'his Grace's tharborough'[20] (*Love's Labour's Lost*, I. 1). His official duties are fulfilled conscientiously, if unimaginatively, but a proposal to present the Nine Worthies to the visiting Queen of France finds him out of his depth. When Holofernes points out that he has not spoken a word all the while, Dull replies: 'Nor understood none, neither, sir.'

[20] cf. *Taming of the Shrew*, Introd., Sc. 1:

> *Hostess.* I know my remedy! I must go fetch the third-borough.
> *Sly.* Third, or fourth, or fifth borough, I'll answer him by law.

# 6

## References to Legal
## Personalities and Cases

The Falconbridge legitimacy case in *King John* (I. 1)
appears to be tried by the King in person. The parties are
introduced by the Earl of Essex to the King for the case
'to be judged by you'. Essex was Geoffrey Fitzpeter, the
mighty and formidable Chief Justiciar, and, as Lord Campbell observes,[1] the action would be tried by the Council in
the King's presence. Fitzpeter was regarded in his day as
the chief pillar of the State, so that when John heard of his
death he exclaimed, 'Now I am again King and Lord of
England'.

Another famous Chief Justiciar, Hubert de Burgh,
appears in the same play, though when John gives him the
custody of Arthur (IV. 1) he is Lord Chamberlain. As Lord
Campbell says,[2] 'It is not easy to discover the view taken
by our immortal dramatist of the character of Hubert de
Burgh, whom he represents with a very tender heart, but
who, when solicited to rid the usurper of the 'serpent in his
way', is made to say "He shall not live"; and who deliber-
ately and seriously makes preparations for putting out the
poor young Prince's eyes with hot irons.' Lord Campbell
points out that Hubert's aside shows that he intended to act
quickly so that his mercy should not be aroused, and that
when he tells Arthur he is going to spare him he admits he
has changed his mind.

[1] *Lives of the Chief Justices,* pp. 41-3.
[2] ibid., p. 47.

In a paper read to the New York State Bar Association in 1881, James D. Teller[3] expressed the opinion that there is perhaps no play of Shakespeare which is more open to the criticism of lawyers than *King John*. Apart from the omission of Magna Carta, Teller found the treatment of the Chief Justiciar, Hubert de Burgh, inexcusable. Although Hubert was faithful to John, he was an upright and wise judge who gave good advice, and perhaps did more than any other person to persuade the King to assent to the Charter. Teller gives Shakespeare credit, on the other hand, for collecting and giving prominence to the facts in the life of Sir William Gascoigne, Chief Justice of the King's Bench under Henry IV; and he contrasts Shakespeare's tributes to the nobility of the law and its most worthy expounders, with his exposure of the weak complacency and mistaken ambition of such justices as Shallow and Silence.

Gascoigne was attorney for Hereford, who succeeded his father, John of Gaunt, as Duke of Lancaster; and Lord Campbell[4] thought that the Duke of York's plea to Richard II not to confiscate the Lancastrian estates followed pretty closely Gascoigne's advice:

> If you do wrongfully seize Hereford's rights,
> Call in the letters-patent that he hath
> By his attorneys-general to sue
> His livery, and deny his offer'd homage,
> You pluck a thousand dangers on your head. . . .
>
> (*Richard II*, ii. 1)

Incidentally, the certificate testifying to the embarkation of the banished Duke of Norfolk in 1398 appears to be the earliest recorded use of the term 'attorney-general', at a time when private persons could have a general attorney;[5] and

---

[3] James D. Teller, 'The Law and Lawyers of Shakespeare', *New York State Bar Association Report* 1881, vol. 4, pp. 162-70.

[4] *Lives of the Chief Justices*, pp. 122-3.

[5] H. H. L. Bellot, 'The Origin of the Attorney-General', (1909) 25 *Law Quarterly Review*, 400, at p. 403.

the passage quoted above from *Richard II* is cited in the leading monograph on the Law Officers of the Crown.[6]

*2 Henry IV* repeats the old tradition, found in Hall's *Chronicle*, that Gascoigne sent Prince Hal to prison for contempt because he tried to take a prisoner from the bar of the King's Bench. The Chief Justice's speech on obedience to law is regarded as a model of its kind, and a fair representation of that good man's character. The prisoner is identified in Act I, Scene 2, as Bardolph, one of Falstaff's friends. The Chief Justice may seem to us to overstep the bounds of his office in accosting Falstaff in the street and warning him, but Chief Justice Coke assisted in taking the Earl and Countess of Somerset into custody on a charge of murdering Sir Thomas Overbury, and examined the witnesses against them, writing the depositions with his own hand. Later still Chief Justice Holt acted as a magistrate, quelling riots, taking depositions and committing for trial. According to Shakespeare, Henry V confirms Gascoigne in his office. Gascoigne was in fact summoned in that capacity to Henry V's first Parliament, but he did not attend, having been dismissed nine days after the death of Henry IV. By that time he was old and due for retirement.

Lord Campbell[7] accepted the tradition of Gascoigne punishing Prince Hal for contempt largely on the authority of Shakespeare himself, though he was aware that — if there was any truth in the story at all — there were several other claimants for the position of the fearless and upright judge. He says that Shakespeare never minded anachronisms in the secondary events of English history, *Henry VIII* abounding with them, and one illustration of this is that the dramatist represents the committal of Prince Hal as having taken place before Archbishop Scroop's insurrection of 1405, whereas it was more probably later in Henry IV's reign. Lord Campbell goes on to exonerate Shakespeare from the

[6] J. Ll. J. Edwards, *The Law Officers of the Crown* (1964), p. 12.
[7] *Lives of the Chief Justices,* pp. 126-34.

charge of another historical error in making Henry V, who succeeded to the throne in 1413, come on to the stage with Gascoigne, who was thought on the evidence of a scarcely legible tombstone to have died in 1412. The discovery of the Chief Justice's will, however, shows that he lived until 1417.

The story of Chief Justice Gascoigne and Prince Hal has been accepted uncritically both on the bench and by legal authors. The report of a Scottish appeal to the House of Lords in a case of commitment without notice for contempt, *Watt v. Ligertwood* (1874),[8] contains the note:

Lord Selborne, in the course of the argument as to notice, referred to the case of Chief Justice Gascoigne, who, without a moment's hesitation, and without any prior notification, sent the Prince of Wales instantly to the Fleet Prison for a contempt of Court committed *in praesentia*; the heir of the Crown submitting patiently to the sentence and making reparation for his error by acknowledging it.

Lord Selborne was probably following Lord Campbell's *Lives of the Chief Justices*, where the story is narrated from Sir Thomas Elyot's *The Governor* (1534), Hall's *Chronicle*, the play *Henry the Fyfte, his Victories*, and Crompton's *Authoritie et Jurisdiction des Courts* which cites a case in Elizabeth's reign in which Chief Justice Catlyne and another judge of the Queen's Bench refer with approval to a Year Book account of the incident. J. H. Beale, the distinguished American lawyer,[9] on the other hand, in an article on contempt of court refers directly to the passage in *2 Henry IV*, v. 2, 'I keep here the place of the King, your sovereign lord and father, to whom ye owe double obedience', as being correct law. The violation of an injunction, Beale explains,

---

[8] *Watt v. Ligertwood* (1874) L.R. 2 H.L. Sc. App., at p. 367.
[9] J. H. Beale, 'Contempt of Court, Criminal and Civil', (1908) 21 *Harvard Law Review*, 161, at p. 162.

# Shakespeare and the Lawyers

is an offence against justice and so punishable by a court other than that which issued the order.

Whether the story is true or not, writes Keeton,[10] affects neither the value of the play nor the character of the Chief Justice, to which Shakespeare has paid such a noble tribute. However, it may seem a pity that so admirable a person as Sir William Gascoigne should twice be worsted by Falstaff in a battle of wits (*2 Henry IV*, i. 2, and ii. 1), especially on the second occasion when Falstaff, arrested on mesne process for debt at the suit of Mistress Quickly, gains his discharge by saying to the Chief Justice: 'My lord, this is a poor mad soul; and she says up and down the town that her eldest son is like you.'[11]

Many scholars believe that Shakespeare collaborated in writing *Sir Thomas More*, and that three pages of the British Museum manuscript (147 lines of Scene 6) are in his handwriting or in a similar hand.[12] In this scene More, as Sheriff of London, with the Lord Mayor helps to quell the riot against the Lombard and French aliens on Evil May Day, 1517, at the gate of St Martin's-le-Grand. He is described by Lincoln as 'a sound fellow', and by Lincoln's wife, Doll, as 'a good housekeeper.' Doll says: 'A keeps a plentiful shrievalty, and a made my brother Arthur Watkins Sargeant Safe's yeoman.' More makes a speech to the people urging obedience to authority, and condemning disobedience to the King as a sin against God. The dramatic significance of this would no doubt appear later in the play when More determines to obey his conscience rather than the King.

The Clown in *The Winter's Tale*, iv. 3 says: 'Advocate's

---

[10] *Shakespeare's Legal and Political Background*, p. 181.

[11] Lord Campbell, *Shakespeare's Legal Acquirements Considered*, pp. 67-71.

[12] R. W. Chambers, Preface to *Shakespeare's Hand in the Play of Sir Thomas More*, by A. W. Pollard, W. W. Greg, E. Maunde Thompson, J. Dover Wilson and R. W. Chambers (Cambridge University Press, 1923). Richard O'Sullivan, Q.C., a devotee of More, says categorically that 'three pages of 150 lines have been identified as the actual composition and handwriting of Shakespeare': *The Spirit of the Common Law*, p. 22; reprinted from vol. 213, *Law Journal* (1952).

the court-word for a pheasant.' There was a notable family of advocates with the name of Feasant or Phesant at Gray's Inn and in the courts in the sixteenth and seventeenth centuries. Peter Feasant, Senior, was Reader of Gray's Inn in 1582, and became Queen's Attorney-General in the North. Peter Feasant, Junior, was called to the Bar by Gray's Inn in 1608, and became a bencher in 1623.[13] *The Winter's Tale* was produced in about the year 1611, soon after the death of Peter Feasant, Senior. Barton thought this identification 'possible' though not generally accepted.

The records of the Star Chamber for 1591-2 in the Public Record Office show that Chief Baron Manwood was accused of intimidating a goldsmith into handing over a gold chain, which he had acquired from Manwood's son, under threat of sending him to the Marshalsea. The evidence was that the goldsmith had acquired the chain in open market, and Manwood was ordered to deliver up the chain or its value. The Chief Baron of the Exchequer's predicament is supposed by some to have inspired Shakespeare's elaboration of the story taken from Plautus' *Menaechmi* to form part of the plot of *The Comedy of Errors* (1594). This identification also has not found general acceptance.

In *Twelfth Night*, III. 2, Sir Toby Belch incites Sir Andrew Aguecheek to challenge Cesario to a duel, saying: 'If thou thou'st him some thrice, it shall not be amiss.' Sir Andrew writes his provocative challenge, which begins: 'Youth, whatsoever thou art, thou art but a scurvy fellow' (III. 4). The suggestion has been made, and is repeated in Lord Campbell's *Lives of the Chief Justices*,[14] that here in the First Folio of 1623 is a reference to Coke's vituperative prosecution of Sir Walter Raleigh for treason in 1603, in which the Attorney-General repeatedly used the contemptuous 'thou',[15]

---

[13] W. R. Douthwaite, *Gray's Inn, its History and Associations* (1886).
[14] *Lives of the Chief Justices*, p. 259.
[15] 'All that he [Lord Cobham] did was by thy instigation, thou viper; for I *thou* thee, thou traitor.'

but if this is so it must be an interpolation, for the play was produced in Middle Temple Hall in 1602. According to the editor Boswell, this parody is supposed to have been Shakespeare's revenge for Coke's charge to the grand jury as Recorder of Norwich in August 1606. The Bankside Company having opened a theatre in the City, Coke declaimed against stage players as vagrants who ought to be hounded out of town. Coke is said by Lord Campbell,[16] presumably on the same evidence, to have shunned the society of Shakespeare and Ben Jonson as of vagrants. A Canadian lawyer has conjectured that Shakespeare may have been revenging himself for Coke's charge to the grand jury when he made Lear constitute Mad Tom 'the robed man of justice'.[17] In fact, when *The Lord Coke his Speech and Charge* was published in 1607 Coke denied its authenticity and attributed it to Robert Pricket; but a letter sent by Chief Justice Popham to two of his judicial colleagues in Norfolk in June 1605, instructing them to bind over certain players to appear before the next Assizes, gives reason to believe that the report of Coke's charge is authentic, if not literally accurate.

If Polonius was intended as a burlesque of any particular public figure, one of the candidates is Sir Thomas Egerton, who was Lord Keeper when *Hamlet* appeared. Later, as Lord Ellesmere, he was Lord Chancellor from 1603 to 1617. Dr Bellario in *The Merchant of Venice* may represent Ottonello Discalzio, Professor of Law at the University of Padua in the time of Shakespeare. A very learned lawyer, he was often consulted by the Government of Venice.[18]

The grave-digger's argument over the death of Ophelia in *Hamlet*, v. 1, must be a skit on the case of *Hales v. Petit*

---

[16] *Lives of the Chief Justices*, pp. 337-8.

[17] R. F. Fuller, 'Shakespeare as a Lawyer', (1863) 9 *Upper Canada Law Journal*, 91, at p. 95.

[18] Suggested by Th. Elze, see *Merchant of Venice* (New Variorum ed., 1888), pp. 458-9.

(1563), reported by Plowden.[19] Sir James Hales, a puisne Judge of the Common Pleas, was indicted on the accession of Mary Tudor for having taken part in the plot to put Lady Jane Grey on the throne. He was pardoned, but so frightened that he went out of his mind. He attempted suicide unsuccessfully by stabbing himself with a penknife, and then walked into a river. At the 'crowner's' inquest a verdict of suicide (*felo de se*) was returned,[20] and his estates were forfeited to the Crown. His widow then brought an action in the Court of Common Pleas claiming an estate that she held as joint tenant with Sir James. Subtle arguments and prolonged litigation followed on the question whether her right of survivorship took priority over the forfeiture. Serjeant Walsh, for the defendant, argued[21] that the act of self-destruction consists of three parts, namely, the imagination, the resolution and the perfection; and the perfection consists of two parts, namely, the beginning (i.e. the doing of the act that causes death) and the end (i.e. the death, which is the sequel of the act). Sir James Hales's act was the throwing of himself into the water, and his death was but the sequel of the act.

The widow appears to have lost her case, according to F. L. Wyndolph, American legal practitioner,[22] although Dover Wilson in his edition of *Hamlet* seems to think she won it. Judgment was given by Chief Justice Sir James Dyer, Mr Justice Weston and Mr Justice Brown, the last-named saying:[23]

---

[19] 1 Plowden 253. The case is summarised in Lord Campbell, *Shakespeare's Legal Acquirements Considered*, pp. 84-8; C. G. Moran, *The Heralds of the Law* (1948), pp. 30-33; and J. W. Wallace, *The Reporters* (4th. ed.), pp. 147-53. It is also discussed in 'Shakespeare as a Lawyer', (1885) 2 *Pump Court*, pp. 139-40; (1885) *Canada Law Journal*, 189.

[20] There is evidence that Sir James was drowned accidentally by falling over a narrow bridge into the river at the age of 85: Edmund Foss, *Judges of England*, V, p. 373.

[21] 1 Plowden, at pp. 259-60.

[22] F. Lyman Windolph, *Reflections on the Law in Literature* (Philadelphia University Press, 1956), pp. 35-58.    [23] ibid., at p. 262.

Sir James Hales was dead. And how came he to his death? It may be answered, by drowning. And who drowned him? Sir James Hales. And when did he drown him? In his lifetime. So that Sir James Hales being alive caused Sir James Hales to die, and the act of the living was the death of the dead man. And for this offence it is reasonable to punish the living man, who committed the offence, and not the dead man.

The First Grave-digger (or First Clown) varies – and most people would say, improves – the report by making the distinction turn on whether the man goes to the water or the water comes to the man.

The credit for the discovery of *Hales v. Petit* as the source goes to Sir John Hawkins (1719-89), who studied law, was articled to an attorney and became a magistrate. He was also a critic and an authority on the life and works of Dr Johnson. Hawkins's opinion is stated in Malone's edition (1790): 'I strongly suspect that this is a ridicule of the case of Dame Hales, reported by Plowden in his Commentaries, as determined in 3 Eliz. . . . I cannot doubt but that Shakespeare was acquainted with [the case] and meant to laugh at it.' Malone comments that if Shakespeare meant to allude to this case, which seemed not improbable, he must have heard of it in conversation, for it was decided before Shakespeare was born and Plowden's reports, published in Law French in 1571-8, were not translated into English till late in the eighteenth century. 'Our author's study', remarks Malone, 'was probably not much encumbered with old French Reports.' Such legal argument and judgment would long be a conversational joke in the Inns of Court and the City taverns, although the actual case may have been generally forgotten by the time *Hamlet* was written.[24]

The two chief points of interest in the report of *Hales v.*

[24] cf. John W. Draper, 'Ophelia's Crime of *Felo de Se*', (1936) 42 *West Virginia Law Quarterly*, 228. The author of this article was a Professor of English.

*Petit,* comments Richard O'Sullivan,[25] are, first, that the judgment of Chief Justice Dyer on the wrongfulness of suicide is taken straight from the *Summa Theologica* of Aquinas (*Utrum aliqui liceat seipsum occidere*); and secondly that Shakespeare came to know the ultra-metaphysical arguments that were used by counsel, and made fun of them in this scene.

When Shakespeare was revising the grave-diggers' scene, he may also have had in mind William Underhill and his double purchase of New Place.[26] William Underhill was a lawyer as well as landowner, with a reputation for covetousness and craft, who can hardly have been ignorant of the fact that the first fine did not include the orchards. The second skull dug up is the skull of a lawyer, a great buyer of land: 'will his vouchers vouch him no more of his purchases, and *double* ones too, than the length and breadth of a *pair* of indentures?'

A correspondent to the *Times Literary Supplement*[27] drew attention to another case reported by Plowden, *The Queen v. Saunders & Nichols* (1572),[28] tried at Warwick Assizes, in which the facts are curiously suggestive of *Hamlet,* v. 2, where the poisoned sword and the poisoned cup are changed in the course of the duel between Hamlet and Laertes. In that case it was held that if *A* persuades *B* to poison *C,* and *B* accordingly gives poison to *C,* who eats part of it and gives the rest to *D* who is killed by it, *A* is not accessory to the murder of *D.* Sir Donald Somervell, for many years a Law Officer and later a Lord of Appeal, replied[29] that he did not think Shakespeare would have read Plowden. A

[25] Richard O'Sullivan, *The Spirit of the Common Law* (1965), p. 50. Reading on 'Edmund Plowden' given at Middle Temple Hall in 1952.

[26] P. R. Watts, 'Shakespeare's "Double" Purchase of New Place', (1947) 20 *Australian Law Journal,* 330; *ante,* pp. 6-7.

[27] C. H. Norman, 'Shakespeare and the Law', *Times Literary Supplement,* 30 June 1950, p. 412; and 4 August 1950, p. 485.

[28] 2 Plowden 473.

[29] *Times Literary Supplement,* 21 July 1950, p. 453.

famous case of forty years earlier would be common knowledge. So Mistress Page in *The Merry Wives of Windsor* talks of fee simple, fine and recovery. No modern playwright would make a Mistress Page joke about the Law of Property Act 1925, but he might well show familiarity with some famous trial of forty or more years ago.

It is highly probable, in Mr Justice Barton's opinion, that certain proceedings which took place in the Star Chamber between two members of Gray's Inn just before the production of *Twelfth Night* in Middle Temple Hall in 1602, inspired the noisy scene in which Sir Toby Belch and his friends indulge in late revelry in Olivia's house and ridicule the puritan, Malvolio. The dispute heard by the Star Chamber was between Sir Posthumus Hoby, a puritan, who had incurred unpopularity by prying officiously into the activities of alleged Popish recusants, and William Eure, who with his friends had created a disturbance in Lady Hoby's house by playing cards and other disorderly behaviour.

In *Macbeth*, II. 3, the porter after the third knocking at the gate says: 'Faith, here's an equivocator, that could swear in both the scales against either scale; who committed treason enough for God's sake, yet could not equivocate to heaven.' It is widely held that this is a reference to Father Henry Garnett, Superior of the Jesuits, who was executed in 1606 for complicity in the Gunpowder Plot. Like Campion in 1581 and Robert Southwell in 1595, Garnett had practised the art of equivocation in his defence.

Mr Justice Barton,[30] who was an authority on the land law, also suggested that certain of Shakespeare's legal allusions familiar to real property lawyers may be traced to three leading cases: *Taltarum's Case*, *Shelley's Case* and *Chudleigh's Case* (*Case of Perpetuities*).

*Taltarum's Case* (1472)[31] was the culmination of the

[30] *Links Between Shakespeare and the Law*, pp. 69 et seq.
[31] *Hunt v. Smith*, also known as *Talcarn's Case*, Y.B. 12 Edw. 4, Mich., fo. 19, pl. 25.

earlier cases laying down the law relating to the circum-
vention of the statute *De Donis* by barring entails. Fines and
recoveries were well known to litigants and those who
frequented the courts. Conveyancers in Shakespeare's time
were trying to get round *Taltarum's Case*, but they were
eventually foiled by *Mary Portington's Case* (1613).[32] In *The
Comedy of Errors*, ii. 2, Dromio of Syracuse says to his
servant Antipholus that there is no time for a bald man to
'recover' his hair.

> *Ant. S.* May he not do it by fine and recovery?
> *Dro. S.* Yes, to pay a fine for a periwig and recover
> the lost hair of another man.

In *The Merry Wives of Windsor*, iv. 2, Mistress Page says
of Falstaff: 'if the devil have him not in fee-simple, with
fine and recovery, he will never, I think, in the way of
waste, attempt us again.' And in the churchyard scene in
*Hamlet*, v. 1, Hamlet makes some multiple puns: 'This
fellow might be in's time a great buyer of land, with his
statutes, his recognizances, his fines, his double vouchers,
his recoveries; is this the fine of his fines, and the recovery
of his recoveries, to have his fine pate full of fine dirt?'

Shakespeare uses the term 'purchased' of property or
qualities acquired by some way other than inheritance. For
example, Henry IV tells his son that the Crown which 'in
me was purchas'd, Falls upon thee in a more fairer sort'
(*2 Henry IV*, iv. 5); and Lepidus says that Antony cannot
change his faults because they are 'hereditary rather than
purchas'd' (*Antony and Cleopatra*, i. 4). The rule in *Shelley's
Case* (1581)[33] distinguished between estates acquired by
'purchase' and those acquired by inheritance or descent.
Coke in his reports says that this legal meaning of 'purchase'
was generally known.

[32] 10 Co. Rep. 35b.
[33] 1 Co. Rep. 88b, at 104a.

*Chudleigh's Case*[34] contains the first use of the word 'perpetuity' in the law books. This case stopped the device of creating successive contingent remainders by way of use. The Queen's Bench considered the case for six years, Bacon being briefed on the second argument. It was eventually heard by all the judges, who gave their decision in 1595. Parolles in *All's Well That Ends Well*, IV. 3, says that Captain Dumain for a trifle 'will sell the fee-simple of his salvation, the inheritance of it; and cut the entail from all remainders, and a perpetual succession for it perpetually.' This may be a topical allusion.

In *King Henry VIII*, I. 3, which dates from 1612-13, Shakespeare pokes fun at a royal proclamation forbidding courtiers to follow French fashions. This would have appealed to the audience so soon after the *Case of Proclamations*,[35] the judges' opinion in which was delivered in 1608.

Falstaff, Prince Henry and Poins plan to carry out a robbery at Gadshill, where: 'There are pilgrims going to Canterbury with rich offerings, and traders riding to London with fat purses' (*1 Henry IV*, I. 2). Pilgrims would no longer be going to Canterbury in Shakespeare's day, but Gadshill was a favourite place for staging robberies in the sixteenth century. Leonard reports a case in 1577[36] where three men who had been robbed joined in an action under the Statute of Winchester[37] against the inhabitants, in which Serjeant Harris, counsel for the inhabitants of Gravesend, said that 'time out of mind, etc. felons had used to rob at Gadds Hill'. Mr Justice Manwood is reported as saying:

> When I was a servant to Sir James Hales, one of the Justices of the Common Pleas, one of his servants was robbed at Gadds Hill, in this the hundred of Gravesend

---

[34] *Case of Perpetuities* (1595), 1 Co. Rep. 113b. See also *Corbet's Case* (1600) 1 Co. Rep. 77b.

[35] (1610), 12 Co. Rep. 74; 2 St. Tr. 723.

[36] 2 Leonard 12.

[37] 13 Edw. 1.

in Kent, and he sued the men of the hundred upon this statute; and it seemed hard to the inhabitants there, that they should answer for the robberies done at Gadds Hill, because robberies are there so frequent, that if they should answer for all of them, that they should be utterly undone.

# 7

## *Trial Scenes*

It has been estimated that nearly one-third of the English plays extant at Shakespeare's death contain a trial scene, and that well over one-third of those plays performed in London during Shakespeare's dramatic career contain one or more trial scenes. The proportion in Shakespeare's plays is nearly two-thirds. Such scenes do not necessarily form the central theme or climax, nor is it practicable for the whole trial to take place on stage. Their purpose varies from posing serious problems of justice and mercy to mere burlesque.[1] The great trial scene in *The Merchant of Venice* has attracted far the most attention from legal commentators, and we shall discuss it in a separate chapter.

In the trial of Buckingham for treason in *Henry VIII* the stage proceedings of the Council, sitting as the Star Chamber, merely consist of the evidence of Buckingham's surveyor, and the King's ordering of Buckingham – who is already in the Tower – to be brought to trial. The trial itself is described in a conversation between two Gentlemen, and Buckingham on the way to execution is allowed to make a final speech which, as Lord Campbell remarks,[2] shows that he is content with the justice he received. The Duchess of Gloucester was convicted of witchcraft in 1441 and confined for life to the Isle of Man, but only the sentence of the King is given on stage (*2 Henry VI*, II. 3). *Richard II* opens with an appeal of treason, which would normally lead to trial by

---

[1] D. Smith, *Trial Scenes in the English Drama up to 1615* (unpublished thesis, Birmingham University, 1960). Ben Jonson runs second to Shakespeare.

[2] Lord Campbell, *Lives of the Chief Justices*, I, p. 161.

battle.[3] Thomas Mowbray, Duke of Norfolk, defends himself against the charge brought by Henry Bolingbroke, Duke
of Hereford (afterwards Henry IV). The formal prelimi-
naries are recited according to the book, but the King stops
the proceedings and banishes both parties – Bolingbroke
for ten years and Mowbray for life. In *Henry V* there is no
trial of Cambridge, Scroop and Grey for treason. Although
there are a number of cases of despotic sentencing in Shakespeare's plays, a Canadian lawyer sees 'very few scenes of
impartial justice'.[4]

The trial scene in *King John*, 1. 1, takes place in a Room
of State in the Palace. Essex says to the King:

> My liege, here is the strangest controversy,
> Come from the country to be judg'd by you,
> That e'er I heard.

There follows the trial of the legitimacy of Falconbridge by
the King in Council (*Curia Regis*), the play being based on an
older play, *The Troublesome Raigne of John, King of England*.
Philip, eldest son of the late Sir Robert Falconbridge, has
entered into possession of the estate. Robert, the plaintiff,
describes himself as son and heir of Falconbridge, which
puts Philip's legitimacy in issue. From circumstances and
physical resemblance the King infers that Philip's father
was Richard I, the King's brother. Robert pleads non-
access. Was this a good plea in bastardy in King John's
reign or in Shakespeare's time? As regards the earlier
period, we have the four grounds for the proof of illegiti-
macy given by Bracton, but these were considerably restricted by the time of James I, and the only one in issue
in this case was non-access. The King's judgment in favour
of Philip's legitimacy, Keeton[5] concludes, was good law for

---

[3] See Keeton, *Shakespeare's Legal and Political Background*, chap. 15.
[4] W. S. Herrington, 'The Legal Lore of Shakespeare', (1925) 3 *Canadian Bar
Review*, 537.
[5] *Shakespeare's Legal and Political Background*, chap. 8.

later Plantagenet and early Tudor times. Shakespeare was more correct than *The Troublesome Raigne* in not bringing in the mother, for she would not be allowed by law to give evidence of non-access in such a case. Lord Campbell also says that the dramatist is uniformly right in his law in this scene,[6] and Lord Simon of Glaisdale,[7] bearing in mind the relative dates of Shakespeare's marriage licence and the baptism of his eldest child, suggests that he may well have had occasion to ponder the matters raised in bastardy suits.

*Henry VIII*, ii. 3, gives an accurate description of the divorce proceedings against Queen Katharine up to her withdrawal, except that for aesthetic reasons the reading of the long commission is omitted. The play contains passages from Holinshed's *Chronicles* and Foxe's *Book of Martyrs*, on which large sections of it are based, though Shakespeare changes the emphasis and makes interesting variations. He succeeds in making the proceedings convincing, while gaining our sympathy for Katharine and at the same time preserving Henry from the charge of deliberate injustice. Cranmer eventually arrives armed with the favourable opinions of the Universities of France, Italy and England. The motives of both Henry and Wolsey are shown to be mixed. The later parts of the proceedings are given in outline – character now being more important for Shakespeare than incident, although Wolsey and Campeius (Cardinal Campeggio) are made to appear more solicitous for the Queen than they actually were.[8] The character of the trials in this play, says a recent editor,[9] is at once public, as they affect the State, and personal, as they affect the protagonists.

J. Pym Yeatman's theory[10] was that much of *Henry VIII*

[6] *Lives of the Chief Justices*, I, p. 43.
[7] (1968) 84 *Law Quarterly Review*, at p. 36.
[8] Keeton, *Shakespeare's Legal and Political Background*, pp. 158-64.
[9] R. A. Foakes, *King Henry VIII* (Arden 3rd. ed., 1957), p. lii.
[10] J. Pym Yeatman, *The Gentle Shakspere: A Vindication* (1896), chap. 5.

— the first four acts of which, down to the death of Katharine, tell us more about Shakespeare than all his other works put together — may have been written by Campion, who possibly inspired the play; but that Act V has been added and is not by Shakespeare at all. Yeatman's version of the play omits from iv. 1, the Order of the Coronation and the discussion of the procession by the three Gentlemen; and in iv. 2, after Patience says 'Heaven comfort her!' he omits the entries of the Messenger and Capucius and twenty lines of dialogue in which they take part. His version finishes with Katharine saying 'I can no more' at the end of Act IV.

The scene in *The Winter's Tale*, iii. 2, is in a Court of Justice. The indictment against Queen Hermione reads that she is accused and arraigned of high treason in committing adultery with Polixenes, King of Bohemia, and conspiring with Camillo to take King Leontes' life; the Queen's overt act being, contrary to her faith and allegiance, to counsel and aid Polixenes and Camillo to fly from justice. The Queen refers her case to the oracle — 'Apollo be my judge' — two men having previously been sent to Delphos by the King to obtain the oracle's opinion. The oracle vindicates the Queen, and Polixenes and Camillo. The King at first, however, says there is no truth in the oracle, and the sessions must proceed; and it is only the news that his young son Mamillius has died, followed by the supposed death of Hermione, that makes him relent. The place is supposed to be Sicily, perhaps then a Greek colony. The appeal to the oracle suggests that the time is that of ancient Greece, though the indictment partly follows the English Statute of Treasons. De Montmorency[11] sees no sign of the lawyer's touch in this trial, and suggests that the play may have been written at Stratford in 1610-11 when Shakespeare had no access to the lawyers at the Temple. But Shakespeare's imagination was working on an old legend,

[11] J. E. G. de Montmorency, 'Shakespeare's Legal Problems', *The Contemporary Review: Literary Supplement* (1930), p. 797.

and, as Keeton[12] says, the trial would have been less dramatic if its form had been either English or entirely classical.

Brabantio's charge against Othello (I. 3) rests on the circumstantial evidence that it was against all rules of nature that Desdemona should 'fall in love with what she fear'd to look on'. At least one lawyer has found the trial of Othello very irregular. After Brabantio's accusation, the Duke, without waiting to hear Othello, cries:

> the bloody book of law
> You shall yourself read in the bitter letter
> After your own sense,

thus giving the plaintiff *carte blanche* to perform the judicial function of interpreting the law.[13] On the other hand, Othello in his great defence speech teaches the jury lawyer, according to Herrington,[14] that the simple, straightforward story is more convincing in the end than wild gesticulation and loud declamation.

Of the imaginary trial of Goneril and Regan in *King Lear*, III. 6, Lord Campbell[15] wrote that, although it is conducted in a manner showing a perfect familiarity with criminal procedure, it could not be carried on with perfect regularity on account of Lear's madness. Without waiting for a verdict, Lear himself sentences Regan to be anatomised. Sir Plunket Barton[16] gives a very different picture of the trial. Lear orders his unnatural daughters to be arraigned before a tribunal composed of the deranged Edgar and the Court Fool, who is described as Edgar's 'yoke-fellow of equity'. One of the members of this ill-assorted criminal tribunal opens the proceedings by singing two comic songs.

---

[12] *Shakespeare's Legal and Political Background*, pp. 158-9.

[13] R. F. Fuller, 'Shakespeare as a Lawyer', (1863) 9 *Upper Canada Law Journal*, pp. 91, 95.

[14] Herrington, loc. cit.

[15] *Shakespeare's Legal Acquirements Considered*, pp. 82-3.

[16] Sir Dunbar Plunket Barton, *Links between Shakespeare and the Law* (1929), pp. 147-8.

The King acts as prosecutor, and then gives judgment without consulting the judges. So far from the trial being conducted, as Lord Campbell asserts, in strict conformity with legal procedure, Barton thinks it would be better described as Gilbertian.

There is a magistrates' court scene in a hall in Angelo's house in *Measure for Measure*, ii. 1. Angelo, fearing that the case will outlast the longest Russian night, withdraws, expressing the hope that his colleagues — Escalus and another Justice — will find good cause to whip them all. Escalus conscientiously sifts the circumstantial and irrelevant evidence, and questions the accused with sympathy and patience. Fripp[17] thought that, except for its London features, the scene might be from the Guild Hall at Stratford; but, of course, the homely humour is much more concentrated.

On the level of pantomime we have in *The Merry Wives of Windsor*, v. 5, the commencement of the mock trial of Falstaff at Herne the Hunter's Oak in Windsor Park at midnight:

*Anne.* Crier Hobgoblin, make the fairy oyes.
*Pistol.* Elves, list your names. . . .

This is shortly followed by a parody of ordeal by fire:

*Anne.* With trial-fire touch me his finger-end:
If he be chaste, the flame will back descend
And turn him to no pain; but if he start,
It is the flesh of a corrupted heart.

In the course of a study of the legal process in Elizabethan and Jacobean drama, Professor Moelwyn Merchant[18] points out that, whereas a present-day audience expects such professional details as examination, cross-examination and summing-up to be technically correct, Jacobean audiences were willing to waive technicalities while they explored

[17] E. I. Fripp, *Shakespeare, Man and Artist* (2 vols., 1938), I, p. 144.
[18] W. Moelwyn Merchant, *Lawyer and Actor: Process of Law in Elizabethan Drama* (Edinburgh University Press, 1964).

principles with the utmost subtlety. Jacobean dramatists were preoccupied with the theoretical conflict between strict justice or retribution and mercy, and the overriding divine grace. The full understanding of the problem of human justice demands a submission to legal disciplines which the Jacobean dramatists appear to have had in full command. Some of Shakespeare's plays are themselves potent instruments of legal argument, parodies or analogues of the process of justice, for example, *Measure for Measure*, *Hamlet*, *King Lear* and *The Merchant of Venice*.

Moelwyn Merchant[19] sees *King Lear*, for example, as depending for the structure of its third and fourth acts largely on the formal pattern of trial in a court of justice. Lear himself regards the storm as a cosmic court of judgment — prefiguring the Last Judgment — the thunder-claps being the dreadful summoners of the Gods. Regan is summoned before a 'fully constituted' commission in which two common law judges are joined by a Chancery judge; but after formal arraignment the cause is placed outside the realm of justice in a borderland of fallen nature and ethical, subjective judgment. This mockery of a trial *in absentia* reveals most strongly Lear's madness, and the play alternates between precise legal form and the profound insights of a disordered mind.

Otto Erickson asserted that Shakespeare's trial scenes are void of error either in law or procedure, instancing not only the trial by battle in *Richard II* and the bastardy trial in *King John* but also *The Merchant of Venice*.[20]

[19] Moelwyn Merchant, op. cit., pp. 120-23.
[20] Otto Erickson, 'Shakespeare and the Law: A Tercentenary Obiter'. (1916) 20 *Law Notes*, 4.

# 8

## *The Trial in*
## The Merchant of Venice

There is a fair measure of agreement among Shakespeare scholars that the trial scene in *The Merchant of Venice* (IV. 1) expresses the perennial conflict between law or strict justice on the one hand and mercy on the other, while the play itself (classed as a comedy) is primarily about a usurer rather than a Jew. Usury was condemned by Christian doctrine, though Christians practised it. Hebrew law forbad usury among Jews, but not between Jews and Gentiles. The main source of the story of Shylock's bond was probably Giovanni Fiorentino's *Il Pecorone* (1558), although we do not know of an English translation in Shakespeare's time. A recent influence on the play would be Marlowe's *Jew of Malta*. The Bond of Flesh and the Casket Choice both had long traditions, and they were linked together in some versions anticipating Shakespeare's union of the two themes.

There is a mass of lawyers' comment and criticism in various languages on the bond and the trial. Not all the pre-1888 legal writings are referred to in the New Variorum, and there have been many since the publication of that invaluable edition. The judgments reached have varied from the high-flown philosophy of German jurists, through some not always very imaginative technical commentary, to a view not unlike that expressed by Professor Russell Brown concerning Portia: 'Shakespeare at his most irresponsible.'[1]

---

[1] *The Merchant of Venice* (New Arden, 1955), p. xlix.

91

The main arguments or discussions of the lawyers have turned on the questions:

> (i) By what law are we to test:
>   (*a*) the validity of Shylock's bond?
>   (*b*) the soundness and fairness of the legal proceedings arising out of the forfeiture?

Should it be Venetian law at the period of the play, i.e., at the time of the trial? or English law of Shakespeare's day, or of the present day? or by natural justice?

> (ii) What is Portia doing at the trial? Is she judge, or advocate, or expert jurist consulted by the Court? She is the wife of Bassanio, the principal debtor for whom Antonio (the defendant) went surety; and she is housing Shylock's daughter, Jessica, who has eloped taking Shylock's jewels with her. Her position is thus most prejudicial.
> (iii) What is our judgment on the validity of the bond?
> (iv) What is our judgment on the soundness and fairness of the trial and sentence?

The following references to the writings of lawyers are arranged for convenience mainly in chronological order, although it is evident that later writers have not always been familiar with the work of their predecessors.

Lord Campbell[2] expressed the opinion that the trial is conducted according to the strict forms of legal procedure. Of the pre-trial proceedings he said: 'All this has a strong odour of Westminster Hall', where the Common Law courts used to sit.

R. F. Fuller, writing to a Canadian law journal in 1863,[3] thought that the grant of the pound of flesh next the heart, if valid, would imply whatever was requisite to obtaining

---

[2] *Shakespeare's Legal Acquirements Considered*, pp. 49-51.
[3] R. F. Fuller, 'Shakespeare as a Lawyer', (1863) 9 *Upper Canada Law Journal* 91, 96.

the flesh; but this bond would be against public policy and void. In an action at law, he continued, the judgment would be not to recover a specific article but its value in money; as the merchant's heart would have no market value in money, 'the Jew would be jewed in his suit'. In equity specific performance might be granted, but equity would not enforce an unconscionable contract.

Ezek Cowen, of New York, published in 1872 a fictitious report of an appeal in the Supreme Court of New York[4] which anticipated some of the points brought forward later in the same year by the great German jurist, Rudolf von Ihering. Ihering, himself a Jew, commented on the trial in *Der Kampf ums Recht*, first published in 1872,[5] without knowing that he had been anticipated by Cowen. Ihering concludes that justice was not done to Shylock. The bond was void as being contrary to good morals, and the judge should have refused to enforce it on this ground from the first. The weakness of Portia's judgment lies juridically in this, that as she did not decide against the validity of the bond on the ground of its being *contra bonos mores*, it was a wretched subterfuge, a miserable pettifogging trick, to forbid the shedding of blood that necessarily accompanied it. We might as well say that a person entitled to an easement may not leave footmarks on the land because this was not expressly mentioned in the grant. If the end ever justifies the means, why was the denial of right not revealed until after the sentence? In defeating Shylock's claim Portia abused the law of Venice. Ihering admits, however, that the poet is free to build up his own system of jurisprudence, and we need not regret that Shakespeare has done so here.

The editor of the *Albany Law Journal*, which in the 1870's seems to have retained a continuing interest in this subject,

[4] Ezek Cowen, 'Shylock v. Antonio' (1872) 5 *Albany Law Journal*, 193.
[5] Rudolf von Ihering, *The Struggle for Law* (trans. J. J. Lalor, 2nd. ed., Chicago, 1915), pp. 86-8. In the preface to the 8th edition, 1886, Ihering discusses the criticisms of Kohler and Pollock.

wrote in January 1875[6] that it is evident from the spirit of the play that the judge regarded the contract as void, even civilly, and he doubtless adopted the legal fiction of so strictly construing the contract that, without nominally declaring it void, he nullified it practically. The case may, then, be evidence of Shakespeare's legal ingenuity. 'In considering Shakespeare's law', he wisely observed, 'we must always take into account the conditions of the time, place and circumstance, and how much is intended for dramatic effect.'

If Shakespeare had been a Chancery lawyer, wrote Senator Cushman Davis,[7] he might have caused an injunction to be served on Shylock. But surely the Chancery would not issue an injunction to restrain the commission of a crime? Sureties to keep the peace would have been more appropriate.

Pietscher, a German judge (Landsgericht-Präsident), wrote a pamphlet in 1881[8] strongly critical of Ihering's views on *The Merchant of Venice*. The play is not a tragedy about a Jew, says Pietscher, but a comedy about a merchant usurer. Shylock typifies the person who mercilessly insists on his legal rights. He cares nothing for the law, but is actuated by envy, hatred and greed. It is doubtful whether the contract would have been void as against good morals by the law of Venice at that time, but it is permissible to meet chicanery with chicanery. Thus the rogue is caught in his own snare. What Shylock really wanted was not the pound of flesh but Antonio's life, though he dared not say so. Anyway, a bargain of this nature must be strictly construed. In the end the outraged State of Venice demands atonement for abuse of private rights.

One of the best known German jurists of the late nine-

---

[6] (1875) 11 *Albany Law Journal*, 45.

[7] C. K. Davis, *The Law in Shakespeare* (St Paul, Minnesota, 2nd. ed., 1884), p. 19.

[8] A. Pietscher, *Jurist und Dichter: Studie über Iherings 'Kampf um's Recht' und Shakespeares Kaufmann von Venedig* (Dessau, 1881).

teenth century, Josef Kohler,[9] always an opponent of Ihering's jurisprudence, accused Ihering of completely failing to understand the history of law. Nor did Kohler agree with Pietscher that cunning may be met with cunning. Portia's judgment may not be justifiable before the Forum of Jurisprudence, but it is an expression of the judge's feeling for right, a manifestation of the (late nineteenth-century) free-law movement. Mercy or equity prevails over the inhuman laws of older times. The moral and legal consciousness of a people must in time prevail over rigid formalism. The judgment was right; but the reasons were faulty, because a right granted to do something includes the right to do anything that is necessarily incidental thereto; also, a creditor is allowed to take less than that to which he is entitled. Although we would not dare openly to oppose an outdated legal rule, we may in a comedy evade it in a thousand ways. Thus the kingdom of Sarastro overcomes the powers of night. Shylock's catastrophe consists, first, in the injustice of being required to become a Christian; and secondly in the forfeiture of all his property. The forfeiture of some of his property would have been justifiable, but the sentence goes rather far. Shylock does not succumb, as Ihering said, under the weight of an unjust sentence. He crumbles because he knows in his conscience that his wrongful motives have been exposed. His demand was within the strict law of his own time, but it was an abuse of right.

An abuse of legal right is morally wrong, and to seek to take a person's life through abuse of right is against law as attempted murder. Shylock's criminality is somewhat lessened, however, by the fact that the court itself is not clear that it is an abuse of right. The only injustice done to Shylock is in treating him as if he had directly sought Antonio's life, whereas he merely made use of legal forms and judicial process. But, Kohler concludes in his Hegelian

---

[9] Josef Kohler, *Shakespeare vor dem Forum der Jurisprudenz* (1st. ed., Würzburg, 1883; 2nd. ed., Berlin, 1919), Preface and Book I.

manner, a severe punishment is justified: even if we think the sentence unjust as being oppressive to the individual, yet it is all part of world history and the universal development of law, because the law on which Shylock relied was obsolete and the representatives of obsolete ideas must be crushed. Here Shakespeare, as a historian of law and right, surpassed even himself.

In lighter vein the author of an article on 'Shakespeare's Lawyers', twice reprinted in 1885,[10] wrote that Portia furnished the eloquence, but the point of law which non-suited Shylock came from the brain of the old professor after he and Portia had 'turned o'er many books together'. Thus the case furnishes a striking and perhaps solitary instance in which the leader did all the work and the junior got all the pay.

Another imaginary appeal by Shylock was published in an American magazine in 1886 by C. H. Phelps,[11] an American Professor of Law and expert on equity and later a State judge, who argued that Shylock did not have that fair and impartial trial to which he was entitled. This is how the case looks to appellant's counsel. The Duke opens the tribunal in the presence of the magnificoes for the purpose of determining the dispute, yet before Shylock arrives the Duke, presumably to show his impartiality, tells Antonio that the plaintiff is:

> A strong adversary, an inhuman wretch,
> Uncapable of pity, void and empty
> From any dram of mercy.

As soon as Shylock comes in, the court urges him not only to 'lose the forfeiture' but to 'forgive a moiety of the principal'. When Shylock says he has sworn a holy vow to pursue

[10] 'Shakespeare's Lawyers', 32 *Albany Law Journal*, 24; (1885) *Irish Law Times*, 422; 79 *Law Times*, 287.
[11] Charles Henry Phelps, 'Shylock vs. Antonio: Brief for Plaintiff in Appeal', (1886) 57 *Atlantic Monthly*, 463.

his claim, the Duke asks him: 'How wilt thou ask for mercy, rendering none?' Pending the arrival of Bellario's substitute, Gratiano – one of the men who plundered Shylock's treasure and abducted his daughter – gives the proceedings an added judicial flavour by calling to the man he has so cruelly wronged: 'Be thou damned, inexorable dog.' Portia's earlier statement of the law, probably furnished by Bellario, is sound, but the infinitesimal hair-splitting that follows is the subtle inspiration of the young disciple. As for the blood, if one has a right to something, one has a right to what necessarily accompanies it; and as to not taking less than a pound of flesh, a creditor may lawfully take less than his due. Anyway, the judgment should be executed by an officer of the court. Shylock is now denied even the principal. Then the Venetian statute is trumped up; but Shylock has not sought the life of any citizen, he has merely asked the court to decree what are his rights. When the court proposes to forfeit his life and property, the Duke relents to the extent of pardoning his life and limiting the forfeiture to half his property, on condition of renouncing his religion. Of this illogical tangle of inconsistencies there seems to be no explanation, until the fact emerges that the so-called youthful doctor of Rome is really a young woman in disguise; and is, in fact, none other than the wife of Bassanio, the principal debtor on the bond, who has left her home in charge of Shylock's runaway daughter – who is in possession of Shylock's plundered property – in order to come to Venice and accomplish the downfall of Shylock himself.

Two peculiarities of Spanish legal procedure which may have obtained in Italy during Spanish domination – consultation by the court with a jurist and the transformation of a civil into a penal action – were illustrated by John T. Doyle[12] with reference to two cases in Central America in the mid-nineteenth century. The first was a commercial

[12] John T. Doyle, 'Shakespeare's Law – The Case of Shylock', *The Overland Monthly* (San Francisco, July 1886).

dispute in Nicaragua in 1851-2, in which the judge heard counsel on each side, then, after stating the facts, submitted the question of law to a jurisconsult. A few days later the jurist returned the papers to the judge with his opinion, which was in favour of the defendant. Afterwards the jurisconsult, whose services were gratuitous, intimated that he expected an honorarium from the successful party according to the custom of the country. So after the trial in *The Merchant of Venice*, the Duke says: 'Antonio, gratify this gentleman.' Mr Justice Barton[13] later pointed out that the reference of the case to a Doctor of Laws (Bellario of Padua) came from the Italian source, and follows the procedure of medieval Italy and Spain.

The other case recounted by Doyle, a somewhat later one in Mexico, began with the matter of the disposition of the estate of the deceased, who had been killed in a quarrel with his partner over the accounts. The cause of death was investigated by the court of first instance, and the surviving partner exonerated. On appeal by the State Fiscal the judgment of the court below was reversed, the defendant sentenced to death and the judge fined for partiality.

The American lawyer and legal author, Appleton Morgan,[14] thought the trial scene in *The Merchant of Venice* showed a most consummate ignorance of all or any legal procedure. Another legal member of the Shakespeare Society of New York, William C. Devecmon[15], agreed that the trial was riddled with legal mistakes. Portia, as *amicus curiae*[16] or referee, makes a number of rulings which are bad in law, in logic and in morals. In the result, her effort

[13] *Links between Shakespeare and the Law* (1929). But Portia ascribes the English doctrine of binding precedent to the courts of Venice.

[14] J. Appleton Morgan, LL.D., *Shakespeare in Fact and in Criticism* (New York, 1888), p. 180.

[15] W. C. Devecmon, *In Re Shakespeare's Legal Acquirements*, Shakespeare Society of New York, No. 12 (1899), pp. 41-50.

[16] The feminine form *amica curiae* is not used by commentators, either because Portia was disguised as a man, or because women were not until recent years admitted to the Bar, or perhaps because *amica* can mean mistress or concubine.

to vest Jessica with Shylock's property was as abortive and ridiculous as any or all of her judicial pronouncements. In this play Shakespeare not only manifests his lack of knowledge of the technique of the legal profession, Devecmon continues, but he shows a profound ignorance of law and of the fundamental principles of justice; unless we assume that the trial scene disregards all ideas of law, justice and morality for mere dramatic effect, although equal dramatic effect could have been attained without such sacrifice.

Of a similar opinion was C. M. Brune,[17] who also asks why Shylock could not at least recover the interest. If anyone was guilty of conspiracy it seems to be Portia. The trust by 'deed of gift of all he dies possess'd' is defective and ineffective. That expression would include all property Shylock acquired between the trial and his death. This would fail either as a gift *mortis causa* or as a will because it was not voluntary; and if it was by will, Shylock would have the right to alter it at any time or to revoke it by making another will.

James M. Love, Professor of Law at Iowa University and an expert on the law of contract, regarded the statements of law about Shylock's bond as a tissue of absurdities from a legal point of view. He thought that in any event Antonio would have a good defence of fraud, as Shylock pretended to treat the transaction as a jest and clearly intimated that the bond would not be enforced. Incidentally, Jessica committed theft, and Lorenzo knowingly received the stolen goods. Love was convinced that Shakespeare, although probably indifferent about the law of the case, intended to hold up for reprobation the then existing English law relating to penal bonds. A bond was not then, as it later became, a mere security for the payment of a debt, to be discharged whenever the actual sum due was paid; but, when the debtor made default by non-payment at the exact day, the bond was forfeited and the holder recovered – not, as

[17] C. M. Brune, LL.D., D.C.L., *Shakespeare's Use of Legal Terms* (1914), 19-34.

later he would, the actual sum due under the debt – but the whole amount of the penalty. Shakespeare probably intended by the metaphor of the pound of flesh to place the strict and literal construction of penal bonds in an odious light.[18]

Italian contributions have been inspired by the comments of Ihering and Kohler. Azzolini[19] in his account of the story of the pound of flesh, or bond story, made much of a case described in Gregorio Leti's *Storia di Sisto V* and showed how ancient and widespread the story was. He also compared it with the Roman law of the Twelve Tables relating to the enforcement of debt, as preserved by Aulus Gellius. Adolfo Ravà,[20] jurist and Professor of Law at Rome, illustrated the second part of a long article on 'Rights over one's own person' with reference to passages from Shakespeare's plays. The *Merchant of Venice* provided him with the story of the pound of flesh, in discussing which he followed Kohler's book on Shakespeare and Azzolini's reference to Leti's *Life* of Sixtus V. As the case of Secchi the Merchant and Ceneda the Jew is not as well known to English as to Italian readers, it may be helpful to recount it here.[21]

A report reached Secchi that Drake had plundered St Domingo and carried off a great deal of booty. Secchi had large concerns in those parts, so he sent for the insurer, Ceneda, a Jew, and told him the report. The Jew, whose interest it was to have such a report thought to be false, said: 'I'll lay you a pound of my flesh it is a lie.' To which

[18] J. M. Love, 'A lawyer's commentary on Shylock v. Antonio', (1891) 25 *American Law Review*, 899.

[19] G. Azzolini, *'Shylock e la leggenda della libbra di carne'* (Reggio Emilia, 1893), a revised and amplified offprint from *L'Italia Centrale* of an article entitled 'Il Contratto di Shylock nel "Mercante di Venezia" dello Shakespeare', first published in *Fanfulla della Domenica*, 31 July and 7 August 1892.

[20] Adolfo Ravà, 'I diritti sulla propria persona', (1901) 32 *Revista italiana per le scienze giuridiche*, I, at pp. 28-30. There is a short bibliography at p. 30.

[21] Gregorio Leti, *The Life of Pope Sixtus the Fifth*, translated by Ellis Farneworth (1754), Book VII, pp. 293-5.

Secchi replied: 'I'll lay you 1,000 Crowns against a pound of your flesh that it is true.' The Jew accepted the wager, and an agreement was drawn up to the effect that if Secchi won he should himself cut the flesh, with a sharp knife, from whatever part of the Jew's body he pleased. The truth of the report from the West Indies was confirmed, and the action for the enforcement of the contract was referred by the Governor of Rome to Pope Sixtus V. The Pope said it was important that contracts should be performed, and he therefore directed Secchi to take a knife and cut a pound of flesh from any part of the Jew's body he pleased, but added: 'if you cut but a scruple, or a grain, more or less than your due, you shall certainly be hanged.' The Merchant, trembling like an aspen, besought the Holy Father to give him his Benediction and to tear the contract in pieces. The Jew for his part expressed himself content to come out of it so easily. Sixtus, however, was far from content. 'The subjects of Princes', said he, 'are the property of the State, and have no right to dispose of their bodies, or any part of them, without the express consent of their Sovereigns.' Both parties were immediately sent to prison, and the Governor was ordered to proceed against them with the utmost severity of the law. The Governor suggested that a fine of 1,000 Crowns might be appropriate. This did not nearly satisfy the Pope, who pointed out that the Jew had actually sold his life by consenting to have a pound of flesh cut from his body, which was direct suicide, and that the Merchant was guilty of premeditated murder in making a contract that he knew must cause the death of the other party if he insisted on its being performed, as he had said he did. So they were both condemned to death. Intercession was made on their behalf, however, by their influential friends and relations; and Sixtus, who did not really intend to put them to death but to deter others from such practices, changed the sentence into that of the galleys; and even this they were allowed to buy off by paying 2,000 Crowns each

to the Hospital which had lately been founded. The translator of Leti's book has a note that the scene between Shylock and Antonio in Shakespeare's *Merchant of Venice* seems
to be borrowed from this story, though the playwright has
inverted the persons and altered some of the circumstances.[22]
Sixtus V would certainly be well known in England, for
he was the Pope who excommunicated Elizabeth I and
encouraged Philip II to send the Armada.

One of the most thoughtful and least accessible articles
on the subject is that by Professor Paul Huvelin,[23] of the
Faculty of Law at the University of Lyon. The denouement
of the play is Portia's judgment.[24] But in what society does
the process take place? We have to place ourselves at different points of view: the plot of the pound of flesh is derived
from a primitive Germanic culture; the scene is laid in
sixteenth-century Venice; the form of the bond and the
legal procedure belong to late sixteenth-century England.
By strict common law the object of the debt, after the three
months have passed, is not the 3,000 ducats but the forfeit
only. Equity, on the other hand, would not allow the creditor to take more than the principal, interest and fruits. The
penalty of the pound of flesh would be illegal in modern
law, but not in primitive law. Disagreeing with Ihering
and Kohler, Huvelin inclines to think that Portia's judgment is right by strict law. The case is evidently tried by a
court of common law. Shylock bungled in not stipulating
in the bond that he might spill Antonio's blood, and that he
might take from him a piece of flesh weighing a pound,
*more or less*. Portia's decision is not only in accordance with
law, it is also fundamentally equitable and humane. But the

[22] Leti, op. cit., p. 293.

[23] Paul Huvelin, 'Le procès de Shylock dans *Le Marchand de Venise* de Shakespeare', *Bulletin de la Société des Amis de l'Université de Lyon*' (1901-2), 173-98.

[24] cf. M. D. H. Parker, *The Slave of Life: A Study of Shakespeare and the Idea
of Justice* (1955), p. 71: the play is constructed on a sudden reversal of situation,
which is one of the traditional weapons for dramatic surprise. And see pp. 51 et seq.
for a discussion of mercy and clemency.

final condemnation of Shylock is arbitrary and without any juridical character. Portia, having rejected Shylock's arguments on grounds of strict law, could not apply equitable principles in sentencing him. The sentence is the work of vengeance rather than justice. But Shylock takes on a symbolic character, his humiliation clothing him with a sort of majesty. He falls, in beauty, like some legal Prometheus, thunderstruck. The feeling for dramatic beauty rather than the sense of legal right guided the dramatist in the latter part of the litigation. And Shakespeare was right because beauty, and not law, was required of him.

Dr Homer B. Sprague in a discussion of Shakespeare's alleged legal blunders,[25] holding that Shylock's contract was *contra bonos mores*, said it was high time that someone should show that when man's law squarely conflicts with God's law, man's must give way. On the other hand, E. J. White[26] asserts that illegal reasons are assigned for giving judgment against Shylock, and that no scientific lawyer could have written this play and delivered the judgment that Portia is made to deliver.

Robertson[27] thought an equity lawyer would probably have set aside Portia's 'blood' argument and Shylock's 'bond' argument, and would have given a simple decree for payment of the debt. We can imagine, he writes, what Bacon would have thought of the proposition that if *A* lends money on condition of being allowed to cut off half a newly killed pig belonging to *B*, he may not cut off less than half and is precluded from taking any blood. But it is the utterly unlawyerlike punishment of the miscreant for his *intentions* that finally makes the theory that a lawyer wrote this play so preposterous.

[25] H. B. Sprague, 'Shakespeare's Alleged Blunders in Legal Terminology', (1902) 11 *Yale Law Journal*, 304. The author was ex-President of the University of North Dakota.

[26] E. J. White, *Commentaries on the Law in Shakespeare* (St Louis, 2nd ed., 1913), pp. 123-4.

[27] J. M. Robertson, *The Baconian Heresy* (1913), pp. 60-61.

Sir George Greenwood[28] emphasised *Il Pecorone* as a main source, and never relied on *The Merchant of Venice* as an argument in favour of the dramatist's knowledge of law. Also, he thought the parallel between Portia's great speech and Seneca's *De Clementia* so striking that it could hardly be disputed. As for the bond, although Shylock talks about 'the condition', it was a *simplex obligatio* or single bond. The force of a 'condition' is that if the obligor does some particular act the obligation shall be void, but in the case of Shylock's bond Antonio was to repay the money in any event under *penalty* of losing a pound of flesh if he did not.

Dr Julius Hirschfeld, writing in the *Law Quarterly Review*[29] on Portia's judgment and German jurisprudence in the year of the 350th anniversary of Shakespeare's birth, wisely came to the conclusion that Shakespeare cannot be discussed juridically. Hirschfeld's psychological answer to the problem of the play is that Shylock was a coward; he never intended to try to get his pound of flesh, though he might have pretended — if he had the chance — to give way magnanimously. But if one reads III. 1, it is impossible to agree with Hirschfeld. Salanio and Salarino are talking of the loss of Antonio's argosies, when they are joined by Shylock. 'Let him look to his bond', Shylock reiterates. Salanio asks, surely he won't take Antonio's flesh; what is it good for? 'To bait fish withal', replies Shylock, 'if it feed nothing else, it will feed my revenge.' Another of the tribe, Tubal, enters and confirms Antonio's loss. 'I thank God, I thank God!' Shylock exclaims, 'good news, good news! ha, ha!' And when Tubal says that Antonio will almost certainly go bankrupt, Shylock cries: 'I am very glad of it: — I'll plague him; I'll torture him: — I am glad on't.' Then he tells Tubal to bespeak an officer a fortnight beforehand, saying: 'I will have the heart of him if he forfeit.' Shylock adds: 'Were

[28] *The Shakespeare Problem Restated*, pp. 94-6; *Is There a Shakespeare Problem?* pp. 90-98.
[29] Julius Hirschfeld, 'Portia's Judgment and German Jurisprudence', (1914) 30 *Law Quarterly Review*, 167.

he out of Venice, I can make what merchandise I will.' It is therefore evident that the Jew's motives are jealousy, revenge and trade rivalry.

Sir Frederick Pollock, who founded and edited the *Law Quarterly Review*, in the same issue[30] disagreed with Hirschfeld that Shylock was a coward, or that he ever intended to make a theatrical gesture of generosity. Shakespeare may have known very little about Jews at first hand, but he intended to make a play out of the popular legend about Jews. Pollock thought German jurists took Shakespeare far too seriously. His own view was that no court in any civilised country would ever administer any such specific remedy as Shylock demands. If Roman creditors ever did cut up a debtor (which Aulus Gellius did not believe) they did so without the aid of the Court. The Shylock theme confuses two different stages in the development of law, those of sanctioned self-help and of judicial execution. Shakespeare must have known that the Doge's procedure was absurd from beginning to end, but he would have replied to his critics: 'I am a maker of plays, not of law-books; I wanted a good scene, not justice.' The English Court most nearly analogous to the Doge's would have been the Star Chamber, which used civilian procedure (including interrogatories) and inflicted fines and corporal penalties without a jury.

The proper judgment, Pollock suggests, would have been something like the following:

Declare the bond void at law, involving as it does consent to be maimed. (There is no question of equity in the technical sense.) Judgment for the plaintiff for 3,000 ducats and interest at the current rate, as on a simple contract debt; but, tender of this having been refused in

---

[30] Sir Frederick Pollock, K.C., 'A Note on *Shylock v. Antonio*', (1914) 30 *Law Quarterly Review*, 175; partly reprinted in *Essays in the Law* (1922), pp. 196-8. Among Pollock's writings was a pioneer text-book on the principles of the Law of Contract.

Court, costs to be paid by the plaintiff. Plaintiff is in contempt for abusing the process of the Court, and liable to summary fine and imprisonment; but his contempt is pardoned at the defendant's suggestion on terms of making a proper settlement on Jessica.

Elsewhere Pollock wrote that in the catastrophe of Shylock all reason, justice and probability are violated with a superb audacity that never fails to carry the spectator on a magic flood of illusion in even a passable performance.[31]

Kohler, in the second edition of his *Shakespeare vor dem Forum der Jurisprudenz*,[32] did not agree with Pollock and Hirschfeld that Shakespeare was unacquainted at first hand with Jews, because of the celebrated case of Dr Roderigo Lopez, Court physician to Elizabeth I, who was hanged at Tyburn in 1594 for treason. Curiously enough, his enemy too was an Antonio – Don Antonio Perez, a Spanish refugee.[33] Also, says Kohler, Shakespeare must have had intercourse with Italians, especially Venetians. Venice included many Jews. Would there not be Venetian Jews in London?

Theodor Niemeyer,[34] Professor at the University of Kiel and President of the German Branch of the International Law Association, who studied the origins of the ancient story of the bond for human flesh, disagreed with Kohler and Huvelin and agreed partly with Ihering. He thinks the decision is wrong, and the reasoning pettifogging and insufficient, for where there is a right there is also a way to exercise it. Also, the confiscation of Shylock's property and

---

[31] Sir Frederick Pollock, *Outside the Law* (1927), p. 105.

[32] 2nd. ed. (Berlin, 1919), p. 5. And see James T. Foard, 'On the Law Case: *Shylock v. Antonio*', (1899) *Manchester Quarterly*, 268.

[33] Sir Sidney Lee, *Life of William Shakespeare* (1898), p. 68.

[34] Theodor Niemeyer, *Der Rechtsspruch gegen Shylock im 'Kaufmann von Venedig': ein Beitrag zur Würdigung Shakespeares* (1912); revised version translated by W. Herbruch as 'The Judgment against Shylock in the Merchant of Venice', (1915) 14 *Michigan Law Review*, 20. In the revised version Niemeyer refers to Pollock's note in (1914) 30 *Law Quarterly Review*.

forcing him to become a Christian are brutalities contrary to both justice and law. We therefore find true tragedy in Shylock's fate. Nor does Niemeyer agree with other writers that the 'merry bond' was intended only as a joke. Shakespeare did not necessarily consider Portia's judgment to be a correct application of Venetian law. We do not know whether he thought it either juristically correct or in itself satisfactory. He probably concerned himself only with the victory of reason and justice. The pettifoggery of the procedure would be well known to the sharp-witted man of the world, the shrewd jurist, that Shakespeare was. The dramatist did not identify himself in any way with the judgment. After the civil case of Shylock *v.* Antonio comes the criminal case against Shylock. The whole course of the *criminal* proceeding is according to any standard illegal, unjust and immoral. About the *civil* case there is much doubt.

In order to judge the civil action, Niemeyer asks: according to what standard is this question of law to be judged? – by German law of the present time, by the law of England when Shakespeare wrote in 1594, or by the law of Venice at the time of the action? Under the German civil code the penalty of the pound of flesh would be void as *contra bonos mores*. Concerning English law of the sixteenth century there is some doubt, though Shylock's case would have been allowable to a certain extent. But a common law court could only enforce the payment of money, that is, a debt or damages; and the Court of Chancery would not have enforced a claim of this kind; so the whole legal conflict would have been impossible by English law. There are therefore only two standards applicable, either the law of Venice or natural justice. The law of nature is ruled out by the specifically Venetian setting; therefore the law of Venice is the only valid standard. This means, not the actual law of Venice (whatever that may have been), but Venetian law as presented to us in the play. Contracts with penalties similar to that contained in Shylock's bond—involving forfeiture of a

hand, a foot, the nose and even the head – are found throughout the Middle Ages in Italy, Germany and Scandinavia,
and in some cases they were held valid. Thus Shylock's
contract was possible and, according to the law of that
time, valid. On the other hand, there is no record that any
creditor from Roman times onwards actually exercised the
right to kill or mutilate his debtor. Shakespeare (following
his sources) then addresses himself to the question, what
would happen if the creditor did lay hands on the debtor?
Niemeyer's conclusion is: 'How right becomes wrong and
wrong becomes right, as in the eternal conflicts between the
Ideal and the Real – how through exaggeration, arrogance
and breach of law that one is crushed who believed in the
inflexibility of the law: – all this is reflected in the tragic
fate of Shylock.'

An American Lawyer, J. O. Boyd,[35] asking what is the
legal effect of the deceit practised on the Duke and the litigants by Portia (Bassanio's wife), gives four reasons against
the decision of the case. First, with regard to the punishment, there was no warrant of law requiring the deed of gift,
or authorising the placing of part of the property in trust,
or requiring Shylock to become a Christian. Secondly, there
was no authority, nor any wording of the bond, that required
Shylock to do the carving of the flesh. It is invariable in
civilised countries for the officers of the court to exercise
the mandates of the court. Incidentally, when tender of
payment was made, which Portia holds was legal and
sufficient, then the security was discharged. Thirdly, it was
foolish to say that Shylock could not take less than the
amount specified in the bond. Lastly, the bond – in recent
times at least – would be void as against public policy.
However, the reasonable part of the bond might have been
enforced, and judgment given for the ducats. 'Such a

[35] J. O. Boyd, 'Shylock Versus Antonio: or Justice Blindfolded'. (1915) 21
*Case and Comment*, 994. The author, after general legal practice in Memphis,
Missouri, became attorney for the Mississippi River Power Co. of Keokuk, Iowa.

picture', Boyd concludes, 'truly presents the classic idea of
the embodiment of justice: namely, a woman with her eyes
completely blindfolded, holding the power of decision in a
thing whereof she knows nothing.'

One of the most substantial writings by a lawyer on *The
Merchant of Venice* is that published in 1924 by H. J.
Griston,[36] a member of the New York, Cleveland and
Federal Bars and one-time partner of S. A. Tannenbaum.
Griston thought it necessary to fix the period of the play
before it could be understood and appreciated. The action
of the play must be after A.D. 311 when Constantine made
Christianity an official religion, and before A.D. 320 when
the right to seize the body of an insolvent debtor was
abolished. The scene is laid, not in Venice, but in the State
of the Veneti (Aquileia) where Roman law applied in the
fourth century. The Duke is not the Doge but the *Dux* or
military governor acting under a 'charter' of authority, and
Portia is an *arbiter*. *The Merchant of Venice*, then, is one of
the 'Roman' plays. Anachronisms include references to the
Rialto (built in 1590), a ship bound for Mexico (discovered
in the sixteenth century), ducats and Magnificoes (which
are medieval), but these do not affect the play. In his discussion of the law of the play, Griston lays emphasis on
Roman law; the bond is drawn under the Twelve Tables
(*nexum*). He thinks Shakespeare could have had little first-
hand acquaintance with Jews: Shylock is not a Jew, but a
human being. The trial and execution of Dr Lopez must
have influenced Shakespeare in writing this tremendous
indictment against barbarous laws and the way they are
applied.

Lord Darling,[37] a Chancery judge, in saying that Portia's
speech would perhaps more closely resemble the addresses to
which juries are privileged to listen if it contained more false

[36] Harris Jay Griston, LL.B., *Shaking the Dust from Shakespeare* (New York,
1924; 2nd. ed., 1924).
[37] Foreword to G. W. Keeton, *Shakespeare and his Legal Problems* (1930).

points than it did, seemed to imply that Portia was acting as counsel for the defence. E. D. Armour, K.C.,[38] law lecturer, author on property law and editor of the *Canadian Bar Review*, inclined to the view that she was an advocate, though he admitted there was some ground for the opinion that she was acting as judge. Chief Justice Campbell[39] called Portia the Podestà, or judge called in to act under the authority of the Doge. Pollock said Portia acts as judicial assessor not as advocate. She speaks throughout on behalf of the Court, and her appeal to Shylock's sense of mercy is a fine stroke of dramatic irony.[40]

Lord Normand,[41] who became President of the Court of Session, asserts positively that Portia is not Antonio's advocate but the judge in the action of Shylock against Antonio. He goes on to contend that it is incorrect to say that Portia resorted to a quibbling construction of the bond. Portia's decision was not based on an interpretation of the bond, nor was there a quibble. Her decision was based expressly on a Venetian statute. But was Shylock treated fairly by the court? Portia accepted a gift from Antonio's friends; but this was not necessarily considered to be bribery at the time when the play was written, if – as Bacon told James I a little later – the case was ended and the gift was not related to a previous promise. Portia was, however, biased in favour of Antonio, her husband's friend. The ground on which Portia can be blamed, in Lord Normand's view, is that – although she knew from Bellario's opinion that Shylock's case was bad by statute – she justified her plea for him to show mercy by repeatedly assuring him that he would

[38] E. Douglas Armour, K.C., D.C.L., 'Law and Lawyers in Literature – IV', (1926) 4 *Canadian Bar Review*, 315 (lectures delivered at Osgoode Hall Law School, Toronto).

[39] *Shakespeare's Legal Acquirements Considered*, p. 50. According to Elze, the Doge did not preside after 1367 (New Variorum Edition, 1888, p. 189).

[40] Sir Frederick Pollock, *Essays in the Law* (1922), p. 198.

[41] Lord Normand, 'Portia's Judgment', (1939) 10 *University of Edinburgh Journal*, 43.

succeed if he persisted in his legal rights. Shakespeare makes her do this, of course, in order to keep the audience in suspense. At the end of the play, then, there will be some sympathy for Shylock for his unfair treatment at the hands of a Christian court.

There is support for the view that Portia, deputising for Bellario, is neither judge nor defending counsel but *amicus curiae*; and the common medieval practice of a lay court making use of professional advisers has been likened to the former practice (now obsolescent) of the House of Lords taking the opinion of the Judges.[42] If she were an advocate she would hardly come in and ask: 'which is the merchant here and which the Jew?'[43] On the other hand, it is objected that Portia would be disqualified as a woman from acting as assessor, and anyway the decision would be liable to be set aside on the ground that the assessor was not impartial.[44]

A lawyer and dramatic critic writing under the initials 'E. F. S.' thought that one of the absurdities of the affair was that Portia did come as Judge: the position of arbitrator, as in Fiorentino's story, would have suited her better. The provisional judgment for specific performance was absurd because 'specific performance' was an equitable remedy granted only where the common law remedy of damages was considered inadequate, and it is ridiculous to suppose that a pound of the debtor's flesh was a more adequate remedy than the payment of 3,000 ducats.[45]

Shylock certainly looks on Portia as judge, though he may not have been familiar with whatever legal procedure

[42] 'Portia's Status', (1923) 87 *Justice of the Peace*, 108, 115.

[43] W. A. Dennis, 'Portia as an Exemplar', (1914) 21 *Case and Comment*, 580.

[44] J. B. Mackenzie, 'The Law and Procedure in "The Merchant of Venice" ', (1904) 16 *Green Bag*, 604.

[45] E. F. S., 'Portia as a Judge', *Weekly Westminster Gazette*, 3 February 1923, p. 12.

was operating. 'Most rightful judge!' 'Most learned judge!' he cries:

> A Daniel come to judgment! Yea, a Daniel!
> O wise young judge, how I do honour thee!

Daniel was the young judge in the apocryphal story of Susannah and the Elders. Moelwyn Merchant[46] in his edition of the play suggests that Portia's youthfulness accords better with Daniel than with Solomon, whom Shylock might have been expected to cite; but Portia's methods are very different from those of Solomon, who called the bluff of one of the parties by proposing a compromise.

There has been much discussion[47] on the meaning of 'single' bond in Shylock's statement to Antonio in 1. 8:

> Go with me to a notary, seal me there
> Your single bond: and, in a merry sport,
> If you repay me not on such a day . . .

then he will be entitled to a pound of his flesh. The explanation given by Pollock and Maitland is acceptable: 'Shylock first offers to take a bond without a penalty, and then adds the fantastic penalty of the pound of flesh, ostensibly as a jesting afterthought.[48]

A correspondent in the *Irish Law Times*[49] offers the explanation that a bond stipulates for the payment of a sum, usually double the amount of the debt, which is called the 'penalty'; and the 'condition' of the bond is the relief of the penalty, stipulating that on payment of the debt (not the penalty) the bond shall be void. The 'condition' in Shylock's bond, however, is not in relief of the penalty, but imposes a

---

[46] W. Moelwyn Merchant, *The Merchant of Venice* (New Penguin edn.), p. 201.

[47] See e.g. C. M. Brune, LL.D., D.C.L., *Shakespeare's Use of Legal Terms* (1914), p. 21; E. D. Armour, loc. cit.; T. M. Wears, 'Shakespeare's Legal Acquirements', (1938) 16 *Canadian Bar Review*, 28, 24-41.

[48] Pollock and Maitland, *History of English Law*, II, 225n. This note was probably written by Pollock, or else Maitland wrote it as a result of Pollock's statement.

[49] 'Was Shakespeare a Lawyer?', (1931) 65 *Irish Law Times*, 258, 264.

penalty in the event of default of payment at the specified date. Such a stipulation would be unsustainable in law. Portia therefore was a bad lawyer. She missed the vital point that the bond itself 'is the thing', and that the 'condition' annexed to it is in relief of the penalty, and cannot impose a penalty in default of payment of the bond according to the tenour.

The German legal philosopher, Gustav Radbruch,[50] in his discussion on law and morals, cites Shylock as typifying the case where the fight for right sinks to the level of a naked struggle of interests without any moral background, even to the mere struggle for power of an empty self-righteousness bare of the substance of an interest. Further on Radbruch says:

> We speak of chicane (*der Schikane*) when the right is . . . to be realised for its own sake alone, with no regard to its moral or even utilitarian purposes; and *The Merchant of Venice*, if indeed it is to be mounted upon a philosophical formula after famous models, resembles many another story of the wise judge in showing how the law, contradicting itself in a chicane, restores itself as it were by a counter-chicane — so strong is its inherent moral purposiveness.[51]

A monograph written by an American law student, Mark Edwin Andrews, in 1935 was found nearly thirty years later in a law library, and permission to publish it was obtained in 1965 from the author,[52] who meanwhile had been a law teacher, an industrialist and Assistant Secretary of the United States Navy. Justice Harlan F. Stone of the American Supreme Court, after examining the manuscript in 1937, wrote: 'Often in listening to *The Merchant of Venice*,

[50] Gustav Radbruch, *Rechtsphilosophie* (3rd. ed., Leipzig, 1932), p. 86; translated by Kurt Wilk in *The Legal Philosophies of Lask, Radbruch and Dabin* (1950).

[51] Radbruch, op. cit., p. 136.

[52] M. E. Andrews, *Law versus Equity in 'The Merchant of Venice'* (University of Colorado Press, 1965).

it has occurred to me that Shakespeare knew the essentials of the contemporary conflict between law and equity. But until I read your manuscript I had never realised how completely the play harmonised with recognised court procedure of the time.' The author sees the trial scene in this play as a treatise on the attributes and qualities of mercy, providing a universal moral lesson. Shakespeare was depicting the dramatic climax of the old conflict between the strict justice of the Common Law courts and the equity of the Court of Chancery, the former giving 'judgments' and the latter pronouncing 'decrees'. So Shylock says: 'There is no force in the decrees of Venice. I stand for judgment.' The author cites a somewhat similar case on a bond, *Glanvill v. Courtney* (1615),[53] in which Glanvill had sold to Courtney for £360 a jewel worth £20, and three other jewels for £100, taking a bond for the payment in the name of one Hampton. He then procured an action to be brought on the bond in Hampton's name. Chief Justice Coke gave judgment for Hampton, but an injunction was issued by Lord Chancellor Ellesmere against its enforcement. After the *Earl of Oxford's Case*[54] in the same year, James I appointed Bacon, Attorney-General, to head a Commission to advise him whether the Chancellor had this power, and Bacon advised that he had. Thus Shakespeare not only dramatised the struggle but rightly predicted the victory for equity. Andrews thinks that, just as the dramatist must have been aware of the conflict between the Courts of common law and equity, so this play may have influenced the process of thought leading up to the decision in *Glanvill v. Courtney*, if not the decision itself, and also Bacon's advice to the King on the *Earl of Oxford's Case*. Shylock's property is disposed of under sixteenth-century equitable principles.[55]

---

[53] Cro. Jac. 343. See W. S. Holdsworth, *History of English Law*, I, 461-2.

[54] (1615) 1 Chancery Reports, 1.

[55] A full analysis is given in Andrews op. cit. at pp. 74-5, by Professor William Arthur, of the University of Colorado Law School.

An attempt has been made, in that kind of lighter legal literature that turns real or imaginary historical events into law cases, to write a judgment in a supposed appeal from the decision of Mr Justice Shakespeare to the English Court of Appeal.[56] By the principles of private international law or 'conflict of laws', a contract is presumed to be governed by the *lex loci contractus* (the law of the country where the contract was made), i.e. in this case the mercantile law of Venice, according to which the contract was not illegal; but the judgment is not enforceable in England (by the *lex fori*) because the procedure of the Venetian court infringed the principles of natural justice. No valid defence was raised to the action on the bond, but the penalty clause is not one that an English court would specifically enforce, although relief against the penalty will be granted only on equitable terms. Antonio must repay to Shylock the full amount of the loan, with interest at four per cent per annum from the date of the bond, and costs.

Recent criticism of Portia's conduct of the case has come from an American practitioner, F. Lyman Windolph.[57] Although Portia delivered a homily to Shylock on the subject of mercy, she shows no mercy to him. With regard to the Venetian law concerning an alien seeking the life of any citizen, Shakespeare 'got mixed up about the two halves of Shylock's goods, as he nearly always got mixed up when he had to deal with figures.'[58] In the trial scene the main question is whether Shylock was entitled to a pound of flesh. Injunctions were granted in the Court of Chancery in Shakespeare's time restraining moneylenders from collecting more in judgment debts than the principal and interest at the lawful rate. Equity was more generous than Portia, who refused to

---

[56] A. L. Polak, *More Legal Fictions: A Series of Cases from Shakespeare* (1946), pp. 113 et seq. ('Shylock v. Antonio'). The other 'cases' are not of great interest.

[57] F. L. Windolph, *Reflections on the Law in Literature* (Philadelphia University Press, 1956), pp. 46-57.

[58] Windolph, op cit., p. 51.

let Shylock have even his principal. The later dialogue between Lorenzo and Jessica, however, suggests that we are neither in England nor Italy, but in an enchanted country with an ethical and legal system all its own. For that ardent but dogmatic Baconian, Edward D. Johnson,[59] on the other hand, the trial scene in this play was in exact accordance with the rules of procedure that formerly obtained in the courts of Venice.

Professor Keeton,[60] a leading authority on equity and the history of the Court of Chancery, considers the trial scene largely in terms of the relation between common law and equity, which in Shakespeare's day were still administered in separate courts, and the conflict between whose principles was not settled until the reign of James I. Keeton also suggests other courses of conduct that Antonio might have taken. First, Antonio might have borrowed the money from his friends, and tendered the amount due *before* the day appointed in the bond.[61] (But then, of course, there would have been no trial scene.) It would in Shakespeare's time be too late to tender the debt after that date, even before action commenced. Antonio signed a single bond, with an express condition, not a conditional bond.[62] Secondly, as many legal commentators have suggested, Antonio could have argued that the bond was void as being contrary to public policy. Further, Shylock would have to commit a crime (inflicting grievous bodily harm) in order to exact

[59] E. D. Johnson, *Francis Bacon of St Albans* (1955), p. 45. The author was a Birmingham solicitor.

[60] *Shakespeare's Legal and Political Background*, chap. 9. For a survey on somewhat similar lines, see Maxine MacKay, 'The Merchant of Venice: a Reflection of the Early Conflict Between Courts of Law and Courts of Equity', (1964) 15 *Shakespeare Quarterly*, 371. Dr MacKay, of the English Department of Jacksonville University, is a law graduate of Wayne State University.

[61] This point is missed by Otto Erickson, 'Shakespeare and the Law', (1916) *Law Notes*, 4.

[62] See Keeton, *Shakespeare's Legal and Political Background*, pp. 135-6. This view agrees with F. F. Heard, *Shakespeare as a Lawyer* (Boston, 1883), pp. 67-8, and appears to have been first suggested by W. L. Rushton, *Shakespeare a Lawyer* (1858)

the penalty. Thirdly, Antonio might have tried the defence
of fraudulent misrepresentation, since he only executed the
bond after Shylock had indicated that it would have no
legal significance. The penalty on a common money bond
was fully enforceable at common law, but not necessarily in
equity. The trial scene is in two stages: (*a*) common law
and (*b*) equity. Portia is technically a judge, though she is
far from being unbiased. Indeed, the fact that she was
Bassanio's wife ought by itself to have disqualified her from
hearing the case. She appeals to a Divine law, superior to
human law. The common law cannot help, so she moves to
equity, in which also she is well versed. Portia then follows
the Chancery practice with regard to claiming an estate as
security for a debt: the creditor may take possession, but a
strict account must be rendered of the profits, which must
go in satisfaction of the debt without any further loss to the
debtor's estate. Shylock then falls back on demanding the
principal, being prepared to let the interest go, and begins
to sharpen his knife. It is then, and not until then, that
Portia raises the point of the illegality of the bond. The
criminal attempt by Shylock was not the bringing of the
judicial proceedings, but the attempt to exact the penalty by
force himself. Such an attempt was a felony, and therefore
punishable by death. Another Venetian statute is now revealed which says that, Shylock being an alien, half his
estate shall go not to the State but to Antonio. Shakespeare
ultimately prevents us from feeling too sorry for Shylock
by allowing the Duke to spare his life, and enabling an
adequate fortune to be settled on the romantic couple,
Jessica (Shylock's daughter) and Lorenzo. Antonio is
willing that the half of Shylock's estate to which he is entitled shall be conveyed to him (Antonio) 'to the use of'
Shylock for life and on his death 'to the use of' Lorenzo and
Jessica absolutely. The effect of this conveyance under the
Statute of Uses 1535 would be to vest a life estate in
Shylock, with remainder to the young couple.

That Shylock's harshness goes far to render his defeat dramatically acceptable to modern audiences is the opinion of Lord Simon of Glaisdale,[63] although it is unlikely that Elizabethan audiences would have felt much difficulty in view of the public reaction to the execution of Dr Lopez. Yet Antonio's proposed settlement of the property after judgment certainly contributes to the final effect.[64]

[63] Sir Jocelyn Simon, Q.C., in 84 *Law Quarterly Review*, at p. 40.
[64] A point made in 'Was Shakespeare a Lawyer?' (1871) 6 *Law Journal*, 81.

# 9

## *Criticism of Shakespeare's Law*

Lawyers, as one would expect, have come forward from time to time to consider and explain the legal terms used and the procedure described by Shakespeare in his plays and poems. This may be called 'criticism' in its wider sense. Another kind of criticism has also been indulged in by lawyers, that of judging whether or not Shakespeare's use of legal terms or his treatment of legal problems is 'correct'. The latter activity is often, though not necessarily, related to the question of Shakespeare's legal qualifications discussed below in chapter 12, or the authorship question which is outside the scope of this book.

For the explanation of legal terms the churchyard scene in *Hamlet*, v. 1, has been a rich quarry for the lawyers:

> *Hamlet.* Why may not that be the skull of a lawyer? Where be his quiddities now, his quillets, his cases, his tenures, and his tricks? . . . This fellow might be in's time a great buyer of land, with his statutes, his recognizances, his fines, his double vouchers, his recoveries. . . .

Malone and Steevens in their editions of the text, Rushton and Lord Campbell in their books, and a line of later commentators in books and periodicals have furnished explanations of these various terms, from 'quiddities' (Malone: quiddities, from Middle Latin *quiditas*; Steevens: subtleties) and 'quillets' (Malone: nice and frivolous distinctions) to the technical terms of land law and procedure – 'recognizances', 'fines', 'double vouchers', 'recoveries' and so on. Fines and recoveries were two highly technical methods for the conveyance of land before 1833 by entry on the rolls of the court. The fine (*finalis concordia*) put an end by agreement to an actual or fictitious suit for the possession of land. The common recovery, another collusive lawsuit, was used by tenants in tail for the purpose of barring their entails and conveying the fee simple (the nearest thing to ownership of land in English law), involving at one stage 'vouching to warranty' a third party who was supposed to have warranted the tenant's title, and often a double voucher. Malone said that by 'statutes' here is meant, not Acts of Parliament, but a species of security for money affecting real property, and Ritson[1] suggested that they were statutes merchant and staple. This was repeated by Heard,[2] who gives it the same meaning in Sonnet 134:

> The statute of thy beauty thou wilt take,
> Thou usurer, that putt'st forth all to use,
> And sue a friend came debtor for my sake.

Sir Arthur Underhill,[3] pointing out that statutes and recognisances have no evident connection with the buying of land, reminds us that the words are spoken by a gravedigger. 'Is not parchment made of sheepskins?' Hamlet asks a little later. 'Ay, my lord', Horatio answers, 'and of calfskins too.' Then, replies Hamlet, 'They are sheep, and calves, which seek out assurance in that.' Deeds, which were usually written on parchment, were called common assurances. Malone pointed out the intended pun.

First after the early lawyer-editors of Shakespeare (discussed in the next chapter) we have the youthful Rushton's little book *Shakespeare a Lawyer*, published in 1858. Among his numerous explanations of legal terms found in Shake-

---

[1] Joseph Ritson, *Remarks, Critical and Illustrative, on the Text and Notes of the Last Edition of Shakespeare* (1783).

[2] F. F. Heard, *Shakespeare as a Lawyer* (Boston, 1883), p. 61. And see W. L. Rushton, *Shakespeare a Lawyer* (1858), pp. 7-11.

[3] In *Shakespeare's England*, I, 406.

speare's works, we may take the following as being less obvious examples.[4]

Rushton drew attention to the double meanings – legal and ordinary – in these lines from *Hamlet*, v. 1:

> Is this the fine of his fines, and the recovery of his re-coveries, to have his fine pate full of fine dirt? . . . The very conveyance of his lands will hardly lie in this box. . . .

Hamlet likened a grave to a box because conveyancers and their attorneys kept their deeds in boxes. The *fine* of his fines means the *end* of his penalties. And his pate is filled, not with fine dirt, but with the *last* dirt that will ever occupy it, leaving a satirical inference to be drawn that even in his lifetime his head was filled with dirt.

When Othello says he will tell the Duke and the Senators with 'What conjuration, and what mighty magic' he won Brabantio's daughter (*Othello*, I. 3), Shakespeare was following closely the statute 33 Henry VIII, cap. 8 (1541-2), against conjuration, witchcraft, enchantment, sorcery and provoking any person to unlawful love.

The difference in English land law between a 'remainder', which on the termination ('determination') of a previous estate will go to a third person, and a 'reversion' which will return to the grantor himself, is explained with reference to such passages as:

> *Parolles.* For a quart d'écu he will . . . cut the entail from
>          all remainders. . . .
>
> > (*All's Well*, IV. 3)

and:

> *Queen.* 'Tis in reversion that I do possess.
>
> > (*Richard II*, II. 2)

The description of an individual in a legal document, e.g. esquire, gentleman or yeoman, was called his 'addition'. So when Lear divests himself of all his property and kingly

---

[4] *Shakespeare a Lawyer*, pp. 5-46.

power, he says: 'Only we retain The name and all th' addition to a king' (*King Lear*, I. I).

'Widowhood' formerly meant the estate settled on a widow, with which a dowager was endowed. In *The Taming of the Shrew*, II. I, Petruchio asks what dowry will be provided if he wins the love of Baptista's daughter. So on receiving a satisfactory promise, Petruchio replies:

> And, for that dowry, I'll assure her of
> Her widowhood, be it that she survive me.

Later in the same scene, when Baptista says to Tranio:

> I must confess your offer is the best;
> And, let your father make her the assurance,
> She is your own;

he seems to refer to dowment by the father's assent (dower *ex assensu patris*). Whereas in IV. 4, of the same play, when Biondello says to Lucentio, 'they are busied about counterfeit assurance. Take you assurance of her, *cum privilegio ad imprimendum solum*: to the church; — take the priest, clerk, and some sufficient honest witnesses', he seems to refer to dowment at the church door (*dower ad ostium ecclesiae*).

'Replication' in common law pleading was the plaintiff's reply to the defendant's answer. So Hamlet asks: 'What replication should be made by the son of a king?'

*Hamlet*. For who would bear the whips and scorns of
time,
> The oppressor's wrong, the proud man's
contumely,
> The pangs of dispriz'd love, the law's delay,
> The insolence of office, and the spurns
> That patient merit of the unworthy takes,
> When he himself might his quietus make
> With a bare bodkin?

(III. I)

'Quietus' means freed or acquitted, and was used by the Clerk of the Pipe (the Great Roll of the Exchequer) and auditors in the Exchequer, in their discharges given to those who rendered account, which usually concluded with the words: *Abinde recessit quietus*, generally termed a *Quietus est*.

Prince Hal accuses the red-faced Bardolph: 'O villain! thou stolest a cup of sack eighteen years ago, and wert taken with the manner, and ever since thou hast blushed extempore'. The old law phrase, 'to be taken as a thief with the mainour' (old French *manoevre*, *meinor*; Latin *a manu*), signifies to be taken in the very act of stealing venison or wood, or being taken with the thing stolen in one's hands or possession.

Duke Frederick in *As You Like It*, III. 7, tells his officers to 'Make an extent upon his house and lands'. The writ of 'extent' directed the sheriff to seize and value lands and goods of a judgment debtor to the utmost extent, and execution of judgment under the statute of 1532 concerning recognisances for debt was called an 'extent'.

Further explanations of legal expressions will be found in Rushton's later books. From *Shakespeare Illustrated by Old Authors* (1867-8) we may take these examples. York's epithet 'Base dunghill villain' (*2 Henry VI*, I. 3) is not pointless vituperation, for a typical service to be performed by a villein for the lord of the manor was to carry and spread dung. Although Glanvill in the twelfth century called judicial officers *Justitii*, Bracton in the thirteenth century changed the word in writs of commission to *Justiciarii*, hence Lear's 'Justicers' in:

Come, sit thou here, most learned justicer.

False justicer, why hast thou let her scape?
(*King Lear*, III. 6)

Dogberry asks the watch whether they are 'good men and true', and afterwards tells them: 'You are thought here to be

123

the most senseless and fit men for the constable of the watch'
(*Much Ado*, III. 3). The common law required a constable
to be *idoneus homo*, apt and fit to execute his office.

Obscure passages may be explained in the light of early
statutes, for example:

> *Gadshill.* I am joined with . . . no longstaff sixpenny
> strikers . . . ; but with nobility and tranquillity,
> burgomasters and great *oneyers* such as can hold
> in, such as will strike sooner than speak.
>
> (*1 Henry IV*, II. 1)

Statutes of Edward VI provided for the punishment of
cutting off one ear for maliciously striking any person in
a churchyard; and if the offender should have *none ears* he
was to be branded. Later statutes dealt with the offence
of cutting off another's ear or ears. 'Oneyers' is therefore
probably a misprint for 'one ears'.[5]

Next comes the septuagenarian Lord Campbell, Chief
Justice, with his *Shakepeare's Legal Acquirements Considered*,[6]
which was published in 1859 and owed much to the notes
of Malone, Steevens and other Shakespeare editors. The
context of the passage in which Dromio of Syracuse says
to Adriana: 'he is 'rested on the case' (*Comedy of Errors*,
IV. 2) is explained as a graphic account of an English arrest
by a sheriff's officer on mesne process (i.e. before judgment)
in an action on the case for the price of a gold chain. In the
second scene of the Induction to *The Taming of the Shrew*,
the First Servant tries to persuade Sly that he threatened to
present the hostess to the leet 'Because she brought stone
jugs and no seal'd quarts'; this would be understood as a
reference to the statute against false measures by which ale
should be sold only in sealed vessels of standard capacity,
concerning which Malone cited the well-known treatise
*Kitchen on Courts*. Henry IV says that Richard II 'Enfeoffed

---

[5] W. L. Rushton, *Shakespeare Illustrated by the Lex Scripta* (1870).

[6] The examples given here are taken from pp. 39 et seq.

himself to popularity' (*2 Henry IV*, III. 2), and Malone explained that this meant he gave himself up absolutely to popularity, feoffment with livery of seisin being the method of conveying a fee simple until 1630.

Sir William Gascoigne's use of the apparently vulgar expression to Falstaff, 'To punish you by the heels would amend the attention of your ears' (*2 Henry IV*, I. 2), is justified by the fact that 'to lay by the heels' was the technical expression for committing to prison (putting in irons or in the stocks).[7] Lord Campbell cites a petition heard in the Court of Chancery before Lord Chancellor Jeffreys against a great city attorney who had given him many briefs at the Bar, and who, threatened with being brought before the Lord Chancellor, exclaimed: 'My Lord Chancellor! I made him.' On hearing this Jeffreys said: 'Then I will lay my maker by the heels', and issued a warrant of commitment under which the attorney was sent off to the Fleet prison.

Gloster says to Edmund, his illegitimate son:

> of my land,
> Loyal and natural boy, I'll work the means
> To make thee capable.
>
> (*King Lear*, II. 1)

In forensic discussions about legitimacy, the question was whether the person concerned was 'capable', i.e. capable of inheriting. So Gloster was considering ways of legitimising Edmund. Later Edmund says of Cornwall: 'If I find him comforting the King, it will stuff his suspicion more fully' (III. 5). Dr Johnson noted that the word 'comforting' was used in the legal sense for supporting or helping; and Lord Campbell added that an indictment against an accessory after the fact for treason charged that the accessory 'comforted' the principal traitor after knowledge of the treason.

[7] cf. Sir Dunbar Plunket Barton, *Links between Shakespeare and the Law*, p. 103.

In *Hamlet*, I. I, Marcellus asks: 'Why such impress of shipwrights?' This passage has been quoted, both by text-writers and by Judges on the Bench, as an authority on the legality of the press gang, and on the debated question whether shipwrights as well as common seamen were liable to be pressed into the navy.

Lepidus says of Antony:

> His faults in him seem as the spots of heaven,
> More fiery by night's blackness; hereditary
> Rather than purchas'd.
>
> (*Antony and Cleopatra*, I. 4)

The distinction between inheritance or descent and 'purchase' as modes of acquiring property — brought out also in Henry IV's speech to Prince Hal in *2 Henry IV*, IV. 3 — is amusingly illustrated (except that 'purchase' is not confined to buying) by two stories told by Lord Campbell. A Law Lord who suffered much from hereditary gout, although very temperate in his habits, said: 'I take it by descent, not by purchase'. On another occasion Lord Chancellor Eldon, a very bad shot, went out to shoot alone and boasted that he had brought home a heavy bag. Lord Stowell (his judicial brother), insinuating that Eldon had filled it with game bought from a poacher, remarked: 'My brother took his game not by descent, but by purchase.'

The central imagery of two of the Sonnets is entirely legal. In Sonnet 46 ('Mine eye and heart are at a mortal war'), a lover is supposed to have made a conquest of (i.e. to have gained by purchase) his mistress: his eye and his heart, holding as joint-tenants, have a contest as to how the fair lady is to be partitioned between them — each moiety then to be held in severalty. There are pleadings as in an action for partition of land between co-owners, the heart being represented as plaintiff and the eye as defendant. Issue is joined, and a jury (in the nature of an inquest of thoughts that are tenants to the heart) is impanelled to decide. By their verdict the lady's outward beauty is apportioned to the eye, and her inward love is allotted to the heart. This has been commented on by Lord Campbell and others,[8] but Clarkson and Warren have also enquired into its more obscure allusions to common law pleading and practice.[9] Elsewhere these learned authors admit that the amazing feature of this Sonnet is not Shakespeare's knowledge of English legal procedure, but that imagery of such far-fetched extravagance could ever have been popular.[10]

Indeed, a Canadian lawyer writing in 1863[11] found much to criticise in the poet's use of legal terms in Sonnet 46. First, Shakespeare calls the allegation of the Heart the 'plea' instead of the 'declaration'. Then the case is represented as a *real* action, though it does not relate to real property. The plaintiff is not (as he should be) a demandant complaining of disseisin, but avers that he already has that for which he brings the action. The jury consists of the 'tenants to the heart'; but, apart from the fact that a 'tenant' was the defendant in a real action, these tenants derive title from and are the party identical in interest with the plaintiff. Lastly, the verdict is only applicable to a suit for partition, and is not relevant to the issue framed.

Another Sonnet whose imagery is entirely legal is No. 134 ('So now I have confess'd that he is thine'). The poet says he has mortgaged himself to a friend, and as a collateral security has executed a bond with a surety. He forfeits the estate to the mortgagee, and his surety is sued for the debt. Thus he finds himself in default to both

[8] e.g. Lord Campbell, *Shakespeare's Legal Acquirements Considered*, pp. 102-3; Barton, *Links between Shakespeare and the Law*, pp. 13-14.

[9] P. S. Clarkson and C. T. Warren, 'Pleading and Practice in Shakespeare's Sonnet XLVI', *Modern Language Notes*, vol. 62 (1947), p. 102.

[10] P. S. Clarkson and C. T. Warren, *The Law of Property in Shakespeare and the Elizabethan Drama* (Baltimore, 1942), p. 170.

[11] R. P. Fuller, 'Shakespeare as a Lawyer', (1863) 9 *Upper Canada Law Journal*, 91, 95.

friend and surety: 'He pays the whole, and yet I am not free.' It has been suggested[12] that if 'write' in line 7 ('He learn'd but surety-like to write for me') is taken as 'underwrite' the lines acquire a significance different from that propounded by Dr A. L. Rowse,[13] who says that Shakespeare tells us he got his young friend to write to her on his behalf.

The question has been raised whether copyhold tenure is alluded to in the following lines:

*Macbeth.*     Thou know'st that Banquo, and his Fleance, lives.
*Lady Macbeth.* But in them Nature's copy's not eterne.

(III. 2)

Clarkson and Warren,[14] after reviewing the state of the law with regard to copyholds, the context of the passage, the use of the word 'copy' by other dramatists and by Shakespeare himself elsewhere, conclude that Shakespeare was not alluding here to copyhold tenure. Copyholds in Shakespeare's day were not terminable at the will of the lord; they were held according to the custom of the manor and were protected in the King's Courts. If Shakespeare were alluding to an inherent uncertainty of the duration of copyhold tenure, then his usage would be unique in Elizabethan drama and uniquely wrong. In Macbeth's time, shortly before the Norman conquest, copyhold tenure did not exist. The copyhold interpretation is not confirmed by the contrasting passage: 'our high plac'd Macbeth Shall live the

---

[12] S. M. Gibson, 'Shakespeare in the Sonnets', (1964) 61 *Law Society's Gazette*, 23. Mr Gibson is mistaken in saying that allusions and images derived from English law are rare in Elizabethan poetry, especially if we include sonnets and poetic drama.

[13] A. L. Rowse, *William Shakespeare, A Biography* (1963), p. 191.

[14] P. S. Clarkson and C. T. Warren, 'Copyhold Tenure and *Macbeth*, III, ii, 38', in vol. 55 *Modern Language Notes* (1940), 483, at pp. 490-93. This article is included in their book, *The Law of Property in Shakespeare and the Elizabethan Drama*, (Baltimore, 1942), which is mentioned in chapter 11.

lease of nature' (IV. 1); and in any case that interpretation would not fit the passage, because Nature (not Macbeth) would be the lord.

Henry V claims the French throne 'by gift of heaven, By law of nature and of nations' (*Henry V*, II. 4); and Hector, speaking of the captured Helen, says:

> 'these moral laws
> Of nature and of nations, speak aloud
> To have her back return'd'.
>
> (*Troilus and Cressida*, II. 2)

We also find references to the laws of war in *Henry V* when Bardolph is to be executed for robbing a French church (III. 6), and the King orders reprisals against prisoners for the attack by French soldiers on the English baggage, which was guarded only by boys (IV. 7). The use of the expression 'the law of nations' with its modern meaning of international law gained currency during the sixteenth century. Shakespeare did not take it from Holinshed. *Henry V* was written in 1599, and a lawyer is tempted to detect the influence, however indirect, of Alberico Gentile, perhaps the greatest of the forerunners of Grotius. Gentile was an Italian protestant who came to England in 1580. He knew Leicester, the Chancellor of Oxford University, and was appointed Reader and then in 1587 Regius Professor of Civil Law at Oxford by Walsingham. In 1600 he became a member of Gray's Inn and began forensic practice, his academic duties at Oxford being discharged by a deputy. His chief work, *De Jure Belli Libri Tres*, dedicated to Essex, was published in 1589. Other publications on the laws of war, some translated from the French, followed in its wake.[15]

---

[15] See Coleman Phillipson's introduction to Alberico Gentile, *De Jure Belli Libri Tres*, vol. II, translated by John C. Rolfe (1933). These publications included *Instructions for the warres* (1589); *Discourse of law and single combat* (1591); Matthew Sutcliffe, 'The practise, proceedings and lawes of armes' (1593, dedicated to the Earl of Essex).

Also, Hooker in his *Ecclesiastical Polity*, first published in 1594, says:

> there is a third kind of law which toucheth all such
> several bodies politic, so far forth as one of them hath
> public commerce with another. And this third is the Law
> of Nations. . . . Primary laws of nations are such as con-
> cern embassage. . . . Secondary laws in the same kind
> are such as this present unquiet world is most familiarly
> acquainted with, I mean laws of arms, which yet are much
> better known than kept.[16]

At any rate, Shakespeare's source does not appear to have
been the *Chronicles*, although there is a reference to the 'law
of nations' as early as the first edition of Hall's *Chronicles*
in 1548.[17] With regard to Hector's words, the editor of
the Third Variorum edition does not think the reference
to Gentile is proved;[18] first, because the terms 'laws of
nature and of nations' were too common in the sixteenth
century to require accounting; and secondly because,
whereas Gentile identified *ius naturae* and *ius gentium*,
Hector distinguishes them in the preceding lines:

> If this law
> Of Nature be corrupted through affection, . . .
> There is a Law in each well-order'd Nation,
> To curb those raging appetites.

Keeton's opinion is that *ius gentium* in this play is not international law in the modern sense, but the custom observed
among the Greek states.[19]

Judge Phelps[20] of Baltimore, a practising and academic

[16] Hooker, *Ecclesiastical Polity*, Bk. I, s. 10.

[17] Hall, *Chronicles*, Edw. IV, 229.

[18] *Troilus and Cressida* (New Variorum, ed. Harold N. Hillebrand, 1953),
p. 108n.

[19] *Shakespeare's Legal and Political Background*, p. 71.

[20] Charles Henry Phelps, *Falstaff and Equity: An Interpretation* (Boston, 1901).
He was Professor of Law at the University of Maryland, Judge of the Supreme
Bench of Baltimore, and author of *Juridical Equity*.

expert on equity, wrote that the word 'equity' occurs only four times in Shakespeare's works, and each time with a different meaning. First, equity means justice in the Biblical sense:

> Foul subornation is predominant,
> And equity exiled in your highness' land.
> > (*2 Henry VI*, iii. 1)

Secondly, equity is used in the technical sense as meaning the equity of the Court of Chancery:

> Thou robed man of justice, take thy place,
> And thou, his yoke-fellow of equity,
> Bench by his side.
> > (*King Lear*, iii. 6)

Thirdly, equity is used figuratively for an equitable right or cause of action:

> For this down-trodden equity we tread
> In warlike march these greens before your town.
> > (*King John*, ii. 1)

Judge Phelps's book is a monograph on the fourth passage, the words of Falstaff at the climax of the Gadshill incident: 'An the Prince and Poins be not two arrant cowards, there's no equity stirring' (*1 Henry IV*, ii. 2). He thinks that 'equity' is used here in all three senses, the second with a twofold application. The first sense was the previously accepted meaning, but it may be questioned whether it is applicable here. For the rest, the war between the courts of common law and equity was a burning controversy at the time when the play was published in 1598.

In *Throckmorton v. Finch* (1597)[21] Throckmorton, who appears to have been related to the Ardens, having lost an action in the common law courts concerning title to land, filed a bill for relief in Chancery. Queen Elizabeth, who on this occasion had special reason to favour the common law

[21] Co. Inst. 124; 4 Co. Inst. 86.

decision, intimated to Lord Chancellor Ellesmere that the case should be referred to all the judges. The case occupied the judges during the latter part of 1597, and they eventually decided that after judgment at law the party could not be relieved in equity. This was three months before *1 Henry IV* was entered at Stationers' Hall. In *Mylward v. Weldon* (1597)[22] Lord Chancellor Ellesmere made an order punishing the scrivener, Richard Mylward, for 'the inordinate length and prolixity of his replication'. The order was that the warden of the Fleet should cut a hole in the engrossed replication, put Mylward's head through the hole and lead him round the courts in Westminster Hall. The Chancery suit *Shakespeare v. Lambert* was also pending 1597. This suit was for the redemption of a mortgage on Mary Arden's maiden property, the family estate Asbies, against her brother-in-law. John and Mary Shakespeare filed a new bill in equity nine days after the decision of the judges was announced in *Throckmorton v. Finch*. In Falstaff's reference to 'equity stirring', Judge Phelps concludes, Shakespeare has one meaning for posterity and for all time; two other meanings for his immediate audience, for stage effect, and for contemporaries; and still another meaning for Shakespeare himself, his family, his friends, and his Stratford neighbours.

Sometimes knowledge of the law of Shakespeare's time is useful, or even essential, for understanding the plot. Marriage pre-contract underlies much of the plot in *Measure for Measure*, and the confusion between the statements made by Friar Ludowick and the Duke as to whether pre-contract involved the right of marital cohabitation had been seen to reflect the confusion in English law on the subject from the twelfth to the mid-eighteenth centuries.[23]

---

[22] The case is referred to in Lord Campbell's *Lives of the Lord Chancellors*, vol. II, chap. 47; Spence, *Equitable Jurisdiction in Chancery* (1846), vol. I, p. 376.
[23] 'Shakespeare and the Law of Marriage', *Contemporary Review*, November 1911, pp. 733-7.

In Sir Arthur Underhill's view[24] pre-contract (*verba de praesenti*) constituted a valid marriage, so that Angelo's condemnation of Claudio for alleged fornication was, and was intended by Shakespeare to be, absolutely tyrannical and illegal. Another view is that Claudio seduced his betrothed Juliet, which was a technical breach of law in England as in Vienna. Although their formal union had not been completed because there was a dispute about dower, a betrothal was regarded as almost equivalent to marriage and neither party was free to marry another.[25] Shakespeare gives examples of informal marriage by simple consent (*per verba de praesenti*) in the conversation between Biondello, Lucentio and Bianca in *The Taming of the Shrew*, IV. 4; also in Regan's declaration of marriage with Edmund, and an ironical comment on the doctrine of pre-contract in the last scene of *King Lear*. Formal marriage after publishing of banns, mentioned twice in *The Taming of the Shrew*, is referred to in *1 Henry IV*, IV. 2, where Falstaff collects money by releasing men pressed for the King's service, seizing on 'contracted bachelors, such as had been asked twice in the banns'. Marriage *per verba de futuro*, or troth, is indicated in *Henry V*, II. 1, when Nym says to Bardolph of Falstaff: 'It is certain, corporal, that he is married to Nell Quickly; and certainly she did you wrong; for you were troth-plight to her.'[26]

There are references to 'divorce' in *Henry VIII*, although that play raises the question of nullity. When Queen Margaret says to Henry VI, 'I here divorce myself, Both from thy table, Henry, and thy bed' (*3 Henry VI*, I. 1) she is referring to divorce *a mensa et toro*. The term 'divorce' is used loosely in *Richard II* for the separation between the King and Queen; but Desdemona uses the term in a rather

[24] *Shakespeare's England*, I, pp. 407-8.

[25] cf. Ernest Schanzer, 'The Marriage-Contracts in *Measure for Measure*', 13 *Shakespeare Survey* (1960), 81.

[26] 'Shakespeare and the Law of Marriage', *supra*.

more technical sense when she says she fears that Othello will 'shake her off to beggarly divorcement' (*Othello*, IV. 2).

With regard to Mariana's right to dower on Angelo's death for treason (*Measure for Measure*, v. 1), Shakespeare gets the subtle point of law right, apparently by accident.[27] Down to the reign of Edward VI a widow was not protected against escheat of the property on the husband's treason or felony. A statute of 1549 provided that in the case of felony escheat should not affect the widow's dower, but this did not apply to high or petit treason, Angelo's offence being the latter.

For adverse criticism of Shakespeare's law we have already quoted Fuller's comments on Sonnet 46. Lord Campbell[28] points out that, although the main plot of *All's Well* is from Boccaccio, the wardship of Bertram is English common law; and he asks whether Bertram might not have refused to marry Helen (II. 3) on the ground that she was not of noble descent, for Coke upon Littleton states that a lord could not 'disparage' his ward by *mésalliance*. Again, a lawyer might object that the condition about the caskets in the will of Portia's father would be void as being 'in restraint of marriage.'[29]

Maria's remark: 'My lips are no common, though several they be' (*Love's Labour's Lost*, II. 1), Underhill pointed out,[30] contains two technical errors: (i) What is common or several is not the lips but the right to kiss them; and (ii) 'though' should be 'but' as the right cannot be both common and several. That Shakespeare was aware of the distinction be-

<hr />

[27] ibid. Greenwood suggests on the contrary that the passage may indicate the dramatist's knowledge of law: *Is There a Shakespeare Problem?* pp. 98-101.

[28] *Shakespeare's Legal Acquirements Considered*, p. 58.

[29] E. F. S., 'Portia as a Judge', *Weekly Westminster Gazette*, 3 February 1923, p. 12.

[30] Underhill, op. cit., I, pp. 382-3. Maria's remark has also been commented on by Kohler, *Shakespeare vor dem Forum der Jurisprudenz*, p. 244, and Ravà, op. cit., p. 26.

tween these two terms, however, seems to be indicated by Sonnet 137:

> Why should my heart think that a several plot
> Which my heart knows the world's wide common place.[31]

Criticism of this kind may be carping, such as the objection that the word 'date' in 'summer's lease hath all too short a date' is not accurately used, as it signifies commencement and not continuance.[32]

Such criticism also has often been misguided. Thus it has been objected that the Queen in *Richard III*, iv. 4, uses 'demise' of honours; Hamlet uses 'replication' as meaning reply (*Hamlet*, iv. 4), which strictly was the plaintiff's answer to the defendant's plea; Thaliard in *Pericles*, i. 3, says 'he is bound by the indenture of his oath'; in *The Comedy of Errors*, v. 2, Dromio of Syracuse says: 'he's 'rested on the case'; and Antony says that Caesar has 'left' all his walls, arbours and orchards on this side Tiber 'to you And to your heirs forever' (*Julius Caesar*, iii. 2), when he should have said 'devised' and omitted 'to your heirs forever'. But these criticisms ignore the supposed place and time of the action, the persons by whom and to whom the words are spoken, and the dramatic effect intended.[33]

There is what we may call a 'conflict of laws in time and place' involved in the study of Shakespeare's law. If we want to consider whether Shakespeare's use of legal expressions in the plays is 'correct', assuming that question to be meaningful, we must ask what legal system (if any) is appropriate. This will depend on the place and the period

---

[31] Rushton, *Shakespeare a Lawyer* (1858), p. 39.

[32] R. F. Fuller, 'Shakespeare as a Lawyer' (1863), 9 *Upper Canada Law Journal*, 91, at p. 95.

[33] See H. B. Sprague, 'Shakespeare's Alleged Blunders in Legal Terminology', (1902) 11 *Yale Law Journal*, 304, replying mainly to Devecmon. Sir George Greenwood in *Shakespeare's Law* (1920) replies to Judge Allen's chapter on 'Bad Law in Shakespeare' in *Notes on the Bacon-Shakespeare Question* (Boston, 1900), arguing that the law was good from the Elizabethan point of view.

in which the action is supposed to be laid. Many legal writers have fallen down on this, by assuming that the law — whatever its context — ought to be what English law was in Shakespeare's time. Where it is relevant, this is a question on which legal historians and comparative lawyers might be most helpful. With regard to the references in the preceding paragraph, the words from *Pericles* were spoken by a lord of Antioch at Ephesus some centuries before the Christian era, and those from *The Comedy of Errors* by a clown in Ephesus a thousand or more years ago. Amleth, Prince of Jutland, is thought to have lived centuries before Shakespeare. And in *Timon of Athens* was Shakespeare thinking of Timon's indebtedness in terms of English law, Greek law, Roman law, or any particular legal system at all?

This question of what legal system governs the case has been raised with regard to Ophelia's funeral. In a study of the ecclesiastical law in *Hamlet*, Guernsey[34] states the general rule of English law that there is a presumption in favour of the *lex fori*, i.e. that the law of England applies whatever the country in which the case arises, unless the contrary is shown by proof; and that the law has always been the same as at present unless some reason appears to the contrary. *Hamlet* was written for an English audience and to be performed in England: Hamlet himself is supposed to be living in England at the time the play was produced. It is more likely, however, as Professor Dover Wilson suggests,[35] that the reason for the 'maimed rites' was theatrical convenience. The Priest thinks it was *felo-de-se*, but that 'great' (i.e. royal) command has persuaded the coroner to bring in a verdict of Christian burial. The Grave-diggers think it was *se offendendo*, and that it is because she is a gentlewoman that she is receiving Christian burial. The dramatist probably chose a Protestant (Anglican)

---

[34] R. S. Guernsey, *Ecclesiastical Law in Hamlet: The Burial of Ophelia* (New York, 1885), p. 49.

[35] J. Dover Wilson, *What Happens in 'Hamlet'* (Cambridge, 1935), App. B.

funeral because he wanted a simple procession without ceremony.

Then, if we want to consider what light a legal reference may throw on Shakespeare the man, there is the question whether Shakespeare himself wrote the passage, for example, in *Pericles* or *Timon*. On this problem, lawyers are not competent to speak.

There is the further question, how far was Shakespeare merely following his sources? The intensive study of Shakespeare's sources still continues among literary historians, and the fruits will be found in the collections of sources edited by Geoffrey Bullough and Kenneth Muir, and in recent editions of the texts. Few legal critics since Malone have had the equipment to tackle this problem, even where it occurred to them.

Let us take Antony's speech about Caesar's will (*Julius Caesar*, III. 2):

> *Antony.* Here is the will and under Caesar's seal.
> To every Roman citizen he gives,
> To every several man, seventy-five drachmas. . . .
>
> Moreover, he hath left you all his walks,
> His private arbours, and new-planted orchards,
> On this side Tiber; he hath left them you,
> And to your heirs for ever. . . .

Greenwood was willing to justify the expression 'and to your heirs for ever' as dramatic oratory;[36] and Homer B. Sprague[37] called the omission of 'devise' and the insertion of the heirs felicitous rather than unfortunate. What did Shakespeare find in his sources? North's *Plutarch* in the *Life of Julius Caesar* merely says: 'But when they had opened Caesar's testament, and found a liberall legacie of money

---

[36] Sir George Greenwood, *Shakespeare's Law.*
[37] Homer B. Sprague, loc. cit.

bequeathed unto every citizen of Rome. ...'[38] The *Life of Marcus Brutus* is much fuller: 'Caesar's testament was openly red amonge them, whereby it appeared that he bequeathed unto every Citizen of Rome, 75 Drachmas a man, and that he left his gardens and arbors unto the people, which he had on this side of the river Tyber.'[39] From Suetonius' *History of the Twelve Caesars* we get: 'He bequeathed in his legacies unto the people his hortyards about Tiberis to be common; and three hundred Sesterces to them by the Poll.'[40] It will be seen how closely North's translation of Plutarch's *Brutus* is followed here, with two emphatic (but strictly redundant) additions: 'To every several man,' and 'he hath left them you, And to your heirs for ever.' Again, it has been observed[41] that the Duke of Suffolk in addressing Wolsey about praemunire (*Henry VIII*, III. 2) mentions forfeiture before outlawry, following Holinshed, whereas Coke would put outlawry before forfeiture.

Sir Frederick Pollock for one was aware of these problems. In his correspondence about fifty years ago with Justice O. W. Holmes, of the American Supreme Court, he referred more than once to questions of sources and texts. 'Some really dull stuff is not Shakespeare at all', he explains to Holmes,[42] 'but the residual *corpus vile* of older plays which he either patched up (as *King Henry VI*) or recast (as *King John*). . . . Then in the historical plays there are chunks of versified chronicle (e.g. opening of *Henry V*), mistakes and all.' And of *Troilus and Cressida* he writes[43] that the 'depreciation of the Greek heroes merely follows

---

[38] Geoffrey Bullough, *Narrative and Dramatic Sources of Shakespeare*, vol. V (1964), p. 87.

[39] ibid., pp. 104-5.

[40] ibid., p. 155 (transl. Philemon Holland, 1606).

[41] F. F. Heard, *Shakespeare as a Lawyer* (Boston, 1883), pp. 19-21. The reference is to Co. I Inst. 129b.

[42] *The Pollock-Holmes Letters* (ed. Howe, 2 vols., Cambridge University Press, 1942), letter dated 10 Sept. 1922; vol. II, pp. 101-3.

[43] Letter dated 24 Feb. 1925; ibid., II, 154.

medieval romances.' On the matter of texts, Pollock says:[44]

> it is to be remembered that the text we read in modern editions is (except where the first Folio is the sole ultimate authority) a conflation of the folio and quarto texts and therefore does not represent, as it stands, any Shakespearean acting copy. . . . As to corruption and emendations, no one who is acquainted with the general carelessness of 16th-17th century printers, not to mention the scribes of prompt copies, will doubt that the corruption is extensive. . . .

Holmes took a somewhat austere New England attitude: 'the only edition of Shakespeare seems to me that which reproduces the folio first and notes the variations.'[45] In 1906 he had admitted that 'Whenever I read S. I am struck with the reflection how a few golden sentences will float a lot of quibble and drool for centuries, e.g. Benedick and Beatrice';[46] and twenty years later he was still bothered by the triumph of poetry or rhetoric over dramatic sense.[47]

Lord Simon of Glaisdale[48] also warns us that, since Shakespeare generally followed his sources closely, it is unsafe to assume that a given speech or image represents the dramatist's own view. Although the prominence given to Menenius in *Coriolanus* has no authority in North's *Plutarch*, yet it is an example of Shakespeare's practice of introducing a neutral character with whom the audience could readily identify itself, a *punctus indifferens* or Greek chorus – for example, Kent, Enobarbus, Horatio and Alcibiades. On the other hand, says Lord Simon, when in *Julius Caesar*, III. 3, the dramatist makes the citizens kill Cinna the poet although

---

[44] Letter dated 19 Sept. 1922; ibid., II, 102-3.

[45] Letter dated 9 Aug. 1926; ibid., II, 188.

[46] Letter dated 6 Sept. 1906; ibid., I, 134.

[47] See letters dated 24 Nov. 1923 and 10 Feb. 1925; ibid., II, 125 and II, 152-3.

[48] Sir Jocelyn Simon, Q.C., 'Shakespeare's Legal and Political Background', (1968) 84 *Law Quarterly Review*, 33, at pp. 41-2.

they know he is not Cinna the conspirator, whereas in North's *Plutarch* they believe him to be the conspirator, we may take this as an indication of Shakespeare's own attitude towards direct action by the mob.

A lawyer may occasionally suggest a worthwhile emendation. One H. T.,[49] for example, blaming the printers of *Measure for Measure* for printing nonsense through their ignorance of law, suggested that in 1. 2, sense could be made of Lucio's 'I had as lief have the foppery of freedom as the morality of imprisonment', if we substituted 'frippery' for 'foppery' and 'reality' for 'morality'; and we could make sense of Claudio's 'propagation' of a dower if we read 'procuration'.

[49] (H.) T., *Was Shakespeare a Lawyer?* (1871), p. 5.

# I O

## *Lawyers' Contributions to Shakespeare Studies*

In surveying the contribution made by lawyers to Shake-speare studies pride of place must be given in this chapter to six legally trained editors of Shakespeare's works who, abandoning the practice of the law, helped to lay the foundations of Shakespeare scholarship.

Nicholas Rowe entered the Middle Temple in 1691, but after his father's death devoted himself to literature. He brought out the first critical edition of Shakespeare's plays in 1709, suggesting a number of useful emendations and inserting lists of *dramatis personae*. The fact that Rowe was himself a dramatist helped him to complete the division of the plays into acts and scenes. He prefaced the plays with the first formal *Life* of Shakespeare, based largely on infor-mation passed on to him by the actor, Betterton, and reporting the tradition that Shakespeare's first performance as an actor was the Ghost in his own *Hamlet*. The second edition in 1714 included the Poems.

Lewis Theobald became an attorney, but finding the law distasteful he abandoned it for literature. His edition of Shakespeare (1773) was the third, and followed his *Shake-speare Restored* (1726) in which he exposed the deficiencies of Pope's edition of 1725, thus becoming, as Tibbald, the original hero of *The Dunciad*. Theobald was the first to draw attention to such sources as the plays preceding *Henry V* and *King Lear*, Holinshed's *Chronicles* and North's *Plutarch*. His famous emendation, 'a' babbled of green fields' (*Henry V*, II. 3), is said by a medical expert to give a perfect clinical picture of Falstaff's death by typhoid or other fever.[1] Malone decried Theobald's scholarship, but Churton Collins called him the Porson of Shakespearean criticism,[2] and wrote that the text of Shakespeare owes more to Theobald than to any other editor.[3]

Edward Capell, a member of the Middle Temple who lived and died in the Temple, produced a scholarly edition of Shakespeare in 1768. This involved the careful study and collation of all available Quartos, and was a landmark in textual criticism. Capell called for a full biography of Shakespeare: meanwhile he passed on the tradition that Shakespeare was lame and not a very good actor.

George Steevens was a man of means who, on going down from Cambridge without taking a degree, appears to have resided for a time in chambers in the Temple. Thereby he has acquired the reputation of being a conveyancer, and on that ground he deserves a place in this survey. Steevens' edition of Shakespeare's plays, first published in 1773, was based on that of Dr Johnson. A second edition was published (after Malone's) in 1793. It was confined to the plays, as he could not bring himself to read the poems. His work emphasises the importance of the Quartos, and displays a wide knowledge of Elizabethan literature. It was enlivened by indecent notes, the authority for which he attributed to two innocent clergymen who had offended him.[4] He did much valuable work on which the First and Second Variorum editions were based, and his notes were retained in the Third Variorum.

Edmond Malone,[5] the younger son of an Irish judge

---

[1] R. R. Simpson, M.B., F.R.C.S., *Shakespeare and Medicine* (1959), p. 56.

[2] J. Churton Collins, *Essays and Studies* (1895), chap. 4.

[3] In *Dictionary of National Biography*.

[4] E. K. Chambers, *William Shakespeare: A Study of Facts and Problems* (1930), II, p. 378.

[5] Sir James Prior, *Life of Edmond Malone* (1860); J. K. Walton, 'Edmond Malone: an Irish Shakespeare Scholar', *Hermathena*, No. XCIX (Autumn 1964),

and nephew of a serjeant-at-law, entered Trinity College, Dublin, in 1757 (not 1756 as usually stated) and graduated in 1762. Admitted to Inner Temple in 1761 he studied law in London from 1763 to 1766, since those wishing to be called to the Irish Bar had to keep part of their terms at one of the English Inns of Court. There he met Dr Johnson, who was living near Inner Temple and working on his edition of Shakespeare. In 1767 Malone returned to Dublin and was called to the Irish Bar. For ten years he continued in practice without great success as a member of the Munster circuit. After the death of his father Malone's income, derived mainly from Irish estates, enabled him to give up the practice of law and to devote himself to the study of Shakespeare and other authors. In 1777 Malone went to live in London where he became friends with Steevens, one of their first joint activities being to go to see Shakespeare's will.

Malone's first major work of scholarship was his 'Attempt to ascertain the Order in which the Plays attributed to Shakespeare were written', which was printed in Steevens' edition of Shakespeare. His 'Historical account of the rise and progress of the English stage' appeared in 1780, as did an edition of Shakespeare's Poems[6] and the doubtful plays of the Third Folio. Malone's important edition of Shakespeare was published in 1790, and contained revised versions of his *Chronology* and *History of the Stage*, and also the first documented *Life* of Shakespeare. For this biography, many times longer than Rowe's, Malone made the first serious search among the official records and documents in London and Stratford-on-Avon, and a review of the known sources that revealed authentic information about

---

pp. 5-26; J. M. Osborn, 'Edmond Malone and Dr Johnson', *Johnson, Boswell and their Circle* (Essays Presented to L. F. Powell, 1965), p. 1; Arthur Brown, *Edmond Malone and English Scholarship* (1963).

[6] Malone's own poetic efforts included an *Ode on the Nuptials of His Majesty George III*.

Shakespeare's life. He even gave a coat of stone-coloured paint to the Shakespeare bust in Stratford parish church.

Malone tells us that his aims were to exhibit the genuine text of the author and to explain his obscurities. This, with other notes left by Malone, became the basis of the Third Variorum edition. In the Preface of 1790 we first meet the authentic note of genuine scholarship with regard to textual theory and first-hand rectification of authorities.[7] Malone has been said to excel other eighteenth-century Shakespeare scholars in two qualities, his well developed historical sense and his critical assessment of theories and evidence.[8]

James Boswell, a son of Dr Johnson's biographer, was a barrister of the Inner Temple and was appointed a Commissioner of Bankruptcy. He lived with Malone for some time, collaborating with him in his work of Shakespeare editorship. Malone gave security of £100 when Boswell was called to the Bar. After Malone's death, Boswell published in 1821 the invaluable Third Variorum Shakespeare, based on Malone's work and sometimes known as 'Boswell's Malone'. Volume I contains a biographical note on Malone by Boswell and Malone's preface of 1790, while Volume II includes Malone's 'Life of Shakespeare' and his essay on the chronological order of the plays.

A name that often occurs in the Third Variorum is that of Sir William Blackstone, who was the first Vinerian Professor of English Law at Oxford and became a Judge of the Common Pleas, but who is best known as the author of the *Commentaries on the Laws of England* first published in 1765. Malone said that the notes Blackstone gave him on Shakespeare showed him to have been a man of excellent taste and accuracy, and a good critic. One example is: 'Portia's referring the *Jew* to the Christian doctrine of salvation, and the Lord's Prayer, is a little out of character' (*The Merchant*

[7] Brown, op. cit., p. 11.
[8] Walton, op. cit., p. 13.

*of Venice*, IV. I).[9] By the grave-digger's scene in *Hamlet*, V. I, it appears that Hamlet was then thirty years old, and knew Yorick who had been dead for twenty-three years; but at the beginning of the play Hamlet is spoken of as a very young man, who intended to return to the University of Wittenberg. 'The poet in the fifth Act', Blackstone comments, 'had forgotten what he wrote in the first.' Again, Blackstone suggested that the Duke in *Measure for Measure* had learned Mariana's story in one of his former periodical retirements; he suspected that Angelo was a hypocrite, and therefore came back in disguise to observe him.

H. H. Furness, the American scholar who began the *New Variorum* edition in 1871 and has been called the greatest of Shakespeare editors, was admitted to the Pennsylvania Bar in 1859. Private means and deafness discouraged him from continuing in practice, but his legal training doubtless helped him in such work as his great edition of *The Merchant of Venice*.

The earliest lawyer to write Shakespeare criticism was Thomas Rymer, official historiographer, editor of the collection of treaties known as *Rymer's Foedera*, and literary critic, who was called to the Bar by Gray's Inn in 1673. His *Short View of Tragedy* (1692) contains a short criticism of *Julius Caesar* and (amounting to nearly half the book) a trenchant attack on *Othello*. '*Shakespears* genius lay for Comedy and Humour', wrote Rymer in this book,[10] 'In Tragedy he appears quite out of his Element; his Brains are turn'd, he raves and rambles, without any coherence, any spark of reason, or any rule to controul him, or set bounds to his phrenzy.' Rymer begins to write very disrespectfully of *Julius Caesar*, but soon passes on to other topics. He accuses Shakespeare of distorting Roman history to serve

[9] Malone's edition (1790), p. 82; New Variorum (1888), p. 213.
[10] *The Critical Works of Thomas Rymer*, ed. C. A. Zimansky (Yale University Press, 1956), p. 169.

his ignoble dramatic purposes, and of putting the same inappropriate language into the mouths of all his senators and orators. Both *Julius Caesar* and *Othello* are improbable, as their Romans and Venetians are not typical. Iago, being a soldier, should be simple and honest, but Shakespeare makes the character improbable and inconsistent.

Rymer says the plot in *Othello* is amoral. Shakespeare altered Cinthio's novel for the worse. The marriage between Othello and Desdemona is absurd, and so is the notion that Venetians would entrust their defence to a Moor. Othello does nothing that befits a general, and his jealousy is no part of a soldier's character. But what is most intolerable is Iago, who is nothing like a soldier, blackamoor or otherwise. Desdemona, on her wedding night, teases Othello on behalf of young Cassio; and on their first sleeping together they get out of bed and go down town to stop a soldiers' fight. From such characters we cannot expect to get worthwhile thoughts, and the expression is limited by thoughts. Shakespeare may have been a master of his craft, but he was too close to the strolling players. Aristotle's unities are not observed, so that the horrible clutter about the missing handkerchief may last one day or seven days. Othello treats Desdemona as some drayman or drunken tinker might possibly treat his drab. The last scenes of the play are nothing but blood and butchery. 'There is in this Play', Rymer concludes, 'some burlesk, some humour, and ramble of Comical Wit, some shew, and some *Mimickry* to divert the spectators: but the tragical part is, plainly none other than a Bloody Farce, without salt or savour.'[11]

Theobald, lawyer-editor, said in his edition of Shakespeare that he did not consider Rymer was to be taken seriously. 'It seems moot Point', he observed, 'whether Mr *Pope* has done most injury to Shakespeare as his Editor and Encomiast; or Mr *Rymer* done him service as his Rival and Censurer.' But Sir Walter Scott, lawyer-novelist, wrote

[11] Rymer (ed. Zimansky), op. cit., pp. 131-64.

of Rymer: 'there is sometimes justice, though never mercy, in his criticism.'[12] In connection with Rymer's criticism of *Othello* it is worth noticing that a recent psychiatric study of morbid jealousy and murder[13] shows that about twelve per cent of all insane murderers admitted to Broadmoor in a given period were men who, through intrinsically illogical ideas and deductions, had become convinced of the infidelity of their wives or mistresses. Morbid jealousy appears to be the delusion associated with more deaths from murder or suicide than any other. All the murderers examined suffered from a definite psychotic illness, if they were not actually schizophrenic.

A legal critic of the Johnson-Steevens edition of Shakespeare was Joseph Ritson, known best as the author of tracts on the Office of Constable and the Jurisdiction of the Court Leet. Ritson was antiquary, atheist, republican and lawyer, who devoted his leisure to literature. After being clerk to a firm of conveyancers in Gray's Inn he worked on his own account in chambers, and was called to the Bar by Gray's Inn in 1789. In 1783 he published a book strongly critical of the Johnson-Steevens edition.[14] Among his comments on the text is one on the lines from *Hamlet*:

> Or that the everlasting had not *fix'd*
> His *canon* 'gainst self-slaughter.

> (I. 2)

Steevens thought 'canon' meant ordnance: Theobald thought it meant an ecclesiastical decree. Ritson saw it as a quibble between the two meanings and exclaims: 'What happiness, what immortal glory, to be the conciliator of such contending chieftains in criticism!' He also points out that

[12] Sir Walter Scott, *Dryden's Works* (1808), vol. 15, p. 379. cf. Nigel Alexander, 'Thomas Rymer and *Othello*', 21 *Shakespeare Survey* (1968), 67, who calls Rymer 'an intelligent and competent neo-classic critic'.

[13] R. R. Mowat, *Morbid Jealousy and Murder* (1966).

[14] *Remarks Critical and Illustrative, on the Text and Notes of the Last Edition of Shakespeare.*

it is rather extraordinary for Hamlet in his soliloquy (III. 1) to say that no traveller had ever returned from that undiscovered country, when he had just had a long conversation with the spirit of his father, which had returned from it for the sole purpose of speaking to him.[15]

Robert Wheler, who was born in Stratford-on-Avon in 1785, was admitted as a solicitor and followed his father into the practice of law. He remained in Stratford and developed local antiquarian and topographical interests which he applied to the study of Shakespeare. Information not previously published about Shakespeare's life and family was contained in his history of Stratford and his guide to that town.[16]

W. L. Rushton wrote a number of short monographs on Shakespeare in the third quarter of the last century. A native of Liverpool, he was called to the bar by Gray's Inn but had chambers in the Temple. In addition to *Shakespeare a Lawyer* (1858), which was written while he was still a bar student, Rushton published *Shakespeare's Legal Maxims* (1859), discussed later, *Shakespeare Illustrated by Old Authors* (1867-8), *Shakespeare's Testamentary Language* (1869), *Shakespeare Illustrated by the Lex Scripta* (1870), *Shakespeare's Euphuism* (1871), and, in his capacity as President of the Mersey Bowmen, *Shakespeare an Archer* (1897).

The purpose of *Shakespeare a Lawyer* was to point out and explain most of the legal terms, allusions and expressions in Shakespeare's works that Rushton could recall, with a view to considering what evidence they together provided that Shakespeare — whether or not he was a member of the legal profession — had a general knoweldge of the English common law. This question is further discussed in chapter

---

[15] This passage may have inspired a facetious correspondent to a legal journal in 1841 to sign his letter 'Ritson's Ghost': 21 *Legal Observer*, 180.

[16] Robert Bell Wheler, *History and Antiquities of Stratford-upon-Avon* (Stratford, 1906); *A Guide to Stratford-upon-Avon* (Stratford, 1814).

12. In addition to his explanations of the particular passages which we have quoted in chapter 9, Rushton explained such legal terms as: — praemunire, fee simple, strays, entail, remainder, reversion, benefit of clergy, indenture, the various parts and contents of a deed, bonds (simple and conditional), purchase (as contrasted with descent), jointure, covenants, articles, premises, homage and fealty, ward, suing out livery, letters patent, attorney, sealing, lease or demise, possessions, plea, issue (in procedure), heir apparent, nonsuit and serjeant.

*Shakespeare Illustrated by Old Authors* was an attempt to explain many obscure words and passages of doubtful meaning by extracts from old authors, not all as old as Shakespeare, such as Puttenham's *Arte of English Poesie* (published by Shakespeare's neighbour, Field, in 1589), St Germain's *Doctor and Student,* Burton's *Anatomy of Melancholy,* Coke's *Institutes,* Holinshed, Aristotle and the ancient Greek dramatists. For example, in *Merry Wives,* I. I, when Falstaff calls to him, Pistol says: 'He hears with ears.' On which Sir Hugh Evans exclaims: 'The tevil and his tam! what phrase is this, "He hears with ear"? Why, it is affectations.' Rushton[17] cites Puttenham: 'The first surplusage the Greekes call Pleonasmus, I call him too full speech and is no great fault, as if one should say, *I heard it with mine ears, and saw it with mine eyes,* as if a man could heare with his heeles or see with his nose.'

*Shakespeare's Testamentary Language* was mainly a comparison of testamentary terms and expressions in the plays (rather than in his will) with *Swinburn's Brief Treatise of Testaments and Last Willes,* which was published in 1590. It shows, for example, that 'devise' and 'bequeath' in Shakespeare's time were applied indifferently to real and personal property.[18] It also explains that Olivia's question,

---

[17] *Shakespeare Illustrated by Old Authors,* Part I (1867), p. 31.
[18] *Shakespeare's Testamentary Language,* pp. 14-23.

'Were you sent here to praise me?' means to appraise or value.[19]

*Shakespeare Illustrated by the Lex Scripta* illustrates and explains obscure passages, words and expressions in Shakespeare with the help of extracts taken from early statutes. In many places Rushton shows himself sensitive to Shakespeare's double meanings. *Shakespeare's Euphuism* gives illustrations comparing passages from Shakespeare with passages from Lyly's *Euphues*, not only from *Love's Labour's Lost* but from a number of other plays as well. It is pointed out that many even of the quibbles and bad puns, for whose use Shakespeare has been censured, were not his own.[20]

Lord Campbell's *Shakespeare's Legal Acquirements Considered* (1859) is discussed fully in chapter 12. Not all its attempts to explain Shakespeare's legal allusions are felicitous. In commenting on Dromio of Syracuse's statement that his master is in the hands of 'One that, before the judgment, carries poor souls to hell . . . he is 'rested on the case' (*The Comedy of Errors*, IV. 2), Lord Campbell talks about arrest on mesne process (i.e. before a personal action is tried) and an action *on the case*; but Robertson[21] objects that 'before the judgment' here refers to the Last Judgment, and suggests that the effect of the passage turns on the naturalness of a servant's fumbling with two legal tags. Lord Campbell's statement that the trial in *The Merchant of Venice* is 'duly conducted according to the strict forms of legal procedure' draws three pages of ironical comment from Robertson's pen.[22] Gratiano's remark to Shylock in *The Merchant of Venice*, IV. 1:

> In christening thou shalt have two godfathers;
> Had I been judge, thou shouldst have had ten more,
> To bring thee to the gallows, not the font,

[19] ibid., p. 38.
[20] *Shakespeare's Euphuism*, p. 106.
[21] J. M. Robertson, *The Baconian Heresy: A Confutation* (1913), pp. 46-7.
[22] Ibid., pp. 57-9.

is described by Lord Campbell as 'an ebullition which might be expected from an English lawyer'; to which Robertson,[23] another Scotsman, retorts that, apart from downright Baconism, this is the worst nonsense ever penned in Shakespearean discussion, which is saying a good deal. Lord Campbell made about ten references to, or quotations from, Shakespeare in his *Lives of the Chief Justices*, the first volume of which was published in 1849.[24] He mentioned some of Shakespeare's anachronisms,[25] and passed on the story that horse-holding was Shakespeare's mode of livelihood on arriving in London.[26]

Continental legal scholarship in the Shakespearean field is led by the distinguished German jurist, Josef Kohler, who brought his immense learning to bear on placing the legal problems involved in Shakespeare's plays within their context in historical and ethnological jurisprudence.[27] This he did with special reference to *The Merchant of Venice* and the law of debt, *Measure for Measure* and the doctrine of pardon, and *Hamlet* and the blood feud. He was specially interested in Shylock and Hamlet, and had lectured on both these characters. Kohler's object was the juristic formulation of Shakespeare's thought about law, to expound in the language of jurisprudence and to put into their general historical framework the thoughts about law expressed by the greatest poet. He was not concerned with the law of Shakespeare's time, nor with the question of Shakespeare's legal qualifications. While the treatment would show the development of legal ideas as part of the evolution of universal history, in the Hegelian manner, Kohler recognised that the juristic notions of a poet also require aesthetic

---

[23] ibid., pp. 59-60.
[24] e.g., vol. I, pp. 42, 47, 123, 130, 135, 161, 259 and 338; vol. II, p. 25.
[25] *Lives of the Chief Justices*, I, p. 133.
[26] ibid., III, p. 266.
[27] Joseph Kohler, *Shakespeare vor dem Forum der Jurisprudenz*, (1st. ed. Würzburg, 1883; 2nd. ed. Berlin, 1919). Kohler prepared the second edition, but died before it was published.

analysis. Among the many subsidiary topics discussed are the doctrine of abuse of rights, bondage or imprisonment for debt (*The Merchant of Venice*), forgiveness as a matter of divine grace and pardon as a royal prerogative (*Measure for Measure*), the problem of the ghost, self-defence, political crimes, and kinship and marriage (*Hamlet*). *Shakespeare vor dem Forum der Jurisprudenz* was one of Kohler's earlier works; and it is not surprising, in view of the range he attempted to cover, that his statements of fact are sometimes inaccurate and some of his theories exaggerated.

In a shorter work, Kohler[28] examined the criminal types in Shakespeare's plays. Among criminals of a social character, four commit crimes of passion: Macbeth and Richard III act under self-seeking impulse, Macbeth out of simple passion and Richard out of lust for political power; the motive of the fanatics, Brutus and Cassius, is altruistic. Othello's crime, on the other hand, is committed on the impulse of the moment. Unscrupulous criminals are Edmund, Iago and Cade, who are cases of moral insanity.

August Goll,[29] a Danish scientist and magistrate, appears to have been the first professional criminologist to apply theories of criminal psychology to certain characters in Shakespeare's plays. Cassius is found to stand for Hatred, the fermenting element in all social revolutions; but he needs the services of the Ideal, Brutus, the revolutionary theorist. Macbeth is the type of man who only becomes criminal through opportunity putting temptation in the way; the defect in his character is not wickedness but weakness: he is led on by the incitement of Lady Macbeth, and the action of instigator or instrument — as Italian criminologists discovered — produces an entirely new character in Lady Macbeth. She herself is the type of altruistic female offender, who commits crimes for the benefit of husband (*Macbeth*), or children (*Cymbeline*) or lover (*King Lear*).

[28] Josef Kohler, *Verbrecher-Typen in Shakespeares Dramen* (Berlin, 1903).
[29] August Goll, *Criminal Types in Shakespeare* (1909).

Richard III is the type of criminal by instinct, whose motive is greed. Iago is another type of the criminal by instinct, whose motive is the lust for destruction: he does not himself desire to be possessed of the treasure, but to rob the possessor of his enjoyment of it. Every genuine criminal is at bottom a cynic. Iago's erotic instinct of cruelty emerges in relation to Desdemona, and his envy of Othello increases: feelings that were at first largely unconscious become fully conscious. In Caliban we have 'the criminal in pure cultivation, the cell which contains the germ of all later creations having like tendencies and inclinations.'[30] Shakespeare, says Goll with reference to Hamlet seeking to trap the guilty King,[31] seems to solve the deepest and most intricate questions of criminology, as if in play.

Dr Julius Hirschfeld,[32] asking what exactly was the crime of which Iago was guilty, argues that Iago neither suggested nor even contemplated the murder of Desdemona, and therefore was not an accessory before the fact. He was scarcely guilty of criminal defamation. He persuaded his wife, Emilia, to steal the handkerchief, but she did not do so – she found it and handed it over to him, and he passed it on. He had 'maimed' Cassio, but no one knew it was he who had done it. He had exploited Roderigo, but the only witness was dead. Iago's only crime, therefore, was the murder of Emilia. This open-handed deed was out of keeping with his character, but was necessary in order to give Shakespeare an excuse for disposing of him.

R. S. Guernsey, American tax lawyer and writer on suicide, who was first Vice-President of the Shakespeare Society of New York, made a study of the ecclesiastical

---

[30] ibid., p. 25. Goll appears to think that *The Tempest*, printed first in the First Folio, was an early play, whereas it is now generally regarded as one of Shakespeare's latest.

[31] J. M. Robertson, *The Problem of Hamlet* (1919), traces the play-within-a-play to Kyd's *Hamlet*.

[32] J. Hirschfeld, 'What was Iago's Crime in Law?' (1914) 14 *Journal of the Society of Comparative Legislation* (N.S.), p. 411.

law in *Hamlet*.[33] He claimed that in *Hamlet* can be found allusions and statements showing the most thorough and complete knowledge of the canon and statute law of England with regard to the burial of suicides that has ever been written. In the dialogue of the Grave-diggers' scene, says Guernsey, the law is not confined entirely to the parallels in *Hales v. Petit*. Shakespeare accurately states the laws of England and of the established Church of England at the time he wrote, and not the laws of Denmark in Hamlet's time. Hamlet lived in about A.D. 700, and Christianity was not introduced into Denmark until about the year 827. The established Church in Denmark had been Lutheran since 1536. The edition of the play before 1604 does not include the full discussion on the burial of suicides. Elizabeth died in 1603, so the play was rewritten in the reign of James I. Also, the canons of the Church of England were being revised in 1603. The parallels between the arguments in *Hales v. Petit* and the Grave-diggers' dialogue are so striking that, in Guernsey's view, there can be no question that the writer was familiar with the report of that case. The coroner's inquest decided whether suicide was voluntary by instigation of the devil: this was binding by statute on the church authorities. Ophelia's burial, Guernsey concludes, was in a rural district where High Church practices prevailed – helped in this case, perhaps, by the fact that Danish royalty were present.

Clement Mansfield Ingleby, son of a Birmingham solicitor, went into partnership with his father and practised for some years, but he found the profession distasteful and devoted his spare time to English literature and other studies. At the age of thirty-six in 1859, the year in which he exposed Collier's forgeries, he severed his connection with the law. He now had leisure to become a Shakespeare scholar, one of his last books being *Shakespeare's Bones*

---

[33] R. S. Guernsey, *Ecclesiastical Law in Hamlet: The Burial of Ophelia* (New York, 1885).

(1883) in which he proposed that Shakespeare's body should be dug up in order that the skull might be examined.

Appleton Morgan[34] – who thought that Shakespeare's own plays had been lost and that the debt we owed to him was as editor of the 'Shakespeare' plays – made a glossary of Warwickshire dialect words. He found examples of the Warwickshire dialect in all the plays, though many other dialects are also found in them. On the other hand, he detected practically no trace of the Warwickshire dialect in *Venus and Adonis*, from which he concluded that it was doubtful whether it was written by the same author.

Sir Dunbar Plunket Barton was a Judge of the Irish High Court who became Bencher and Treasurer of Gray's Inn. Possessing both a historical sense and a cultivated literary taste, he was a student of the Elizabethan period and a specialist on the history of the Inns of Court. His *Links between Shakespeare and the Law*, published in 1929,[35] covers with ease and grace a number of topics dealt with in the present book as they had been written and thought about forty years ago. He distributes the discoverable links between Shakespeare and the law under three principal heads: (i) Shakespeare's relations to the Inns of Court and of Chancery; (ii) Shakespeare's references to great Judges, famous advocates and celebrated trials; and (iii) Shakespeare's legal allusions. This last was a path that had been trodden by previous writers, but Barton adopted a new method of arrangement by classifying the legal allusions from a lawyer's point of view under the various branches of law to which they belong. This kind of arrangement was intended to help the reader to estimate the range of legal allusions, and to observe Shakespeare's methods of transmuting legal ideas into poetry and dramatic dialogue.

[34] J. Appleton Morgan, *A Study in the Warwickshire Dialect* (Shakespeare Society of New York, New York, 4th. ed., 1900).

[35] Sir Dunbar Plunket Barton, *Links between Shakespeare and the Law* (1929), being a reprint of a series of articles in the *Law Journal*, vol. 63, pp. 470, 493, 511, 531, 575, 598 and vol. 64, pp. 30, 50, 70, 90.

Barton's chief contributions to Shakespeare studies lie in the application of his practical and theoretical knowledge of English property law to explaining the texts; and the clarity with which he saw, and the vigour with which he insisted on, the fact that the poet and playwright transmuted legal ideas (as he did other ideas) into poetry and drama.

Barton had previously published *Links between Ireland and Shakespeare*,[36] in which he tells us that *Macbeth* is the only Shakespeare play that can be traced back to an Irish source. Its principal characters – Duncan, Macbeth and Lady Macbeth – are Scottish Gaels of Irish extraction; and the weird sisters are not witches in the usual sense, but like the wizardesses of ancient Irish story. *King Lear* is Celtic, and has its analogue in the legend of the Irish Lir. Why is Hamlet in his dialogue with Horatio made to swear by Saint Patrick? In Shakespeare's day St Patrick's Purgatory, a cave on an island in Lough Derg, was a place of pilgrimage known throughout Europe, and a full account of it was given in the Irish volume of Holinshed's *Chronicles* to which Stanyhurst contributed. It was appropriate that Hamlet, having just seen his father's ghost back from purgatory, should think of that spot where pilgrims contemplated the life after death. Shakespeare's only stage Irishman, Captain Macmorris, is a sound practical soldier, a good fighting man and 'a very valiant gentleman.'

George W. Keeton, for many years a Professor of English Law at London University, published his first book on Shakespeare[37] when he had only just emerged from the student ranks at Gray's Inn. It was a new approach to the soundness of the legal principles that Shakespeare applied in his plays. In this book Keeton expounded with thoroughness and lucidity the legal problems involved in about two-

[36] Sir Dunbar Plunket Barton, *Links between Ireland and Shakespeare* (Dublin, 1919). The book was suggested by an article contributed by Mr Justice Madden to a Shakespeare *Book of Homage*. Barton also mentions at pp. 206-7 the references to Shakespeare in Madden's *Classical Learning in Ireland* (Dublin, 1908).
[37] G. W. Keeton, *Shakespeare and his Legal Problems* (1930).

thirds of the plays, for example: the title to the English crown; the English Kingship; the distinction and relation between common law and equity; crime; local justice; international law; and the trial scenes. On the other hand, he did not concern himself with Shakespeare's law as exhibited in numerous particular passages.

Recently Professor Keeton has published a larger book under the title *Shakespeare's Legal and Political Background*,[38] which includes in a revised form the material of the earlier book (to which it does not refer), but covers a wider field and in greater detail. It is undoubtedly the most significant legal contribution to Shakespeare studies made in recent years. Professor Keeton is well versed in a wide range of law, public and private, including international law, as well as legal history, being a specialist in equity and the history of the Court of Chancery. The purpose of the book is to explain the manner in which Shakespeare employed the language and content of the law in his plays, and to relate this to the political ideas reflected in them. Beyond this limit he expresses no wish to express judgment on the plays themselves. An analysis of Shakespeare's law and politics, he says, adds something to our understanding of the dramatist, although, of course, that is only one among many aspects of his achievement.

Part I of Keeton's Book, headed 'Shakespeare and the Law', contains an analytical explanation of, and a historical commentary on, such topics as the relation between Shakespeare and the law and lawyers; Shakespeare's use of legal terminology; the law of nature in Shakespeare, local justice, the law of debt, bastardy, burial and trial by battle in the plays; trial scenes; and certain legal problems in *Hamlet* and *Richard III*. These last are, in *Hamlet*, the succession to the Danish throne, the Queen's marriage to her husband's

---

[38] George W. Keeton, *Shakespeare's Legal and Political Background* (1967). Reviewed by Sir Jocelyn Simon, Q.C., in 'Shakespeare's Legal and Political Background' (1968) 84 *Law Quarterly Review*, 33-47.

brother, and her complicity in the murder of her husband; and, in *Richard III*, Buckingham's claim to the earldom of Hereford, and the right to sanctuary of Edward IV's widow and children.

In Part II, headed 'Shakespeare's Political Thinking', Keeton discusses the contemporary background to the dramatist's political thought; the title to the Crown in the history plays; Shakespeare's view of the English Kingship; and the political background to such plays as *Henry VI*, *Richard III* and *Henry VIII*, as well as the Greek and Roman plays. The book finishes with a discussion of *Measure for Measure*, in which the central legal problem is found to be that of criminal justice and the evils that necessarily follow when laws are about to fall into disrepute; and the secondary problem, the question how should the law deal with the magistrate who falls short of the standard that he applies rigorously to others?

The most comprehensive contribution made in the nineteenth century to the explanation of legal terms in Shakespeare was Senator Cushman Davis's *The Law in Shakespeare*.[39] The book is a kind of glossary of legal terms found in Shakespeare, with an introduction exaggerating the dramatist's legal knowledge. Cushman Davis, a lawyer who became Governor of Minnesota, found 312 legal terms in Shakespeare, but these include on the one hand cases where the same word is used more than once, and on the other hand a number of words that are not exclusively legal, e.g. traitor, pardon, inheritance and warrant.

This useful exercise was better done by Edward J. White, who first published his *Commentaries on the Law in Shakespeare* in 1911.[40] White was an American lawyer, who also wrote on the law of mines and railroads. This book

[39] C. K. Davis, *The Law in Shakespeare* (St Paul, Minnesota, 2nd. ed., 1884). See W. C. Devecmon, *In Re Shakespeare's 'Legal Acquirements'* (New York, 1899), p. 24.

[40] E. J. White, *Commentaries on the Law in Shakespeare* (St Louis; 1st. ed., 1911; 2nd. ed., 1913).

explains the meaning of the legal terms or propositions found in Shakespeare's plays and poems mainly in the light of English law in Shakespeare's day, not as criticising the rightness or wrongness of the use of the expressions in their context. He deals with over 500 different instances of these without duplication – four times as many as Lord Campbell. The reason why White's book is not so well known as Davis's is probably that Davis was fully commented on in Robertson's *The Baconian Heresy* (1913), whereas White's book was either not available when Robertson was preparing his book (the latter's preface is dated 1912) or else it was passed over because White was not under attack as a Baconian. Richard Bentley accuses White of being ignorant of the literary, as distinct from the legal, commentaries on Shakespeare, and therefore unable to appreciate the literary and dramatic qualities of Shakespeare's works. He also accuses him of not being sufficiently selective, saying: 'although it would be well-nigh impossible to discern a legal allusion which Mr White's scissors have failed to find ... Mr White has let in too much chaff with the wheat.'[41] To this mixed metaphor White replied that Bentley was criticising the first edition although the second edition had been out for ten years. White says he quoted and explained Shakespeare's law terms, not to show that the poet was a lawyer, but to demonstrate that he correctly used law terms.[42]

The most thorough study so far of the use of legal concepts in the plays of Shakespeare and his contemporaries – though it only covers part of the field – is a work by two American legal practitioners, P. S. Clarkson and C. T. Warren, in *The Law of Property in Shakespeare and the Elizabethan Drama*.[43] The authors regard previous commentaries on the law in Shakespeare as inadequate, because:

---

[41] Richard Bentley, 'Diversities de la Ley', (1922) 17 *Illinois Law Review*, 145; 'Shakespeare's Law', (1923) 155 *Law Times*, 34.

[42] Edward J. White 'Shakespeare and the Law', ibid., p. 196.

[43] P. S. Clarkson and C. T. Warren, *The Law of Property in Shakespeare and the Elizabethan Drama* (Baltimore, 1942).

(i) most were selective rather than comprehensive in the passages discussed; (ii) many commentators seemed to be attempting to support pre-conceived theses; (iii) too little attention had been paid to a comparison of legalisms in Shakespeare's works with those in the works of other Elizabethan dramatists; and (iv) their arrangement was defective. Previous commentators either: (*a*) noted their comments play by play, act by act and line by line, e.g. Campbell and White; or (*b*) collected mere lists of legalisms, unconnected and uncorrelated, e.g. Judge Allen[44] and Robertson. The former method had been limited to the plays of Shakespeare, and so lacked the corrective of comparison; also it involves repetition, and especially it precludes orderly and thorough delineation of any particular field of law. The latter method is inexhaustive both as to the authors read and the legal subject-matter included, and it results in an ill-arranged and insufficiently explained miscellany of technical terms. It may, however, be objected that the legal allusions may not fit into arrangement according to subject-matter, for a single passage often involves more than one legal concept.

Clarkson and Warren read not only all of Shakespeare's works but also the plays of seventeen of his contemporary dramatists,[45] and they catalogued on 8,000 index cards the thousands of passages containing legal references. Their method is to group and discuss all legal allusions by all the playwrights surveyed according to legal subject-matter, giving a full presentation of the legal background. They planned a series of volumes on such branches of law as Equity, Marriage and Divorce, and Criminal Law, for which the materials had already been collected, but neither of the learned authors appears to have published a book since 1942. The work under discussion is confined to

[44] Judge Charles C. Allen, *Notes on the Bacon-Shakespeare Question* (Boston, 1900).

[45] Lyly, Peele, Marlowe, Greene, Kyd, Marston, Chapman, Ben Jonson, Dekker, Webster, Beaumont, Fletcher, Tourneur, Heywood, Middleton, Ford and Massinger.

property law. If we take 'Fines' and 'Recoveries' as samples to test Davis, White and Clarkson and Warren, we find that White has much fuller references than Davis to Shakespearean texts and to legal authorities; but on 'Fines' and 'Recoveries', as on other matters connected with property law, Clarkson and Warren give a much fuller exposition than either of the others.

# I I

## *The Lawyers and Shakespeare*

Varying degrees of seriousness have been shown by lawyers in their writings and spoken addresses on Shakespearean topics. At one end of the scale legal authors offer balanced criticism or they comment earnestly on the law of nature in Shakespeare; at the other end they content themselves (if not their readers) with humorous mock trials featuring the playwright or his characters. They have even fallen to the temptation of fabricating manuscripts. If Shakespeare made many references to lawyers, the latter have returned the compliment on numberless occasions by quoting from his plays or alluding to his characters in the courts, in commentaries or legal textbooks and in after-dinner speeches. Addresses are delivered from time to time at learned society meetings in provincial towns or the more remote American States, bringing in familiar Shakespearean quotations without adding new knowledge or insights; while some contributions are simply unclassifiable.

Justice Oliver Wendell Holmes, of the American Supreme Court, in his correspondence with the English jurist, Sir Frederick Pollock, had this to say about Shakespeare's rhetoric:

Shakespeare it seems to me is so full of the mystery of life that anything pulls the trigger and he goes off with splendid talk that we wouldn't for the world give up but that seems to me often to disregard dramatic probability or reason, e.g. Richard II or Macbeth when told of his wife's death, or a broken line from Percy when run through the guts.[1]

And of the language in *Troilus and Cressida* Holmes said that 'when anything suggests to him his magnificent tall talk about life or the ultimate mysteries he fires it off bang, without the slightest regard to dramatic fitness'; but, he adds, we accept it gratefully as we would rather hear Shakespeare talk than Richard II or Achilles or Macbeth.[2] To which Pollock replied: 'Shakespeare was in a mighty bad temper when he wrote *Troilus and Cressida*, and meant it to be a frankly arbitrary satire, not respecting even legend, and wilfully flouting history, for he really must have known that Aristotle came after the Trojan war.' 'However', he adds, 'his depreciation of the Greek heroes merely follows medieval romances.[3]

A survey of natural law in Shakespeare has been made by John Wu, formerly Chief Justice of the Provisional Court of Shanghai and later Professor of Law at Seton Hall University School of Law, as part of a historical study of the scholastic philosophy of law in England.[4] 'Shakespeare seems to know his common law and natural law pretty well', Wu writes. He knows the psychological reason of case law, and the importance of tempering the rigours of the law with equity, as through Portia. He knows the importance of observing degree, proportion, form and order (*Troilus and Cressida*, I. 3), and Hector cites Aristotle (ibid., II. 2). The dialogue between Henry V and the Chief Justice in *2 Henry IV* gives a vivid picture of the majesty and power of law and justice. Shakespeare has such a profound respect for the dictates of natural reason that even a solemn oath is held to be of no binding force if the pledge

[1] *The Pollock-Holmes Letters*, letter dated 24 November 1923; vol. II, p. 125.
[2] Letter dated 10 February 1925; ibid., vol. II, pp. 152-3.
[3] Letter dated 24 February 1925; ibid., vol. II, p. 154.
[4] John C. H. Wu, LL.D., *Fountain of Justice: A Study in the Natural Law* (1959), chap. 6, 'Natural Law in Shakespeare'.

is to do something that is contrary to the basic principles of justice:

> *Salisbury.* It is a great sin to swear unto a sin,
> But greater sin to keep a sinful oath.
>
> (*2 Henry VI*, v. 1)

'The works of Shakespeare', Wu concludes, 'are strewn with grains of human wisdom.'

Another Catholic lawyer refers more than once to Shakespeare in writing about the law of nature. Natural law is the law of reason, which teaches the superiority of the rational nature of man to the animal order. This tradition is seen by Richard O'Sullivan[5] to be reflected by Shakespeare in the passage:

> What is a man, if his chief good and market of
>                                         his time
> Be but to sleep and feed? A beast no more.
> Since He that made us with such large discourse
> Looking before and after, gave us not
> That capability and god-like reason
> To fust in us unused.
>
> (*Hamlet*, IV. 4)

One of the reasons given for the judgment in *Hales v. Petit* was that suicide is an offence against nature, and O'Sullivan[6] asks us to compare the line in *Richard III*: 'Richard loves Richard, that is, I am I'.

Lord Simon of Glaisdale shows a special interest in Shakespeare's Sonnets. He is surely right in interpreting the words of Sonnet 146:

> Why so large cost, having so short a lease,
> Dost thou upon thy fading mansion spend?

as meaning in their context: 'Why do you spend so much

[5] Richard O'Sullivan, Q.C., *The Spirit of the Common Law* (1965), p. 79.
[6] ibid., p. 73n.

money on the adornment of your external person, when you
have such a short time in this world?'[7] and in disagreeing
with Keeton, who (reading 'costs' for 'cost') makes it a
prosaic reference to 'the overcharging which often accompanied verbose leases for short terms'. Lord Simon doubts,
again taking issue with Keeton, whether Sonnet 46 ('Mine
eye and heart are at a mortal war') involves trial by battle.[8]
That mode of trial was exceptionally adopted in *Lowe v.
Paramour* (1571),[9] although the battle never took place as
the demandant made default, but it was almost obsolete by
the end of the thirteenth century.

The only clearly legal image, apart from the common-
place 'lease', that Lord Simon finds in the seventeen initial
'marriage-broking' Sonnets is 'determination' in Sonnet 13:

> So should that beauty which you hold in lease
> Find no determination.

Sonnet 99 (They that 'do not do the thing they most do
show') is suspected of flirting with Machiavellism.[10]

Another distinguished present-day Judge, Viscount Radcliffe,[11] a Lord of Appeal and Fellow of All Souls, has
referred ironically to the attempts made to 'improve' Shakespeare in the eighteenth and nineteenth centuries, for
example, by rewriting *Romeo and Juliet* and *King Lear* with
happy endings. He has also commented playfully on Canon
Plumptre's refinement of Shakespeare's coarseness, e.g.:

> Under the greenwood tree,
> Who lives to work with me?

and in Cloten's aubade in *Cymbeline*:

> With everything that pretty is,
> For shame, thou sluggard, rise.

[7] Sir Jocelyn Simon, Q.C., 'Shakespeare's Legal and Political Background'
(1968) 84 *Law Quarterly Review*, 33, at p. 34.
[8] ibid., pp. 34-5.    [9] Dyer's Reports, p. 301a.
[10] (1968) 84 *Law Quarterly Review*, at p. 47.
[1] Viscount Radcliffe, *Not in Feather Beds* (1968), pp. 156-8.

One of the foremost names among English lawyers who have written about Shakespeare in the present century is that of Sir George Greenwood. His early studies of Shakespeare's law led him to disbelieve that the man of Stratford wrote the works, but later his fixed anti-Stratfordianism coloured his studies of Shakespeare's law. Although a competent lawyer, he sometimes misquoted Shakespeare. With regard to the poems, Greenwood[12] quotes with approval the statement by another lawyer, Appleton Morgan, that *Venus and Adonis* is the most carefully polished production that William Shakespeare's name was ever signed to, and as polished, elegant and sumptuous a piece of rhetoric as English letters have ever produced: but he confessed that *The Rape of Lucrece* seemed to him tedious and pedantic, and he found it hard to discover much real poetic inspiration in it.

In spite of the warning by Mr Justice Trout that 'quotations from Shakespeare (in Court) are generally meaningless and always unsound',[13] we do find in our law reports or newspapers that judges and counsel cite Shakespeare in Court. The practice began in the seventeenth century with Judge Jeffreys. The great eighteenth-century advocate, Erskine, prepared himself for the Bar by learning many of Shakespeare's famous speeches by heart, and he is said to have been so familiar with Shakespeare that he could carry on a conversation for days on all subjects in the language of his characters.

In an action some years ago between a Scottish laird and the Great North of Scotland Railway, the question was whether Queen's Messenger and summer excursion trains were passenger trains, so that the railway company were bound by covenant to stop regularly at a certain station. One of the judges in the Court of Session, Lord Young,[14]

---

[12] Sir George Greenwood, *Is There a Shakespeare Problem?* (1916), pp. 208, 218
[13] A. P. Herbert, *Uncommon Law* (1935), p. 22. The author, later Sir Alan Herbert, was a non-practising barrister.
[14] 11 Court Sess. Cas., 4th. Series, at p. 386.

had cited the familiar case of *Shylock v. Antonio*, and intimated that the pursuer here was going for his pound of flesh. Lord Bramwell on appeal in the House of Lords,[15] expressed the following view:

> Now I am quite certain that I should have decided that case in the way in which dear Portia did, not perhaps entirely on her reasonings, but upon some of them. The learned Lord of Session says – 'The pursuer says it is within the weight of his pound of flesh.' Now, the truth is that Shylock never had a pound of flesh which could be called his; it had never been appropriated to him, and he could only get it by the commission of a considerable crime, no less than that of murder. If indeed the pound of flesh had been appropriated to him and was his, and if Antonio had wished to steal an ounce of it, I should have given the whole pound to Shylock.

'As to the pound of flesh argument', his Lordship concluded,[16] 'the judgment is not that the appellant should have none, but three-quarters of his pound. His right is to all; whether as a reasonable man he should exact all, is another matter.' In the more recent case of *Tsakiroglou & Co. v. Noblee Thorl*[17] the question was whether a contract for the shipment of Sudanese groundnuts to Hamburg was validly rescinded or frustrated by the closure of the Suez Canal. 'Lawyers have ever been more prone than merchants to cling to the letter of the contract', said Mr Justice Diplock, 'see, for example, *Shylock v. Antonio*, a case which might have been decided on grounds of public policy but, in fact, turned on a pure question of construction.'

In *Re Freeman*,[18] an application for the settlement of the property of a lunatic not so found, the question for the

---

[15] *Sir R. Burnett, Bart., v. Great North of Scotland Rly. Co.* (1885) 22 *Scottish Law Reporter*, 456, at p. 459.

[16] 10 *Appeal Cases*, 147, at p. 167.

[17] [1960] 2 Queen's Bench Division Reports, pp. 318, 329.

[18] [1927] 1 Chancery Division Reports, 479, at p. 487.

Court of Appeal was the meaning of 'suffer an injustice' in section 171 of the Law of Property Act 1925. An injustice, declared Lord Hanworth, Master of the Rolls, quoting *King John*, v. 2, must connote unfairness, and impart a sense of grievance at 'the hand of stern injustice and confused wrong.' The question of the prescriptive right of the inhabitants of the County Palatine of Durham to go on to the foreshore and take away sea-washed coal was in issue in the Court of Appeal in *Alfred F. Beckett v. Lyons*.[19] Talking of 'sea-coal', Lord Justice Harman said, it had become a common fuel by the time of Elizabeth I, and it would be remembered that, according to Mistress Quickly, when Falstaff promised to marry her he was 'sitting in my Dolphin-chamber, at the round table, by a sea-coal fire, when the prince broke thy head for liking his father to a singing-man of Windsor.' An American court in *Snyder v. Snyder* (1879),[20] on a question of the custody of the children of a marriage, cited a passage from *The Taming of the Shrew*, v. 2 ('Thy husband is thy lord, thy life, thy keeper . . .'), as correctly stating the law concerning the relation of husband and wife.

Lord Denning, presiding as Master of the Rolls over the Court of Appeal, observed recently in *Allen v. Sir Alfred McAlpine & Sons Ltd.*[21] that 'All through the years men have protested against the law's delay. Shakespeare ranked it among the whips and scorns of time.' But citation of Shakespeare by counsel does not necessarily help to win cases. Lord Denning has told how, in his earlier days at the Bar, he and his leader, Sir William Jowitt, appealed to the House of Lords in the case of a Major Rowlandson who had insured his life for £50,000. The insurance policy provided that no payment would be made if the insured

[19] [1967] Chancery Division Reports, p. 449.

[20] Common Pleas, Lachawanna County, Pa.; see Otto Erickson, 'Shakespeare and the Law: A Tercentenary Obiter', (1916) 20 *Law Notes*, 4. C. K. Davis, op. cit., refers to a number of other American cases and legal textbooks citing Shakespeare.

[21] [1968] Queen's Bench Division Reports, p. 229.

committed suicide in the first year. Being unable to renew the premium, the Major shot himself dead in a taxi two minutes before the expiry of the ninth year. In spite of the inference that the amount would be paid if the insured committed suicide after one year, the House of Lords held the insurance company not liable on the ground that no person, or his representatives, can recover money for the fruits of his own crime. 'We quoted Hamlet and Ophelia,' says Lord Denning,[22] 'including the part about the grave-diggers. None of it did any good. We lost the case.'

In criminal cases Judges and counsel occasionally liken defendants and other parties to such characters as Macbeth, Lady Macbeth and Iago.[23]

Some of the most reputable legal authors in the English-speaking world cite Shakespeare in support of statements of principle. Leading text-writers on the law of evidence have approved of the strict adherence to the procedure of trial by battle in *Richard II*,[24] or the proposition in *Othello*, III. 3, that what a person has been heard to say while talking in his sleep seems not to be admissible as evidence against him.[25] From the same scene in *Othello* comes a quotation in an article by Richard O'Sullivan, Q.C., on 'A Scale of Values in the Common Law.'[26] The law of defamation (on which O'Sullivan edited a standard textbook) guards more jealously a man's right to his reputation than his title to

[22] Lord Denning, '1967 Turner Memorial Lecture', (1967) 2 *University of Tasmania Law Review*, 349, at p. 353. Lord Denning quotes Portia's 'quality of mercy' speech, ibid., p. 359; and also in 'Law and Life in our Time', (1967) 5 *Legal Executive*, 111, at p. 113.

[23] [1967] *Criminal Law Review*, p. 496, note by Professor Brian Hogan.

[24] E.g., J. B. Thayer, 'Law and Fact in Jury Trials', (1891) 4 *Harvard Law Review*, 147, 156.

[25] *Best on Evidence* (3rd. ed.) cited by R. F. Fuller in 'Shakespeare as a Lawyer', (1863) 9 *Upper Canada Law Journal*, 91. This quotation is not in the latest edition of Best (12th. ed., 1922).

[26] Richard O'Sullivan, Q.C., *Spirit of the Common Law*, p. 152: taken from an article in (1937) 1 *Modern Law Review*, 27.

goods – as Iago says, my good name is worth much more to me than my purse. Successive editions of *Lewin on Trusts* began by illustrating the fact that trusts were formerly called 'uses' by quoting the settlement of Shylock's property in *The Merchant of Venice*, iv. 1 ('The other half in use . . .'). Another old textbook, Haynes, *Outlines of Equity*, says: 'It is clear that, had the scene of Shakespeare's play been laid in England, and not in Venice, the proper advice for Portia to have given would have been to file a bill in Chancery.'[27]

The German jurist, Radbruch, in his work on the philosophy of law,[28] heads the section on 'Mercy' with the quotation: 'The quality of mercy is not strained. . . .' Writing of the independence of judges, Professor A. L. Goodhard,[29] for many years Professor of Jurisprudence at Oxford, says it consists in their being bound by law, for if they were free to decide according to discretion we should have only a series of individual orders. Shakespeare, he points out, based the trial scene in *The Merchant of Venice* on this point; for in reply to Bassanio's plea to the Duke to 'wrest once the law to your authority', Portia answers: 'It must not be. There is no power in Venice can alter a decree established.'

The late Professor R. W. Lee, a leading authority on Roman and Roman-Dutch law, in a textbook on Roman law described the procedure of executing judgment in the *Legis actio per manus injectionem* (form of action by laying on of hand), whereby judgment debtors who had not paid by the time fixed were put to death or sold across the Tiber. He went on to explain that if there were several creditors they were entitled to share in the liquidation of the corpse; but that the statute anticipated and avoided the point made

[27] F. O. Haynes, *Outlines of Equity* (5th. ed., 1880), p. 19. This passage is cited by F. L. Windolph, a member of the Pennsylvania Bar, in *Reflections of the Law in Literature*, p. 52.

[28] Gustav Radbruch, *Rechtsphilosophie* (Leipzig, 3rd. ed., 1932), translated by Kurt Wilk in *The Legal Philosophies of Lask, Radbruch and Dabin* (1950), p. 195.

[29] A. L. Goodhart, in *Interpretations of Modern Legal Philosophies: Essays in Honor of Roscoe Pound* (ed. Sayre, New York, 1947), p. 297.

by Portia, by adding: 'If they have cut too much or too little, be it free from blame.'[30] On the other hand, Professor Julius Stone, the distinguished Australian jurist, writing of the *lex talionis* in Jewish law,[31] tells us that the interpreters of the Talmud came to prohibit the *talio* and to substitute money compensation, on the rabbinical arguments including that later used by Portia to check Shylock. 'The talionic exaction', writes Professor Stone, 'had to be no more than the *precise* equivalent, and humans were incapable of such precise exaction.'

Like other educated speakers and writers, lawyers habitually employ Shakespeare quotations to illustrate or adorn their discourse. Sir Norman Birkett, one of the greatest English advocates of the present century and later a Lord of Appeal, who was an enthusiastic lover of literature, in proposing the toast of 'The Immortal Memory' at the Shakespeare Birthday Luncheon at Stratford-on-Avon in 1938 included some well-worn quotations from *Richard II* and *Henry V*.[32] One of these he repeated a few days before he died in a speech in the House of Lords opposing a Manchester Corporation Bill to permit the construction of waterworks in his native Lake District.[33]

Sir Walter Scott, legal practitioner as well as poet and novelist, expressed keen admiration for Shakespeare, whom he introduces as an already successful poet and playwright into scenes of *Kenilworth* that would have occurred when Shakespeare was about fifteen. Scott liked to prefix lines from Shakespeare to chapters of his novels. Thus before chapter 20 of *The Heart of Midlothian* stands a quotation from *Measure for Measure* in which Claudio begs his sister to save his life, indicating that Scott saw Jeanie's problem

---

[30] R. W. Lee, *Elements of Roman Law* (4th. ed., 1956), p. 428.
[31] Julius Stone, *Human Law and Human Justice* (1965), p. 22n.
[32] H. Montgomery Hyde, *Norman Birkett* (1964), pp. 446-7.
[33] ibid., p. 614.

as being similar to Isabella's. At the head of the chapter in *The Antiquary* that contains the graphic account of the cliff rescue from the storm and rising tide, we find lines from *King Lear*, IV. I:

> There is a cliff, whose high and bending head,
> Looks fearfully on the confined deep. . . .

An attempt to add a chapter to the biography of Shakespeare was made by W. G. Thorpe,[34] member of the Middle Temple. Possessing a copy of the First Folio, a manuscript of Essex's *Apologie* against Burghley's policy of peace with Spain and also a lively imagination, he arrived at the conclusion that there was a close intimacy between Shakespeare and Bacon over a period of twenty years, involving large business transactions both in theatrical and money matters. As actor and manager from 1588 onwards Shakespeare would know Bacon, Master of the Revels at Gray's Inn. The playwright had two ways of becoming affluent. One was by gambling, the proceeds of which enabled him to buy New Place, though the money that enabled him to buy more land in 1602 came from the fine Catesby paid to Bacon. The other was by lending money to Bacon, for which he was repaid in part by Bacon getting Shakespeare's plays copied out (with 'scarce a blot') at the Scrivenery at Twickenham Park which Bacon had acquired from Essex. From this Thorpe proceeds to deduce that the epitaph on Shakespeare prefixed to the Second Folio and commonly attributed to Milton ('What needs my Shakespeare for his honoured bones') was in fact written by Bacon, the closing lines of whose *Henry VII* share a common echo of Horace's *Exegi monumentum aere perennius*, though Thorpe does admit that the epitaph is full of 'almost Miltonian music'. Why was it not attached to the First Folio? Because

---

[34] W. G. Thorpe, F.S.A., *The Hidden Lives of Shakespeare and Bacon* (1897). Letters from the author on this topic to *The Academy* dated 1895 are set out in the Appendix to that book.

when Shakespeare died and Ben Jonson and other friends applied to Bacon for help in setting up a monument, all they got was this poem saying that Shakespeare did not need any monument. In Thorpe's (Bacon's?) version, incidentally, the first line has 'hallowed' for 'honoured'.

Mr Justice Madden, who had been the holder of both the Irish Law Offices before becoming a Judge of the Irish Queen's Bench Division, in *The Diary of Master William Silence* (1897)[35] applied to the elucidation of Shakespeare's text the lore of deer-hunting and horsemanship. He pretends to have discovered a diary of the son of Justice Silence, in which are traced the steps of a courtship and marrriage that supplied many of the incidents of *The Taming of the Shrew* and *The Merry Wives of Windsor*. The hunting and hawking described, according to another Irish lawyer who enjoyed the good things of life,[36] give valuable textual criticism of the plays.

Augustine Birrell, K.C., Chancery practitioner and politician, included in his early *Obiter Dicta*[37] an elegant essay on Falstaff. Among a number of 'mock trials' that lawyers have liked to write is a *Trial of Sir John Falstaff*,[38] wherein the Fat Knight is permitted to answer for himself concerning the charges laid against him, and to attorney his own case. The book is a lawyer's jocular fantasy.

We must admit that lawyers have also made their contribution to Shakespeare forgeries or suspected forgeries. Theobald is sometimes thought to have fabricated his ascription to Shakespeare of *The Double Falsehood*, which he produced in an adapted version at Drury Lane in 1727.

[35] D. H. Madden, *The Diary of Master William Silence: a Study of Shakespeare and of Elizabethan Sport* (1897). The author was also Vice-Chancellor of Dublin University, a post equivalent to that of Pro-Chancellor at a modern English University. See also his *Shakespeare and His Fellows: an attempt to decipher the Man and his Nature* (1916).

[36] Maurice Healy, *The Old Munster Circuit* (1939), pp. 36-7.

[37] Augustine Birrell, *Obiter Dicta* (1884).

[38] A. M. F. Randolph, *The Trial of Sir John Falstaff* (New York, 1893).

It is probable that Theobald adapted an old play to which was attached a tradition that Shakespeare was the author.[39] Steevens was accused by Isaac Disraeli on insufficient evidence of forging a letter of Peele's describing a conversation about *Hamlet* between Shakespeare and Alleyn. It has also been suggested that Steevens composed the lines attributed to Jonson and Shakespeare –

*Jonson*
If, but *stage actors*, all the world displays,
Where shall we find *spectators* of their plays?

*Shakespeare*
Little, or much, of what we see, we do,
We're all both *actors* and *spectators* too.

– which he said came from a manuscript of William Oldys. Further, Steevens's statement that the names Othello and Iago occur in John Reynolds's *God's Revenge against Adultery*, indicating that Shakespeare and Reynolds both took them from a lost story, is suspect as these names have not been found in any of Reynolds's works.[40]

William Henry Ireland, a conveyancer's clerk who had access to old deeds, fabricated many Shakespeare signatures, letters between Shakespeare, Anne Hathaway and Southampton, and deeds between Shakespeare and Heminge and Condell; as well as bogus manuscripts of plays. The forgeries were published in good faith by his father[41] in 1796, but were exposed by Malone in the same year.[42]

[39] E. K. Chambers, *William Shakespeare: A Study of Facts and Problems*, (2 vols., 1930), I, pp. 539-42; II, p. 377.

[40] Chambers, *William Shakespeare*, pp. 274-9; 379-80.

[41] Samuel Ireland, *Miscellaneous Papers and Legal Instruments under the hand and seal of William Shakespeare: including the Tragedy of King Lear, and a small fragment of Hamlet, from the original Manuscripts in the possession of Samuel Ireland, of Norfolk Street* (1796); W. H. Ireland, *An Authentic Account of the Shakespearian Manuscripts* (1796); *The Confessions of William Henry Ireland: containing the Particulars of his Fabrication of the Shakespeare Manuscripts* (1805).

[42] *Inquiry into the Authenticity of Certain Miscellaneous Papers and Legal Instruments* (1796). And see Bernard Grebanier, *The Great Shakespeare Forgery* (1966).

John Payne Collier, literary historian, journalist, librarian to the Duke of Devonshire and one of the founders of the Shakespeare Society, was called to the Bar by the Middle Temple in 1829 at the age of forty, his call having been delayed for ten years by a hostile profession after his publication as a Bar student of *Criticisms on the Bar*.[43] Collier's undoubted contributions to Shakespeare scholarship were offset by the uncounted forgeries that sprang from his fertile imagination. The latter related to the history of English dramatic poetry and to Shakespeare's life and works, the most notable being the 'seventeenth-century' marginal emendations to the Second Folio which he published in 1852.[44] These forgeries were exposed seven years later by another lawyer, Ingleby.[45]

[43] J. P. Collier, *Criticisms on the Bar* (1819). The book contained strictures on the principal counsel practicising in the Courts of King's Bench, Common Pleas, Chancery and Exchequer.

[44] Chambers, *William Shakespeare*, II, pp. 384-93.

[45] C. M. Ingleby, *The Shakespeare Fabrications* (1859); *A Complete View of the Shakespeare Controversy concerning the Genuineness of the M.S. Matter Published by Collier* (1861).

# 12

## Did Shakespeare have a Legal Training?

The thought that Shakespeare may have had some legal training does not seem to have occurred to the two earliest lawyer-editors, Rowe and Theobald, but the controversy goes back at least to Malone, who first put forward the suggestion in a footnote to *Hamlet* in his essay on the chronological order of the plays in 1778. Malone expanded the suggestion in his first edition of Shakespeare's works in 1790, where, citing some two dozen passages from Shakespeare, he wrote:

> . . . his knowledge of legal terms is not such as might be acquired by the casual observation of even his all-comprehending mind; it has the appearance of *technical* skill; and he is so fond of displaying it, on all occasions, that I suspect he was early initiated in at least the forms of law, and was employed, while he remained at Stratford, in the office of some country attorney, who was at the same time a petty conveyancer, and perhaps, also, the seneschal of some manor court. . . . Perhaps it may be said that our authour in the same manner may be found to have been equally conversant with the terms of divinity, or physick. Whenever as large a number of instances of his ecclesiastical or medicinal knowledge shall be produced, what has now been stated will certainly not be entitled to any weight.[1]

[1] Edmond Malone (ed.), *The Plays and Poems of William Shakespeare*, vol. I, Part I, p. 307.

## Did Shakespeare have a Legal Training?

Was it the Irish coming out in Malone when he said that he had to brush up his black-letter law to understand Shakespeare's allusions? It would have been more remarkable if Shakespeare had shown some familiarity with the law of Malone's time. Even if Malone was, as Sir Sidney Lee says,[2] 'a laborious and amiable archaeologist, without much ear for poetry or delicate literary taste', he was a lawyer with more than a little practical experience, and his opinion on this question has exerted considerable influence.

Rushton in 1858 published a shilling booklet of fifty pages, *Shakespeare a Lawyer*, in which he sought to show that Shakespeare had acquired a general knowledge of the principles and practice of the law of real property, of the common law and criminal law, that he was familiar with the exact letter of the statute law, and that he used law terms correctly. In support of his thesis, Rushton cited a number of legal expressions from Shakespeare's works and explained them by reference to such legal authorities as Littleton, Coke and Rolle's Abridgment; but he made no reference to Shakespeare's contemporary authors, nor to his sources. He followed this in the next year with another shilling booklet of thirty-four pages, *Shakespeare's Legal Maxims*, arguing that Shakespeare's use of legal maxims indicates legal training, but overlooking the fact that other Elizabethan playwrights frequently employed legal maxims in their plays, usually in a more direct form than Shakespeare.

Meanwhile, early one winter's morning in 1859 at the south gateway of Lincoln's Inn large placards were seen adhering to a bookseller's window, asking in bold red type: 'Was Shakespeare an Attorney's Clerk? by John, Lord Campbell'.[3] This was an advertisement for a short book by

[2] Sir Sidney Lee, *A Life of William Shakespeare* (1898), p. 266. On the other hand, Malone had a keen appreciation of painting, especially portraits, and was a friend of Gainsborough and Reynolds, see Sir James Prior, *Life of Edmond Malone* (1860), pp. 333 et seq. ('Maloniana'.)

[3] (1859) 7 *Law Magazine and Law Review*, 41.

Lord Campbell, *Shakespeare's Legal Acquirements Considered.* Because of the author's position in the legal profession, the book has had a great influence among laymen from Macaulay onwards. It is, therefore, worth while looking into its origin and background. Its origin was a letter from John Payne Collier, literary historian, barrister and fabricator of Shakespeareana, asking his Lordship his opinion on the question whether Shakespeare was a clerk in an attorney's office at Stratford before he joined the players in London. In 1858, when the letter was written, Lord Campbell, Chief Justice of the Queen's Bench, was seventy-nine years of age. Yet he spent the summer vacation at his country estate reading through Shakespeare's works in order to answer Collier's question.[4]

Two things may be said about Lord Campbell which may prepare the reader to judge his book on Shakespeare's legal acquirements. He had a sense of humour, as is shown by the reasons he gave for preferring golf to cricket, that cricket 'is too violent and gives no opportunity for conversation.' Secondly, Lord Campbell's reputation for scholarship, based on his *Lives* of the Lord Chancellors and Chief Justices, as opposed to legal learning, is not high. A reading of his Preface shows that the elderly Chief Justice[5] was not taking the matter very seriously. As he says in his introductory letter to Payne Collier, he had 'glanced at' the subject of Shakespeare's legal acquirements in both his

---

[4] The following entries appear consecutively in his diary for 1858: *Hartrigge: August* 23. 'My amusement is to read once more the whole of Shakespeare's plays marking all the passages in which he introduces legal phraseology or alludes to legal proceedings, that I may consider the question whether the Bard of Avon, before he left Stratford, had not been an attorney's clerk.'

*Hartrigge, October* 28. 'Alas! the long vacation is over, and tomorrow I return to London. . . . I have accomplished my purpose of writing a dissertation on the question of Shakespeare's legal training, which, if it be approved of by a critical friend to whom I shall submit it, I may bring out in the shape of a shilling's-worth for railways.': *Life of John Campbell*, ed. by his daughter, The Hon. Mrs Hardcastle (1881), II, 361.

[5] He became Lord Chancellor in 1859 at the age of eighty.

## Did Shakespeare have a Legal Training?

*Lives of the Lord Chancellors* (1845) and his *Lives of the Chief Justices* (1849). Referring in the latter work to the Falconbridge bastardy trial in *King John*, I. I, Campbell had said: 'This scene corroborates the supposition that Shakespeare, either before he left Stratford or on his coming to London, had been employed in an attorney's office. He is uniformly right in his law and in his use of legal phraseology, which no mere quickness or intuition can account for.'[6] In his *Shakespeare's Legal Acquirements Considered* Campbell found legal phrases and allusions in twenty-three out of thirty-seven plays. Of the indictment against Lord Saye in *2 Henry VI*, IV. 7, he says this shows an experienced hand: it is 'quite certain' that the drawer of this indictment must have had some acquaintance with *The Crown Circuit Companion*, and must have had a full and accurate knowlege of that rather obscure and intricate subject, Felony and Benefit of Clergy.[7] The discussion in the grave-diggers' scene as to whether Ophelia was entitled to Christian burial, his Lordship says, 'proves' that Shakespeare had read and studied Plowden's report of *Hales v. Petit*; while Sonnet 46 'smells as potently of the attorney's office as any of the stanzas penned by Lord Kenyon while an attorney's clerk in Wales.' Kenyon was Chief Justice of the King's Bench at the beginning of the nineteenth century.

In view of the limited time available to an old and busy man on his summer vacation, Lord Campbell's reading was necessarily superficial. He said he had found nothing that fairly bore on the controversy in fourteen of the plays, although these fourteen contain at least 150 legal allusions, including more than 30 in *Richard II* and nearly as many in *Henry VIII*.[8]

Richard Bentley[9] finds Lord Campbell's quotations,

---

[6] *Lives of the Chief Justices*, I, p. 43.

[7] *Shakespeare's Legal Acquirements Considered*, pp. 75-6.

[8] P. S. Clarkson and C. T. Warren, *The Law of Property in Shakespeare and the Elizabethan Drama* (Baltimore, 1942), pp. xix-xx.

[9] See Richard Bentley, 'Shakespeare's Law', (1923) 155 *Law Times*, 34.

though fewer, more convincing than Edward White's.[10] The one startling statement of Lord Campbell's is that Shakespeare wrote a beautiful and business-like hand. 'Let who will say that it is beautiful', Bentley comments, 'I deny that it is business-like!' To his mind one of the most convincing remarks Lord Campbell makes is his failure to remark at all on the ' no jot of blood' quibble in *The Merchant of Venice*; his Lordship ignores it as not worthy of comment in relation to the question of Shakespeare's legal training. Lord Campbell's knowledge of Roman Law, in connection with the Roman plays, was one of his qualifications to write on the subject.

Some of Lord Campbell's notes are undoubtedly useful, but the general tone throughout is that of an indulgent stretching of the case in favour of Collier's brief. His general conclusion, often overlooked, is in fact neutral. There is evidence to go to the jury, he says, but the evidence is 'very far from being conclusive,' and if the jury gave a verdict either way it could not properly be set aside. As for Shakespeare's poems, 'cursory perusal' of them did not discover the propensity to legal thoughts and words which might be expected in an attorney's clerk who takes to rhyming.[11] His Lordship's sense of humour oversteps the bounds of good taste when to the line 'Why so large cost, having so short a lease?' he appends the footnote: 'Taxing an overcharge in the attorney's bill of costs.' Foss,[12] writing shortly after the publication of Lord Campbell's book, said that 'from the trifling nature of some of the passages he produced from the various plays tending to confirm this hypothesis [that Shakespeare spent his youth in an attorney's office], we are left in doubt whether his lordship, though professing to be grave, is not quizzing the theorists and treating the subject ironically.'

[10] E. J. White, *Commentaries on the Law in Shakespeare* (2nd. ed., 1913).
[11] *Shakespeare's Legal Acquirements Considered*, p. 99.
[12] Edmund Foss, *The Judges of England* (1864), vol. 9. The biographer was a solicitor, magistrate and a founder of the Incorporated Law Society.

Looking back over a hundred years we find it difficult to understand why Lord Campbell's book has been taken so seriously in some quarters. A scathing review appeared almost immediately in a legal magazine[13] – written perhaps by a friend of Rushton – openly accusing Lord Campbell of plagiarism. He had, said the reviewer, successfully combined the work of biography with that of the *nisi prius* leader, 'for it is well known to be an essential quality in the latter, that . . . he should skilfully draw upon, and boldly appropriate, the labours of his juniors.' Later Lord Campbell was defended against the charge of plagiarism by T. M. Wears,[14] who pointed out that many quotations in Rushton are not in Campbell, and vice versa, and that the methods of Lord Campbell are more selective and artistic. In a second article,[15] Wears says he examined all passages in the plays propounding legal doctrine and found no bad law. 'It is difficult to prove that Shakespeare had a legal training', he concludes,[16] 'and impossible to believe that he had not.'

Rather more than twenty years after the publication of Lord Campbell's book, an American lawyer named Heard published a work entitled *Shakespeare as a Lawyer*,[17] the object of which was to point out and explain Shakespeare's references to the technical science of the law. The learned author thought there could be no doubt that legal expressions are more frequent and are used with more precision in Shakespeare's plays than in those of any other dramatist of the period. Among the terms picked out is Pistol's '*absque hoc*' in *2 Henry IV*, v. 5, a special traverse (denial, in pleading, of facts alleged by the other party) when proceedings are in Latin. In the absence of any explanation of

[13] (1859) 7 *Law Magazine and Law Review*, p. 41.

[14] T. M. Wears, 'Lord Campbell & Rushton – A Vindication', (1934) 12 *Canadian Bar Review*, 97.

[15] T. M. Wears, 'Shakespeare's Legal Acquirements', (1938) 16 *Canadian Bar Review*, 28.

[16] ibid., p. 41.

[17] F. F. Heard, *Shakespeare as a Lawyer* (Boston, 1883).

this highly technical term of pleading in all reports and treatises extant in the time of Shakespeare, Heard says it seems to justify the conclusion that he must have obtained a knowledge of it from actual practice.[18] Of Shakespeare's will, Heard thinks it was probably written by himself. It is expressed in terms at once apt and concise: the intention is abundantly clear. 'Without professional education and experience,' says Heard,[19] 'the technical language of the law could not have been so appropriately used.' A somewhat circuitous piece of reasoning! Having presented some of the evidence on the question whether Shakespeare was professionally versed in the law, he writes,[20] 'If the verdict is in the affirmative, it may safely be concluded, that neither a motion in arrest of judgment nor a writ of error will lie.'

The question whether Shakespeare had a legal training was raised again some years later by John Light, the Attorney-General of Connecticut.[21] He found that Shakespeare speaks well of lawyers and understands their duty towards their client; that there are very few lawyers who really understand the true spirit and science of the law as well as Shakespeare; and that the dramatist frequently used the language of conveyancing, and never once slipped in its use. On the other hand, Shakespeare's genius is the essential explanation of his accurate knowledge of the law; he had an unrivalled capacity for absorbing and retaining knowledge. 'I incline to the opinion', Light concludes,[22] 'that he never studied law as a science, but that he had a natural aptitude for it, and it is possible he was a clerk in a lawyer's office at Stratford for a number of years before going to London, and that there and in London he frequented the courts and associated with lawyers and judges.'

[18] ibid., p. 48.
[19] ibid., p. 101.
[20] ibid., p. 103.
[21] The Hon. J. H. Light, 'Law and Lawyers in Shakespeare, (1914) 21 *Case and Comment*, 185.
[22] ibid., p. 189.

A member of the Missouri Bar, asking the same question, has expressed the opinion that it is highly probable that Shakespeare, in his quest after knowledge, invaded and encompassed the realm of legal lore, and thereby enriched his amazing mind by acquiring an adequate knowledge and a true understanding of both the spirit and the letter of the common law.[23]

More recently an English solicitor, S. M. Gibson,[24] has expressed the view that Shakespeare probably had some legal experience before he went to London; and has suggested that, during the two barren years when the theatres were closed, he found work in an attorney's office, perhaps as a conveyancer or engrossing clerk in the City, and that he wrote the Sonnets in his spare time – if not in office hours. 'It is with the Sonnets', says Gibson, 'that the poet's vocabulary begins to take on its peculiar legal flavour', and he asks: 'When he wrote (in Sonnet 92): "O what a happy title do I find" was he writing as a lover, a sycophant or a conveyancer?'

Across the Atlantic in 1859 Richard Grant White[25] published a joint review of Rushton's first booklet and Lord Campbell's book. Grant White (1821-85) was an American who was admitted to the Bar but never practised. After helping to edit a short-lived humorous paper called *Yankee Doodle*, he turned to literary criticism and other more serious forms of writing, in spite of which anti-Stratfordians tend to describe him as a distinguished lawyer. His review is strongly critical of the arguments based by Rushton and Campbell on the passages cited from Shakespeare. For example, on the passage about *praemunire* in *Henry VIII*,

---

[23] W. W. Calvin, 'Shakespeare and the Law', (1946) 51 *Case and Comment*, 6.

[24] S. M. Gibson, 'Shakespeare in the Sonnets', (1964) 61 *Law Society's Gazette*, 23.

[25] R. G. White, 'William Shakespeare, Attorney at Law and Solicitor in Chancery', (July 1859) IV *Atlantic Monthly*, 84. Apart from his edition of Shakespeare's *Works*, incorporating 'Memoirs of William Shakespeare', his publications include *Studies in Shakespeare* (Boston and New York, 1886).

III. 2, he points out that there was a somewhat similar passage in an earlier work on Cromwell by Michael Drayton, who is not known to have been an attorney's clerk, and that in fact they were both following Holinshed. By an apparent *volte face* Grant White then reaches a conclusion similar to that of Rushton and Campbell. Yet he is too hardly treated by Robertson.[26] No doubt Robertson acquired a much wider and deeper knowledge of Elizabethan drama, but it was Grant White who – greatly improving on the amateur approach of Rushton and Campbell – pioneered the method of tackling the problem by comparing Shakespeare's works with those of his contemporaries and by adverting to Shakespeare's sources.

Among laymen Churton Collins,[27] in a passage mainly based on Lord Campbell's book, expressed his conviction that Shakespeare had studied law, and he thought it 'quite possible' that the dramatist was in early life employed as a clerk in an attorney's office, for example, attached to the Stratford Court of Record. Anyway, it is more probable that he was in an attorney's office than that he was a butcher. Perhaps the strongest lay supporter of this theory was Fripp, who gives a section of his important work on Shakespeare and Stratford the heading, 'In an Attorney's Office'.[28]

Some of the lawyers who have addressed themselves to this question have remained on the borderline. Three years after Grant White's review, R. F. Fuller,[29] having pointed out that many of Shakespeare's expressions, which in modern times are restricted to legal usage, were in common use in Shakespeare's day and so do not imply an acquaintance with the law, admitted that Shakespeare does seem to have had a knowledge of the forms and phrases of

[26] J. M. Robertson, *The Baconian Heresy* (1913), chap. 4.
[27] John Churton Collins, *Studies in Shakespeare* (1904), pp. 209-40: 'Was Shakespeare a Lawyer?'
[28] Edgar I. Fripp: *Shakespeare, Man and Artist* (1938), vol. I, §16.
[29] R. F. Fuller, 'Shakespeare as a Lawyer', (1863) 9 *Upper Canada Law Journal*, 91. This appears to be reprinted from (1862) 21 *Monthly Law Reporter* (Boston), 1.

real property which he might have acquired in the employ of a conveyancer and would probably not have gained otherwise. Real property is the driest department of law, and would not be studied merely for amusement. However, Fuller thought that Shakespeare never took to the business or imbued his mind with the great principles of jurisprudence. If he was ever connected with the business of an attorney he must have held some subordinate post, because if he had been admitted to practice as an attorney or had been an attorney's clerk, he would probably have attested many deeds, some of which we should expect to be extant.

Also on the borderline was George Wilkes[30] – known in his day as the fighting cock of American journalism – a lifelong reader of Shakespeare who was for a time in his youth a clerk in a law office. Instigated by a conversation with that prominent American lawyer, General B. F. Butler – who had been converted to the Baconian theory by Delia Bacon's book[31]–Wilkes took issue with Lord Campbell and formed the opinion that Shakespeare's plays and poems do not show an unusual legal knowledge. Wilkes's main theme is Shakespeare's respect for royalty and aristocracy, and his contempt for the lower classes. The author calls this an aristocratic tendency, although actually it is rather middle-class. He set out to prove, by internal evidence, that the dramatist could not have been either a statesman or a lawyer. In one place the author says there seems to be little doubt that Shakespeare went into an attorney's office: although he never became a lawyer he acquired the conveyancer's jargon and the phrases of attorneyship.[32]

Against examples of the apt, and apparently understanding, use of legal expressions by Shakespeare, J. B. Mackenzie offset the trial scene in *The Merchant of Venice*

[30] George Wilkes, *Shakespeare, from an American Point of View* etc. (1877), chap. 9, 'Legal Acquirements of Shakespeare'.
[31] Delia Bacon, *Philosophy of Shakespeare's Plays Unfolded* (1857). The American authoress of this diffuse work did not claim any relationship to Francis Bacon.
[32] Wilkes, op. cit., pp. 22-3.

which 'lends judicial methods the guise of opera bouffe', and the arraignment of Hermione in *The Winter's Tale* which makes Leontes judge in his own cause.[33]

The weight of legal opinion, among those who accept William Shakespeare of Stratford as the author of the works attributed to him, is that the internal evidence does not indicate that Shakespeare had legal training or experience. Benjamin F. Washer,[34] of the Louisville, Kentucky, Bar, taking the view that the law was pre-eminently the calling of the wealthy, suggested that the (supposed) bankruptcy of the Shakespeare family would have prevented the young William from adopting it even if he had wished and been qualified to do so, and after Shakespeare arrived in London he had neither time nor opportunity for adopting the law as a profession. Is it likely, asks Washer, that if Shakespeare had had a legal training he would have written thirty-seven plays, not one of which is founded on a legal plot or story? Would even a lawyer's clerk produce scores of acts without making one of them relate to the law? This unusual argument was apparently intended to relate to the profession of barrister, because in a second article Washer goes on to consider another possibility. Those who hold that Shakespeare had, or probably had, a legal training think it was probably in the office of a conveyancer. Washer gives a list of about sixty real property terms found in Shakespeare, but says that if we investigate how far Shakespeare uses the terms to be found in Littleton, we discover that some common and important terms he does not use at all – e.g. mortgage, donor, vendor, grantor, escheat, evict, apportion, contingent, premises, feoffment, abeyance, corody, mort-

---

[33] J. B. Mackenzie, 'Was Shakespeare bound to an Attorney?' (1902) 14 *Green Bag*, 58.

[34] B. F. Washer, 'William Shakespeare, Attorney at Law', (1898) 10 *Green Bag*, 303, 336. D. R. Keys saw no evidence that Shakespeare had any legal training, 'Was Shakespeare bred an Attorney?' (1902) 2 *Canadian Law Review*, 83. No lawyer would have written *The Merchant of Venice*, says E. F. S. in 'Portia as a Judge', *Weekly Westminster Gazette*, 3 February 1923, p. 12.

main, estovers, emblements, alienation, freehold, copyhold, waiver, encumber, easement, occupant and laches. 'Consideration' is never used in the technical legal sense, and 'seal' is used in connection with every kind of agreement. 'Trust' is only once used in a technical sense, when Helicanus says: 'His sealed commission left in trust with me' (*Pericles*, 1. 3). However, it is not clear to us why, even if the dramatist were familiar with Littleton's *Tenures*, he need contrive to bring such words as corody, estovers and emblements into his plays, except perhaps as fodder for his comedians.

William C. Devecmon,[35] a member of the Maryland Bar and of the Shakespeare Society of New York, saw no profound knowledge of law disclosed in the plays. 'Shakespeare's knowledge of law', he says,[36] 'was simply a knowledge of legal expressions, with a fairly correct idea of their application such as any bright man attending court frequently and in daily companionship with lawyers could not fail to acquire; and of the law itself he had no real knowledge, except such little as he could pick up in the manner indicated.' Webster's *The Devil's Law Case* contains more legal expressions, some of them highly technical and all correctly used, than are to be found in any single one of Shakespeare's works. In his last chapter setting out what are called 'Some of Shakespeare's Errors in Legal Terminology', Devecmon, on the other hand, falls into the error of expecting the characters – whatever the time, place or dramatic purpose – to use the technical terms of English law with precision. A similar conclusion is reached in a book by Judge Charles C. Allen,[37] of the Supreme Court of Massachusetts, who thought that Shakespeare's legal knowledge was not extraordinary, or such as to imply that the author was educated as a lawyer or even as a lawyer's clerk: his legal knowledge

[35] W. C. Devecmon, *In Re Shakespeare's 'Legal Acquirements'* (New York, 1899).
[36] ibid., p. 32. See also his conclusion at p. 51.
[37] Charles C. Allen, *Notes on the Bacon-Shakespeare Question* (Boston, 1900).

may be paralleled by many citations from other authors. Judge Allen also has a chapter on Bad Law, or the untechnical use of legal terms, in Shakespeare.

The members of the Vermont Bar Association at their annual meeting in 1903 heard an address delivered by their President, John H. Senter, on the question: 'Was Shakespeare a Lawyer?'[38] expressing the view that no lawyer would write down such nonsense as what is said about Shylock's bond. Shakespeare's legal acumen is seen only in the fact that this law is put into the mouth of a woman, which recalls a passage in *Cymbeline*, II. 3:

> *Cloten.*                                     I will make
> One of the women lawyer to me, for
> I yet not understand the case myself.

August Goll,[39] the Danish criminologist, remarks that Homer is another great writer about whose personal identity doubts are felt, but that Shakespeare had similar opportunities to Dickens for meeting lawyers and finding out about the law. Some hesitation was expressed by Herbert Morse,[40] barrister of Lincoln's Inn and author of 'Where Do We Come From?', writing in 1915 that the indications of legal training found in the plays, and the correct application of legal terms, hardly warrant the assertion that Shakespeare was ever an attorney's clerk, 'at the best it is but a surmise.' Although Mr Justice Madden[41] thought that a good deal could be said in support of the supposition that Shakespeare was employed in his early years in an attorney's office, he pointed out that there is no hint of it in any contemporary writing.

The opinion of Sir Arthur Underhill,[42] in his day the

---

[38] John H. Senter, 'Was Shakespeare a Lawyer?', *Vermont Bar Association* (Montpelier, Vermont, 1903).

[39] *Criminal Types in Shakespeare* (1909).

[40] Herbert Morse, *Back to Shakespeare* (1915), pp. 31-2.

[41] D. H. Madden, *Shakespeare and his Fellows* (1916), p. 221.

[42] In *Shakespeare's England*, vol. I, chap. 13, at pp. 381 et seq.

doyen of conveyancing counsel, was that Shakespeare's knowledge of law was 'neither profound nor accurate,' and that there is no reason to suppose that he had even some training in an attorney's office. Mr Justice Barton[43] wrote that Shakespeare's legal allusions were less numerous and less technical than those of other dramatists of that time, such as Ben Jonson, Dekker, Peele and Nashe. Many of Shakespeare's legal and constitutional allusions in the historical plays, which Lord Campbell took as evidence, were derived from the *Chronicles* and other sources. Also, Shakespeare was often inaccurate in his use of legal expressions. His allusions were of that superficial nature which, in a litigious age, would characterise the common speech of the time. Barton himself is especially critical of Rushton's *Shakespeare's Legal Maxims*, contending that more than thirty of the forty maxims cited by Rushton are either coincidences or have a different point.[44] In the rare cases where Shakespeare does allude to a legal maxim, he does so in an assimilated or applied form, as in *The Merry Wives of Windsor*, II, 2, where the speaker's love is: 'Like a fair house, built upon another man's ground; so that I have lost my edifice, by mistaking the place where I erected it.'

James Montgomery Beck, formerly Solicitor-General of the United States and an honorary Bencher of Gray's Inn, was a keen student of Shakespeare's works. In his Foreword to Barton's book he wrote that Shakespeare's legal terminology fell far short of proving that he was a lawyer at any period of his life. While there is no evidence that Shakespeare was a student in any of the Inns of Court, yet, if he had been a student at Gray's Inn, it would explain several puzzling facts – for example, his intimacy with Southampton and Pembroke and other nobles of the Court, as well as the asserted familiarity with legal phraseology.

[43] *Links between Shakespeare and the Law* (1929).
[44] ibid., pp. 126-7.

Southampton and Pembroke, like Bacon and Burghley, were members of Gray's Inn.

D. B. Somervell, K.C., later a Law Officer and eventually a Lord of Appeal, who did not see any real internal evidence that Shakespeare had studied law in an office, said that this discussion had produced some gems of ineptitude, especially on the other side of the Atlantic. It was assumed, for example, that if a person had at one time been in an attorney's office he would be expected to make no mistakes in law for the rest of his life. One might as well deduce that Shelley could not have been brought up in the country or he would never have written to the skylark: 'Hail to thee blithe spirit, Bird thou never wert.'[45]

F. Lyman Windolph,[46] a legal practitioner of Philadelphia, also thinks that Lord Campbell exaggerated Shakespeare's legal knowledge and greatly underestimated his acquisitive powers. Shakespeare simply kept his ears open, as his custom was. No better ears for picking up information ever existed. When the lawyers talked nonsense he was quick to notice and deride, but when they talked sense he paid no attention whatever.

Professor Keeton's[47] opinion is that Shakespeare's legal knowledge differed little from that of other writers of his time, but his observation was closer and more accurate, and there were prominent lawyers of his day – notably Sir Edward Coke – who interested him greatly. We may observe that Keeton has not been sufficiently interested in this question to pay any special attention to it, and that the emphasis on Coke may represent Keeton's own interest in that massive but unattractive personality of English legal history.

[45] D. B. Somervell, K.C., 'Shakespeare and the Law', *Stratford-on-Avon Herald*, 15 April 1932.

[46] F. L. Windolph, *Reflections on the Law in Literature* (Philadelphia, 1956), pp. 43-4.

[47] *Shakespeare's Legal and Political Background*, Preface.

## Did Shakespeare have a Legal Training?

No more reliable authority could be found on this question than Clarkson and Warren,[48] whose reading of Elizabethan drama revealed that about half of Shakespeare's fellows employed on the average more legalisms than he did, and some of them a great many more. Most of them also exceed Shakespeare in the detail and complexity of their legal problems and allusions, and with few exceptions display a degree of accuracy at least no lower than his. It is accordingly the conclusion of these scholarly American practitioners that what law there is in Shakespeare must be explained on some grounds other than that he was a lawyer, or an apprentice, or a student of the law. 'We do not say, dogmatically', they add, 'that William Shakespeare was not a lawyer, or that he had no legal education. As to that we are agnostic: as a matter of biographical fact, we simply do not know. But on the basis of our comparative studies, we do state categorically that the internal evidence from Shakespeare's plays is wholly insufficient to prove such a claim.'

Of a similar opinion is Judge Donald F. Lybarger, of the Court of Common Pleas, Cleveland, Ohio. Much as lawyers might like to claim the world's greatest dramatist, he admits,[49] they can hardly do so in the absence of one scintilla of external proof to that effect. Nor does he regard the evidence within the plays as clear or convincing in establishing the connection. In the end the Judge rests satisfied with the working of nature or destiny in imparting genius to a few outstanding men.

Where Shakespeare's legal allusions surpassed those of his contemporaries, as Mr Justice Barton[50] well said, was in their quality and aptness rather than in their quantity or technicality. It is questionable whether they are more

---

[48] *Law of Property in Shakespeare and Elizabethan Drama*, pp. 285-6.

[49] Judge D. F. Lybarger, *Shakespeare and the Law: Was the Bard Admitted to the Bar?* (Cleveland, Ohio, 1965). Address given before The Great Lakes Shakespeare Association, and reprinted from *Cleveland Bar Journal*, March 1965.

[50] *Links between Shakespeare and the Law*, p. 159.

surprising than many other facets of his brilliant mind.
When we have put aside the dramatic skill, the characterisa-
tion, the pathos and the humour, there remains the poetry.
In that poetry legal expressions are merely one of many
different elements that are transmuted into a richer substance. The process continues from the early poems and
sonnets:

> When to the sessions of sweet silent thought
> I summon up remembrance of things past,
> > (Sonnet 30)

> Why so large cost, having so short a lease,
> Dost thou upon thy fading mansion spend?
> > (Sonnet 146)

through the dramatic speeches:

> Take but degree away, untune that string,
> And hark! what discord follows . . .
> Force should be right; or rather, right and wrong –
> Between whose endless jar justice resides –
> Should lose their names, and so should justice too.
> > (*Troilus and Cressida*, I. 3)

> But mercy is above this sceptred sway.
> It is enthroned in the hearts of Kings,
> It is an attribute to God himself,
> And earthly power doth then show likest God's
> When mercy seasons justice.
> > (*Merchant of Venice*, IV. I)

down to the late dirge in *Cymbeline* (IV. 2):

> Thou thy worldly task hast done,
> Home art gone, and ta'en thy wages.

# Bibliography

This bibliography does not include works concerning the authorship question, unless they also deal with matters coming within the scope of this book.

The place of publication is London unless otherwise stated.

A. C., 'Shakespeare in his own Age', (1964) 61 *Law Society's Gazette*, 240. (Review of *Shakespeare Survey No. 17*).

ADAMS, JOHN QUINCY, *A Life of William Shakespeare* (London and Cambridge, Mass., 1923).

ADDY, S. O., 'Shakespeare's Will: The Stigma Removed', *Notes and Queries*, 16 January 1926, p. 39.

A. H. R., 'An Appreciation of Shakespeare's Knowledge of Law on this Tercentenary of his Death', (1916) 82 *Central Law Journal*, 133.

ALEXANDER, NIGEL, 'Thomas Rymer and "Othello"', (1968) 21 *Shakespeare Survey*, 67.

ALEXANDER, PETER (ed.), *Studies in Shakespeare: British Academy Lectures* (Oxford University Press, 1964).

ALLEN, SIR CARLETON KEMP, Q.C., J.P., *The Queen's Peace* (1953).

ALLEN, (Judge) CHARLES C., *Notes on the Bacon-Shakespeare Question* (Boston, 1900).

ALPERS, O. T. J., *Cheerful Yesterdays* (Hamilton, N.Z., 1928; 2nd. ed., 1951).

ANDREWS, MARK EDWIN, *Law versus Equity in 'The Merchant of Venice'* (University of Colorado Press, 1965).

ANON.

in (1831) 1 *Legal Observer*, 27.
in (1859) 7 *Law Magazine and Law Review*, 41.
in (1875) 11 *Albany Law Journal*, 45.

'Law and Literature', (1928) 72 *Solicitor's Journal*, 620.

Letter signed 'Ritson's Ghost', (1841) 21 *Legal Observer*, 180.

'Mr W. Shakespeare, Solicitor', *Household Words*, 23 October 1858, p. 454. (A facetious review of Rushton's *Shakespeare a Lawyer*, probably by the editor, Charles Dickens.)

*More from a Lawyer's Notebook*, see Haynes.

'Portia's Status', letter signed *'Amicus Curiae'* in (1923) 87 *Justice of the Peace*, 108, and editorial comment, p. 115.

review of Lord Campbell's *Shakespeare's Legal Acquirements Considered* in (1859) 7 *Law Magazine and Law Review*, 41.

review of Marrian's *Shakespeare at Gray's Inn*, in *Graya*, No. 65, Easter Term, 1967.

ditto, in (1969) 20 *Shakespeare Quarterly*, 477.

review of Rushton's *Shakespeare a Lawyer* and *Shakespeare's Legal Maxims* in *Law Magazine and Review*, May 1869.

'Shakespeare and the Law of Marriage', *Contemporary Review*, November 1911, p. 733.

'Shakespeare a Lawyer', (1885) 2 *Pump Court*, 139; (1885) 21 *Canada Law Journal*, 189.

'Shakespeare's Lawyers', (1885) 32 *Albany Law Journal*, 24; *Irish Law Times*, 422; (1885) 79 *Law Times*, 287.

'Shakespeare's Will and His Wife's Dower', (1841) 21 *Legal Observer*, 166.

'Shylock and the Law', *Times Literary Supplement*, 29 January 1925, p. 68. (Review of Griston's *Shaking the Dust from Shakespeare*.)

'The Law and the Bard', (1964) 19 *Record of the Association of the Bar of the City of New York*, 325.

'Was Shakespeare a Lawyer?', (1871) 6 *Law Journal*, 81.

'Was Shakespeare a Lawyer?', (1931) 65 *Irish Law Times*, 258, 264.

ARMOUR, E. D., K.C., D.C.L., 'Law and Lawyers in Literature – IV', (1926) 4 *Canadian Bar Review*, 315.

ASSERSOHN, D. P., 'Shakespeare in the Sonnets', (1964) 61 *Law Society's Gazette*, 208.

AUDEN, W. H., in *The Listener*, 2 July 1964.

AZZOLINI, G., *Shylock e la leggenda della libbra di carne* (Reggio Emilia, 1893), revised and amplified offprint from *L'Italia Cen-*

*trale* of article entitled 'Il Contratto di Shylock nel Mercante di Venezia dello Shakspeare', *Fanfulla della Domenica*, 31 July and 7 August 1892.

BACON, DELIA, *Philosophy of Shakespeare's Plays Unfolded* (1857).

BARTON, SIR DUNBAR PLUNKET (Mr Justice), *Links between Ireland and Shakespeare* (Dublin, 1919).
*Links between Shakespeare and the Law* (1929); reprinted from *Law Journal*, vol. 63, pp. 470, 493, 511, 531, 575, 598; vol. 64, pp. 30, 50, 70, 90. Reprinted by Benjamin Blom Inc., (New York, 1971).

BEALE, J. H., 'Contempt of Court, Criminal and Civil', (1908) 21 *Harvard Law Review*, 181.

BECK, J. M., Foreword to Barton, *Links between Shakespeare and the Law* (1929).

BELLOT, H. H. L., 'The Origin of the Attorney-General', (1909) 25 *Law Quarterly Review*, 400.

BENTLEY, RICHARD, 'Diversities de la Ley', (1922-3) 17 *Illinois Law Review*, 145.
'Shakespeare's Law', (1923) 155 *Law Times*, 34.

BERMAN, RONALD, 'Shakespeare and the Law', (1967) 18 *Shakespeare Quarterly*, 141.

BLACKSTONE, SIR WILLIAM, *Commentaries on the Laws of England* (1765-9).

BIRRELL, RT. HON. AUGUSTINE, K.C., 'Lawyers at Play' (1905), reprinted in *Selected Essays and Addresses*, vol. 3 (1922), p. 235. *Obiter Dicta* (1884).

BLAND, D. S., 'The "Night of Errors" at Gray's Inn', (1966) *Notes and Queries*, n.s., XIII (vol. 211), 127.

BOND, D. F., 'English Legal Proverbs', (1936) 51 *Publications of Modern Language Association of America*, 921.

BOSWELL-STONE, W. G., *Shakespeare's Holinshed: The Chronicle and the Historical Plays Compared* (1896); reprinted in *The Shakespeare Library*, ed. I. Gollancz (1907).

BOYD, J. O., 'Shylock Versus Antonio: or Justice Blindfolded', (1915) 21 *Case and Comment*, 994.

BRENNAN, ELIZABETH MARY, *The Theme of Revenge in Elizabethan Life and Drama 1580-1605* (unpublished thesis, Belfast University, 1955).

BROWN, ARTHUR, *Edmond Malone and English Scholarship* (1963).

BROWN, BASIL, *Law Sports at Gray's Inn (1594), including Shakespeare's connection with the Inns of Court, with a reprint of the Gesta Grayorum* (New York, 1921).

BROWN, IVOR, *How Shakespeare Spent the Day* (1963).

BRUNE, C. M., LL.D., D.C.L., *Shakespeare's Use of Legal Terms* (1914).

BULLOUGH, GEOFFREY, *Narrative and Dramatic Sources of Shakespeare*, vol. V, *The Roman Plays* (1964).

BURRUSS, W. B., 'Shakespeare, the Salesman', (1932) 37 *Commercial Law Journal*, 603.

BUTLER, SAMUEL, *Shakespeare's Sonnets Considered* (1899).

CALVIN, W. W., 'Shakespeare and the Law', (1946) 51 *Case and Comment*, 6.

CAMPBELL, LORD, *Lives of the Chief Justices* (1849).
*Lives of the Lord Chancellors* (1845).
*Shakespeare's Legal Acquirements Considered* (1859).

CHAMBERLAIN, J. D., 'Legal Experiences of Great Authors', (1914) 21 *Case and Comment*, 207.

CHAMBERS, E. K., *Shakespearean Gleanings* (1944).
*Sources for a Biography of Shakespeare* (1946).
*William Shakespeare: A Study of Facts and Problems*, 2 vols. (1930).

CHARLTON, KENNETH, 'Liberal Education and the Inns of Court in the Sixteenth Century', (1960) 9 *British Journal of Educational Studies*, 25; reprinted with revisions in *Education in Renaissance England* (1965), chap. 6.

CLARKSON, P. S., and WARREN, C. T., 'Copyhold Tenure and *Macbeth*, III, ii, 38', in vol. 55 *Modern Language Notes* (Baltimore, 1940), p. 483.
'Pleading and Practice in Shakespeare's Sonnet XLVI', in vol. 62, *Modern Language Notes* (Baltimore, 1947), p. 102.
*The Law of Property in Shakespeare and the Elizabethan Drama* (Baltimore, 1942; reprinted with corrections, 1968).

COKE, SIR EDWARD, *First Institute (Commentary upon Littleton)* (1628).
*Reports* (1600–55).

COLLIER, J. P., *The Diary of Philip Henslowe from 1591–1609, printed from the Original Manuscript preserved at Dulwich College* (Shakespeare Society, 1845).
*The Plays of Shakespeare: The Text regulated by the Old Copies, and by the Recently Discovered Folio of 1632, containing Early Manuscript Emendations* (2nd. ed., 1853).

COLLINS, JOHN CHURTON, *Essays and Studies* (1895).
*Studies in Shakespeare* (1904).

COOPER, WILLIAM, *Henley-in-Arden* (1946).

COWEN, EZEK, 'Shylock v. Antonio', (1872) 5 *Albany Law Journal*, 193.

COWPER, FRANCIS, *A Prospect of Gray's Inn* (1951).
'The Prince and the Poet', *Graya*, No. 60, Michaelmas Term, 1964, p. 111.

CUNINGHAM, HENRY, 'Shakespeare and a Great War', *The Bookman's Journal*, April 1926, p. 1.

DAVIS, C. K. (Senator), *The Law in Shakespeare* (St Paul, Minnesota, 2nd. ed., 1884).

DAWSON, J. P., review of Andrews's *Law Versus Equity in the Merchant of Venice* in (1967) 18 *Shakespeare Quarterly*, 89.

DENNING, LORD, '1967 Turner Memorial Lecture', (1967) 2 *University of Tasmania Law Review*, 349.
'Law and Life in our Time', (1967) 5 *Legal Executive*, 111.

DENNIS, W. A., 'Portia as an Exemplar', (1914) 21 *Case and Comment*, 580.

DEVECMON, W. C., *In Re Shakespeare's 'Legal Acquirements'*, (Shakespeare Society of New York, No. 12; New York, 1899).

DOBRÉE, BONOMY (ed.), *Shakespeare, The Writer and His Work* (1964).

DOUTHWAITE, W. R., *Gray's Inn, Its History & Associations* (1886).

DOYLE, J. T., 'Shakespeare's Law – The Case of Shylock', in *The Overland Monthly* (San Francisco, July 1886).

DRAPER, J. W., 'Dogberry's Due Process of Law', *Journal of English and Germanic Philology*, vol. 42, (University of Illinois, Urbana, Ill., 1943), p. 563.
'Ophelia's Crime of *Felo de Se*', (1936) 42 *West Virginia Law Quarterly*, 228.

DUKE, WINIFRED, 'The Law in Drama', (1926) 38 *Juridical Review*, 55.

ECCLES, MARK, *Shakespeare in Warwickshire* (University of Wisconsin Press, Madison, 1961).

EDWARDS, J. LL. J., *The Law Officers of the Crown* (1964).

E. F. S., 'Portia as a Judge', *Weekly Westminster Gazette*, 3 February 1923, p. 12.

ELTON, C. I., K.C., *William Shakespeare: His Family and Friends* (1904).

ELZE, KARL, *Essays on Shakespeare* (transl. Schmitz, 1874).

ERICKSON, OTTO, 'Shakespeare and the Law: A Tercentenary Obiter', (1916) 20 *Law Notes*, 4.

FITZHERBERT, SIR ANTHONY, *Boke of the Justices of the Peace* (transl. Redman, 1538).

FOARD, J. T., 'On the Law Case: *Shylock v. Antonio*', (1899) *Manchester Quarterly*, 268.

FOSS, EDMUND, *A Biographical Dictionary of the Judges of England* (1870).
*The Judges of England* (1864).

FRIPP, E. I., *Shakespeare, Man and Artist*, 2 vols., (1938).
(ed.), *Minutes and Accounts of the Corporation of Stratford-on-Avon, vol. I, 1553-1566* (Dugdale Society, vol. I).
ditto, *vol. III, 1577-1586* (Dugdale Society, vol. V).

FULLER, R. F., 'Shakespeare as a Lawyer', (1863) 9 *Upper Canada Law Journal*, 91; reprinted from (1862) 21 *Monthly Law Reporter* (Boston), 1.

GENTILE, ALBERICO, *De Jure Belli Libri Tres*, vol. II (transl. Rolfe, 1933).

# Bibliography

*Gesta Grayorum* (1594), ed. Desmond Bland (Liverpool University Press, 1968).

ed., W. W. Greg (Malone Society, 1914).

reprinted in Basil Brown, *Law Sports at Gray's Inn*.

'Gesta Grayorum: The Prince of Purpoole III', *Graya*, No. XLIV (Supplement, 1956).

GIBSON, S. M., 'Shakespeare in the Sonnets', (1964) 61 *Law Society's Gazette*, 23.

GODWIN, GEORGE, *The Middle Temple* (1954).

GOLL, AUGUST, *Criminal Types in Shakespeare* (1909).

GOODHART, A. L., *Interpretations of Modern Legal Philosophies; Essays in Honor of Roscoe Pound* (ed. Sayre, New York, 1947).

GREBANIER, BERNARD, *The Great Shakespeare Forgery* (1966).
*The Truth about Shylock* (New York, 1962).

GREEN, A. WIGFALL, 'Shakespeare's Will', (1932) 20 *Georgetown Law Journal*, 273.
*The Inns of Court and Early English Drama* (Yale University Press, 1931).

GREENWOOD, SIR GEORGE, *Is There a Shakespeare Problem?* (1916).
*Shakespeare's Law* (1920).
*The Shakespeare Problem Restated* (1908).
*The Shakespeare Signatures* (1924).

GREG, W. W., *The Shakespeare First Folio* (1955).

GRISTON, H. J., LL.B., *Shaking the Dust from Shakespeare* (New York, 1924; 2nd. ed., 1924).

GUERNSEY, R. S., *Ecclesiastical Law in Hamlet: The Burial of Ophelia* (New York, 1885).

HALL, EDWARD, *The Union of the Two Noble and Illustre Famelies of Lancastre and Yorke* (1548).

HALLIDAY, F. E., *Shakespeare and his Critics* (1949; revised ed., 1958).
*The Life of Shakespeare* (1961).

HALLIWELL-PHILLIPPS, J. O., *Outlines of the Life of Shakespeare* (1881; 7th. ed., 1887).

HANLEY, H. A., 'Shakespeare's Family in Stratford Records', *Times Literary Supplement*, 21 May 1964.

HANNIGAN, J. E., 'Shakespeare and the Young Lawyer', (1926) 6 *Boston University Law Review*, 168.

HARDCASTLE, HON. MRS (ed.), *Life of John Campbell* (1881).

HARRISON, G. B., *Shakespeare at Work* (1933).
*Shakespeare under Elizabeth* (1933).
*The Sonnets* (Penguin edition of Shakespeare, 1938).

HAYNES, E. S. P., *More from a Lawyer's Notebook* (published anonymously, 1933).

HAYNES, F. O., *Outlines of Equity* (1858; 5th. ed., 1880).

HEALEY, MAURICE, *The Old Munster Circuit* (1939).

HEARD, F. F., *Shakespeare as a Lawyer* (Boston, 1883).

HENSLOWE'S DIARY, ed. R. A. Foakes and R. T. Rickert (Cambridge, 1961).

HERBERT, A. P. (SIR ALAN), *Uncommon Law* (1935).

HERRINGTON, W. S., 'The Legal Lore of Shakespeare', (1925) 3 *Canadian Bar Review*, 537.

HICKS, F. C., 'List of Books on Shakespeare and the Law', (1916) IX *Law Library Journal*, 20.
'Was Shakespeare a Lawyer?', (1916) 22 *Case and Comment*, 1002, reprinted from *New York Sun*, 16 April 1916.

HIRSCHFELD, JULIUS, 'Portia's Judgment and German Jurisprudence', (1914) 30 *Law Quarterly Review*, 167.
'What was Iago's Crime in Law?', (1914) 14 *Journal of the Society of Comparative Legislation* (N.S.), 411.

HOGAN, BRIAN, Note in [1967] *Criminal Law Review*, 496.

HOLDSWORTH, SIR WILLIAM SEARLE, K.C., *History of English Law*, vol. I.
'The Disappearance of the Educational System of the Inns of Court', (1921) *University of Pennsylvania Law Review*, 201.

HOLINSHED, RAPHAEL, *Chronicle*, see Boswell-Stone and Nicoll.

*Holmes-Pollock Letters*, see *Pollock-Holmes Letters*.

HOOKER, RICHARD, *The Laws of Ecclesiastical Polity* (1593).

# Bibliography

HOTSON, LESLIE, *I, William Shakespeare* (1937).
'*Mr. W. H.*' (1964).
*Shakespeare versus Shallow* (1931).
*Shakespeare's Sonnets Dated* (1949).
*The First Night of 'Twelfth Night'* (1954).

(H.) T., *Was Shakespeare a Lawyer?* (1871).

HUNT, J. H., 'Law, Lawyers and Literature', (1937) 5 *Journal of the Bar Association of Kansas*, 234.

HUVELIN, PAUL, 'Le procès de Shylock dans *Le Marchand de Venise* de Shakespeare', *Bulletin de la Société des Amis de l'Université de Lyon* (1901-02), p. 173.

HYDE, H. MONTGOMERY, *Norman Birkett* (1964).

IHERING, RUDOLF VON, *The Struggle for Law (Der Kampf ums Recht)*, transl. Lalor (2nd. ed., Chicago, 1915).

INGLEBY, C. M., *A Complete View of the Shakspere Controversy concerning the Genuineness of the MS. Matter published by Collier* (1861).
*Shakespeare's Bones* (1883).
*The Shakespeare Fabrications* (1859).

IRELAND, SAMUEL, *Miscellaneous Papers and Legal Instruments under the hand and seal of William Shakespeare; including the Tragedy of King Lear, and a small fragment of Hamlet* (1796).

IRELAND, W. H., *An Authentic Account of the Shakespearian Manuscripts* (1796).
*Inquiry into the Authenticity of Certain Miscellaneous Papers and Legal Instruments* (1796).
*The Confessions of William Henry Ireland: containing the particulars of his Fabrication of the Shakespeare Manuscripts* (1805).

IVES, E. W., 'A Lawyer's Library in 1500', (1969) 85 *Law Quarterly Review*, 104.

'The Law and the Lawyers', in *Shakespeare in His Own Age*, (1964) 17 *Shakespeare Survey*, 73.

JAUDON, V. H., 'Shakespeare and the Law', October 1912, 1 *West Pub. Co. Docket*, 799.

JOHNSON, E. D., *Francis Bacon of St. Albans* (1955).

JOSEPH, MIRIAM (Sister), *Shakespeare and the Arts of Language* (New York, 1947).

KANTOROWICZ, E. H., *The King's Two Bodies* (Princeton University Press, 1957).

KEETON, G. W., LL.D., *Lord Chancellor Jeffreys and the Stuart Cause* (1965).
*Shakespeare and his Legal Problems* (1930).
*Shakespeare's Legal and Political Background* (1967).

KEYS, D. R., 'Was Shakespeare bred an Attorney?', (1902) 2 *Canadian Bar Review*, 83.

KNIGHT, CHARLES, *Pictorial Edition of the Works of Shakspere* (1st. ed., 1839-42).
'Postscript to Twelfth Night: Shakspere's Will', op. cit., vol. 2, p. 187.

KNIGHT, G. WILSON, *The Mutual Flame* (1955).

KNIGHTS, L. C., *The Histories*; reprinted in *Shakespeare, The Writer and His Works*, ed. Dobrée (1964).

KOHLER, JOSEF, 'Die Staatsidee Shakespeares in 'Richard II', (1917) 53 *Shakespeare Jahrbuch*, 1.
*Shakespeare vor dem Forum der Jurisprudenz* (Würzburg, 1883; 2nd. ed., Berlin, 1919).
*Verbrecher-Typen in Shakespeares Dramen* (Berlin, 1903).

LAMBARD, WILLIAM, *Eirenarcha, or the Office of the Justices of the Peace* (1581).
*The Duties of Constables, Borsholders, Tythingmen, and such other low and lay Ministers* (enlarged, 1610).

L(ANDOR), W. S., *Citation and Examination of William Shakespeare, Euseby Treen, Joseph Caudy, and Silas Gough, Clerk, before the Worshipful Sir Thomas Lucy, Knight, touching Deer-stealing* (1834).

LASCELLES, MARY, *Shakespeare's Measure for Measure* (1953).

LEECH, CLIFFORD, *The Chronicles*; reprinted in *Shakespeare, The Writer and his Work*, ed. Dobrée (1964).

LEE, R. W., *Elements of Roman Law* (4th. ed., 1956).

# Bibliography

LEE, SIR SIDNEY, *A Life of William Shakespeare* (1898; 6th ed., 1908).

LETI, GREGORIO, *The Life of Pope Sixtus the Fifth*, transl. Farneworth (1754).

LIGHT, HON. J. H., 'Law and Lawyers in Shakespeare', (1914) 21 *Case and Comment*, 185.

LOVE, J. M., 'A Lawyer's Commentary on Shylock v. Antonio', (1891) 25 *American Law Review*, 899.

LYBARGER, D. F. (Judge), *Shakespeare and the Law: Was the Bard Admitted to the Bar?* (Cleveland, Ohio, 1965; reprinted from *Cleveland Bar Journal*, March 1965).

LYELL, H., 'Shakespeare in the Sonnets', (1961) 61 *Law Society's Gazette*, 133.

MACKENZIE, J. B., 'The Law and Procedure in "The Merchant of Venice"', (1904) 16 *Green Bag*, 604.
'Was Shakespeare Bound to an Attorney?', (1902) 14 *Green Bag*, 58.

MACKINNON, SIR FRANK (Lord Justice), 'Notes on the History of English Copyright', in *Oxford Companion to English Literature* (Oxford University Press, 4th. ed., 1967), App. II.

MACLEAN, R. U., 'La Justicia en las obras de Shakespeare', *Letras* No. 36 (1964), (Universidad Nacional Mayor de San Marcos de Lima, Peru), p. 48.

MCNAIR, LORD, Q.C., 'Why is the Doctor in *The Merry Wives of Windsor* called Caius?', (1969) vol. 13 *Medical History*, 311.

MADDEN, D. H. (Mr Justice), *Passages in the Early History of Classical Learning in Ireland* (Dublin, 1908).
*Shakespeare and his Fellows: an attempt to decipher the Man and his Nature* (1916).
*The Diary of Master William Silence: a Study of Shakespeare and of Elizabethan Sport* (1897).

MAITLAND, F. W., *Constitutional History of England* (Cambridge University Press, 1908).
'The Crown as Corporation', (1901) 17 *Law Quarterly Review*, 131; reprinted in *Selected Essays* (Cambridge University Press 1936).

'The Shallows and Silences of Real Life', in *Collected Papers*, (3 vols., Cambridge University Press, 1911), I, 466.

MALONE, EDMOND (ed.), *The Plays and Poems of William Shakespeare*, vol. I (1790).

ditto, ed. Boswell, vols. I and II (1821).

MARCHAM, FRANK, *William Shakespeare and His Daughter Susannah* (1931). (*William Shakespeare and his Family* on cover and page headings).

MARDER, LOUIS, 'Law in Shakespeare'. *Renaissance Papers* (University of South Carolina Press, 1954), 40.

MARRIAN, F. J. M., *Shakespeare at Gray's Inn – A Tentative Theory* (1967).

MERCHANT, W. MOELWYN, 'Lawyer and Actor: Process of Law in Elizabethan Drama', *English Studies Today*, 3rd. Ser. (Edinburgh University Press, 1964), p. 107.

MINOR, P. S., LL.B., 'Shakespeare on Law and Lawyers' (1901), in *Shakespearian Addresses delivered at the Arts Club, Manchester, 1886-1912* (ed. Fishwick), p. 223.

MONTMORENCY, J. E. G. DE, 'Shakespeare's Legal Problems', in *The Contemporary Review: Literary Supplement* (1930), 797.

MORAN, C. G., *The Heralds of the Law* (1948).

MORGAN, J. APPLETON, LL.D., *A Study in the Warwickshire Dialect* (Shakespeare Society of New York, New York, 4th. ed., 1900). *Shakespeare in Fact and in Criticism* (New York, 1888).

MORSE, HERBERT, *Back to Shakespeare* (1915).

MOWAT, R. R., *Morbid Jealousy and Murder* (1966).

MUIR, KENNETH, *Shakespeare's Sources* (1957).

NICOLL, JOSEPHINE and ALLARDYCE, *Holinshed's Chronicle as Used in Shakespeare's Plays* (1927).

NIEMEYER, THEODOR, *Der Rechtsspruch gegen Shylock im 'Kaufmann von Venedig': ein Beitrag zur Würdigung Shakespeares* (1952); revised version translated by Herbruch as 'The Judgment against Shylock in the Merchant of Venice', (1915) 14 *Michigan Law Review*, 20.

NOEL, F. R., 'Legal Influences in Shakespeare', (1941) 18 *Journal of District of Columbia Bar Association*, 353. (Address delivered before Shakespeare Society of Washington, 12 May 1941).

NORMAN, C. H., 'Shakespeare and the Law', letters in *Times Literary Supplement*, 30 June 1950, p. 142, and 4 August 1950, p. 485.

NORMAND, LORD, 'Portia's Judgment', (1939) 10 *University of Edinburgh Journal*, 43.

O'SULLIVAN, RICHARD, Q.C., *The Spirit of the Common Law* (1965). 'A Scale of Values in the Common Law', (1937) 1 *Modern Law Review*, 27.
*Edmund Plowden*, a Reading given at Middle Temple Hall, 1952, and published for the Honourable Society of the Middle Temple.

OSBORN, J. M., 'Edmond Malone and Dr Johnson', in *Johnson, Boswell and their Circle* (Essays Presented to L. F. Powell, 1965), p. 1.

PARKER, M. D. H., *The Slave of Life: A Study of Shakespeare and the Idea of Justice* (1955).

PATER, WALTER, 'Measure for Measure', in *Appreciations* (1889).

PATHAK, ILA, 'Shakespeare and the Law', (1965) 8 *Vidya* (Journal of Gujarat University).

PHELPS, C. H. (Judge), *Falstaff and Equity: An Interpretation* (Boston, 1901).
'Shylock vs. Antonio: Brief for Plaintiff in Appeal', (1886) 57 *Atlantic Monthly*, 463.

PHILLIPS, J. E., review of Keeton, *Shakespeare's Legal and Political Background* in (1969) 20 *Shakespeare Quarterly*, 101.
*The State in Shakespeare's Greek and Roman Plays* (Columbia University Press, 1940), p. 208.

PHILLIPS, O. HOOD, Q.C., 'Shakespeare and Gray's Inn', *Graya*, No. 72, Michaelmas 1970, p. 107. (Abbreviated version of Address read to Gray's Inn Historical Society on 7 July 1970.)
'The Law Relating to Shakespeare, 1564-1964', (1964) 80 *Law Quarterly Review*, I, 172; II, 399.

PIETSCHER, A., *Jurist und Dichter: Studie über Iherings 'Kampf um's Recht' und Shakespeares Kaufmann von Venedig* (Dessau, 1881).

POLAK, A. L., *More Legal Fictions: A Series of Cases from Shakespeare* (1946).

POLLARD, A. W., W. W. GREG, E. MAUNDE THOMPSON, J. DOVER WILSON and R. W. CHAMBERS, *Shakespeare's Hand in the Play of Sir Thomas More* (Cambridge University Press, 1923).

POLLOCK, SIR FREDERICK, BART., K.C., 'A Note on Shylock v. Antonio', (1914) 30 *Law Quarterly Review*, 175.
*Essays in the Law* (1922).
*Leading Cases Done into English, and Other Diversions* (1892).
*Outside the Law* (1927).
'War and Diplomacy in Shakespeare', *The Cornhill Magazine*, 1916; reprinted in *Outside the Law* (1927), 99.

POLLOCK, SIR FREDERICK and MAITLAND, F. W., *History of English Law* (Cambridge University Press, 2nd. ed., 1898), vol. II.

*Pollock-Holmes Letters, The*, 2 vols. (ed. Howe, Cambridge University Press, 1942). Published in the United States as *The Holmes-Pollock Letters* (ed. Howe, Harvard University Press, 1941).

PREST, W., 'Legal Education of the Gentry at the Inns of Court 1560-1640', in *Past and Present*, No. 38 (1967), p. 20.

PRIOR, SIR JAMES, *Life of Edmond Malone* (1860).

RADBRUCH, GUSTAV, *Rechtsphilosophie* (3rd. ed., Leipzig, 1932); transl. K. Wilk, in *The Legal Philosophies of Lask, Radbruch and Dabin* (1950).

RADCLIFFE, VISCOUNT, P. C., *Not in Feather Beds: Some Collected Papers* (1968).

RADIN, MAX, 'The Myth of Magna Carta', (1947) 60 *Harvard Law Review*, 1060.

RANDOLPH, A. M. F., *The Trial of Sir John Falstaff* (New York, 1893).

RAVÀ, ADOLFO, 'I diritti sulla propria persona', (1901) 32 *Rivista italiana per le scienze giuridiche*, 1; and short bibliography at p. 30.

REA, J. D., 'Shylock and the Processus Belial', (1929) *Philological Quarterly*, VIII, 311.

RITSON, JOSEPH, *Remarks. Critical and Illustrative, on the Text and Notes of the Last Edition of Shakespeare* (1783).

ROBERTSON, J. M., *An Introduction to the Study of the Shakespeare Canon* (1924).
*The Baconian Heresy: A Confutation* (1913).
*The Genuine in Shakespeare: A Conspectus* (1930).
*The Problem of Hamlet* (1919).

ROWSE, A. L., *William Shakespeare, A Biography* (1963).

RUBINSTEIN, H. F., *Night of Errors* (1964).

RUSHTON, W. L., *Shakespeare a Lawyer* (1858).
*Shakespeare's Legal Maxims* (1859).
*Shakespeare Illustrated by Old Authors* (1867-8).
*Shakespeare Illustrated by the Lex Scripta* (1870).
*Shakespeare's Euphuism* (1871).
*Shakespeare's Testamentary Language* (1869).
*Shakespeare an Archer* (1897).

RYDER, E. C. *Law and the Universities* (Inaugural Lecture at King's College, Newcastle-upon-Tyne, 1955).

RYMER, THOMAS, see Zimansky, C. A.


SALZMAN, L. F., 'Shakespeare and the Quarter Sessions', in *The London Mercury*, vol. 15, 1926-7, p. 46.

SCHANZER, ERNEST, 'The Marriage-Contracts in *Measure for Measure*', (1960) 13 *Shakespeare Survey*, 81.

SCHOENBAUM, SAMUEL, *Shakespeare's Lives* (Oxford and New York, 1970).

SCOTT, SIR WALTER, *Kenilworth* (1821).
*The Antiquary* (1816).
*The Heart of Midlothian* (1818).
(ed.) *Dryden's Works*, vol. 15 (1808).

SEASONGOOD, MURRAY, 'Some Law in Shakespeare', (1908) 6 *Ohio Law Reporter*, 327.

SENTER, J. H., 'Was Shakespeare a Lawyer?', *Vermont Bar Association* (Montpelier, Vermont, 1903).

SHANNON, R. W., K.C., 'The Countess of Strathmore *versus* Bowes', (1923) 1 *Canadian Bar Review*, 425.

SIMON, SIR JOCELYN, Q.C., (Lord Simon of Glaisdale), 'English Idioms from the Law', (1960) 76 *Law Quarterly Review*, 283, 429; (1962) 78 *Law Quarterly Review*, 245.
'Shakespeare's Legal and Political Background', (1968) 84 *Law Quarterly Review*, 33.

SIMPSON, R. R., M.B., CH.B., F.R.C.S., F.R.C.S.Ed., *Shakespeare and Medicine* (1959).

SMITH, D., *Trial Scenes in the English Drama up to 1615* (unpublished thesis, Birmingham University, 1960).

SMITH, SIR THOMAS, *De Republica Anglorum* (1583).

SOMERVELL, D. B., K.C., (later Lord Somervell), Letter in *Times Literary Supplement*, 21 July 1950, p. 453.
'Shakespeare and the Law', *Stratford-on-Avon Herald*, 15 April 1932.

SPENCE, GEORGE, *Equitable Jurisdiction in Chancery* (1846), vol. I.

SPENCER, T. J. B., *The Roman Plays*; reprinted in *Shakespeare, The Writer and His Work*, ed. Dobrée (1964).

SPRAGUE, H. B., 'Shakespeare's Alleged Blunders in Legal Terminology', (1902) 11 *Yale Law Journal*, 304.

SPURGEON, CAROLINE, *Shakespeare's Imagery and What It Tells Us* (1935).

STONE, JULIUS, *Human Law and Human Justice* (1965).

STOPES, CHARLOTTE CARMICHAEL (Mrs), *Shakespeare's Industry* (1916).

STYLES, PHILIP, 'The Commonwealth', in *Shakespeare in his own Age*, (1964) 17 *Shakespeare Survey*, 103.

TANNENBAUM, S. A., *Problems in Shakspere's Penmanship, including a Study of the Poet's Will* (1927).

TELLER, J. D., 'The Law and Lawyers of Shakespeare', *New York State Bar Association Report 1881*, vol. 4, p. 162.

THAYER, J. B., 'Law and Fact in Jury Trials', (1891) 4 *Harvard Law Review*, 147, 156.

THOMAS, SIDNEY, 'The Date of *The Comedy of Errors*', (1956) 7 *Shakespeare Quarterly*, 377.

# Bibliography

THORPE, W. G., *The Hidden Lives of Shakespeare and Bacon* (1897).

TILLYARD, E. M. W., *Shakespeare's History Plays* (1944).
*Shakespeare's Problem Plays* (Penguin ed., 1965).

UNDERHILL, SIR ARTHUR, K.C., in *Shakespeare's England* (ed. Raleigh, Oxford, 1916), vol. I, chap. 13 ('Law').

WALLACE, C. W., *Shakespeare and his London Associates as Revealed in Recently Discovered Documents* (1910).
'New Shakespeare Discoveries', *Harper's Monthly Magazine*, vol. CXX, No. DCCXVIII, March 1910, p. 489.
*The Newly Discovered Shakespeare Documents* (1905).

WALLACE, J. W., *The Reporters* (4th ed., Boston, 1882).

WALTON, J. K., 'Edmond Malone: an Irish Shakespeare Scholar', *Hermathena*, No. XCIX (Dublin, Autumn 1964), p. 5.

WASHER, B. F., 'William Shakespeare, Attorney at Law', (1898) 10 *Green Bag*, 303, 336.

WATTS, P. R., 'Shakespeare's "Double" Purchase of New Place', (1947) 20 *Australian Law Journal*, 330.

WEARS, T. M., 'Glamis or Cawdor—Which?', (1923) 1 *Canadian Bar Review* 531.
'Lord Campbell & Rushton — A Vindication', (1934) 12 *Canadian Bar Review*, 97.
'Shakespeare's Legal Acquirements', (1938) 16 *Canadian Bar Review* 28.
'Shakespeare's Will', (1942) 20 *Canadian Bar Review*, 53.

WHELER, R. B., *History and Antiquities of Stratford-upon-Avon* (Stratford, 1806).
*A Guide to Stratford-upon-Avon* (Stratford, 1814).

WHITE, E. J., *Commentaries on the Law in Shakespeare*, (St Louis, 1911; 2nd. ed., 1913).
'Shakespeare's Criminal Types', (1918) 52 *American Law Review*, 347; reprinted in (1940) 74 *New York Law Review*, 505.

WHITE, R. G., 'William Shakespeare, Attorney at Law and Solicitor in Chancery', IV *Atlantic Monthly* (July 1859), p. 84.

WIGMORE, J. H., 'Shakespeare's Legal Documents', (1942) 28 *American Bar Association Journal*, 134.

WILKES, GEORGE, *Shakespeare: from an American Point of View, including An Inquiry as to his Religious Faith and his Knowledge of Law* (New York, 1877; 3rd. ed., 1882).

WILSON, J. DOVER, *What Happens in 'Hamlet'* (Cambridge University Press, 1935).

WINDOLPH, F. L., *Reflections on the Law in Literature* (Philadelphia University Press, 1956).

WU, J. C. H., LL.D., *Fountain of Justice: A Study in the Natural Law* (1959).

YEATMAN, J. PYM, *Is William Shakspere's Will Holographic?* (Darley Dale, 2nd. ed., 1901).
*The Gentle Shakspere: A Vindication* (1896; 4th. ed., Birmingham, 1906).

YOUNG, G. M., 'Shakespeare and the Termers', in *Proceedings of the British Academy*, vol. 33 (1947), p. 81.

ZIMANSKY, C. A., (ed.) *The Critical Works of Thomas Rymer* (Yale University Press, 1956).

# Index

211

# Index

Elton, C. I., 11, 18, 19
equity, 60, 95, 114, 115, 116-7, 131-2
equivocation, 80
Erickson, Otto, 90
Erskine, Thomas, 166
Escalus, 89
extent, writ of, 41, 123

Falstaff, 33, 41, 49, 61, 63, 65, 67, 72, 74,
    82, 89, 131, 132, 133, 142, 149, 168,
    173
Field, Richard, 3
fine, 119-20, 121, 161
Fitzpeter, Geoffrey, 70
*Folio, First,* 1, 14, 21-2, 24, 139, 172
    *Second,* 22, 172, 175
    *Third,* 143
    *Fourth,* 22
Fortescue, Sir John, 33-4, 49, 51
Fortinbras, 50
Foss, Edmund, 180
Fripp, E. I., 20, 89, 184
*Froissart's Chronicle,* 49
Fuller, R. F., 92-3, 134, 184-5
Furness, H. H., 145

Gascoigne, Sir William, 62, 71-4, 163
Gentile, Alberico, 26, 129-30
*Gesta Grayorum,* 24-5, 26-7, 31-2
Gibson, S. M., 183
Goll, August, 152-3, 188
Goodhart, A. L., 170
Gray's Inn, 23-7, 57, 75, 80, 129, 145, 147,
    148, 155, 156, 172, 189, 190
Green, A. Wigfall, 15, 20-21
Greenwood, Sir George, 18, 19, 20, 104,
    134, 135, 137, 166
Griston, H. J., 109
Guernsey, R. S., 153-4

*Hales v. Petit, see* 'cases'
Hales, Sir James, 77-8, 82-3
Hall, John, 14-15, 19, 20-21
Hall, Susanna, 3, 14-15, 19, 20-21, 22
Halliwell-Phillipps, J. O., 8, 9, 17-18
*Hall's Chronicle,* 34, 48, 56, 73, 130, 189
*Hamlet,* 38, 44, 45, 47, 50, 51-2, 53, 61,
    76-9, 81, 90, 119-20, 121, 122-3, 126,
    135, 136-7, 145, 147-8, 151, 152-3,
    154, 156, 157-8, 164, 174
Hanley, H. A., 13-14
Hannigan, J. E., 56
Hanworth, Lord, 167
Harman, Lord Justice, 168
Harrison, G. B., 31-2
Hatcliffe, William, 29-30
Hathaway, Anne, *see* 'Shakespeare, Anne'
Hawkins, Sir John, 78
Haynes, E. S. P., 10
Heard, F. F., 11, 120, 181-2

heirlooms, 16
Heminge, John, 5, 8, 11, 14, 21, 174
Henley-in-Arden, 36
*Henry IV, Part 1,* 33, 45, 49, 52, 61, 63,
    82, 124, 131-2, 133
    *Part 2,* 46, 49, 51, 52, 61, 63, 65, 66,
        67, 72-4, 81, 125, 126, 163, 181-2
*Henry V,* 26, 46, 51, 52, 54, 55-6, 57, 85,
    129-30, 133, 138, 141, 142, 171
*Henry VI, Part 1,* 32, 46, 48, 49, 51, 66,
    138, 158
    *Part 2,* 33, 44, 46, 48, 49, 51, 56, 84,
        138, 158, 164, 179
    *Part 3,* 46, 48, 49, 51, 56, 61, 133, 138,
        158
*Henry VIII,* 49, 50, 56, 72, 82, 84, 86-7,
    133, 138, 158, 179, 183-4
Henslowe, Philip, 4
Herbert, Sir Alan P., 166
Herrington, W. S., 62, 88
Hirschfeld, Julius, 104, 106, 153
Holdsworth, Sir William, 34
*Holinshed's Chronicle,* 9-10, 34, 48-9, 129,
    130, 138, 141, 149, 156, 184, 189
Holmes, Oliver Wendel (Justice), 10, 138,
    162-3
homilies, 50
Hooker, Richard, 21, 49, 130
Hotson, Leslie, 1, 9-10, 13, 27-31, 67
Hunsdon, Lord, 26
Huvelin, Paul, 102-3, 106

Iago, 153, 169, 170, 174
idioms, legal, 43-4
Ihering, Rudolph von, 93, 102, 106
Ingleby, C. M., 154-5, 175
Inner Temple, 24, 65, 143, 144
Inns of Court, 23-34, 65, 78, 189-90
Ireland, W. H., 174

Jeffreys, Lord Chancellor, 125, 166
*John, King,* 37, 49, 52, 61, 70-71, 85-6,
    90, 138, 167, 179
Johnson, E. D., 116
Johnson, Samuel, 78, 125, 142, 143, 144,
    147
Jonson, Ben, 12, 21-2, 76, 84, 160, 173,
    174, 189
Joseph, Miriam (Sister), 44-5
*Julius Caesar,* 52, 56, 57, 135, 137-8, 139-
    40, 145-6
justice, 40, 43, 44, 54, 58-61, 90, 91, 114,
    168, 192

Kantorowicz, Ernst, 53
Keeton, G. W., 50-52, 55, 56, 60, 66, 67,
    74, 85-6, 88, 116-17, 130, 156-8, 165,
    190
Keys, D. R., 186
kingship, 50-6
Knight, Charles, 15-17

212

# Index

# Index

Robertson, J. M., 103, 150-1, 159, 160, 184
*Romeo and Juliet*, 40, 42, 46, 63, 165
Rowe, Nicholas, 4, 141, 143, 176
Rowse, A. L., 128
Rubinstein, H. F., 26
Rushton, W. L., 119, 120-4, 148-50, 177, 181, 183, 184, 189
Russell, Thomas, 13, 21, 22
Rutland, 5th Earl, 23
Ryder, E. C., 35
Rymer, Thomas, 59, 145-7

Scott, Sir Walter, 146-7, 171-2
seal, 40, 47, 149, 187
Seneca, 104
Senter, J. H., 188
Shakespeare, Anne, 2, 15-20, 21, 174
Shakespeare, Hamnet, 3
Shakespeare, John, 7, 22, 35, 132
Shakespeare, Judith, *see* Quiney, Judith
Shakespeare, Mary, 132
Shakespeare, Susanna, *see* Hall, Susanna
Shakespeare, William,
  actor-manager, 3, 5, 25, 26, 141, 142
  and Coke, 35-6
  and Inns of Court, 23-36, 189-90
  choice of plots, 46-7
  coat-of-arms, 3, 26
  descendants, 15
  horse-holder? 151
  legal training? 176-92
  litigation, 8-9
  marriage, 2, 132-4
  monument, 3, 144, 173
  property, 5-8, 172
  opinion of lawyers, 62-4
  records of life, 1-22, 143-4
  sources of works, 9, 26, 48-50, 56, 57, 58, 91, 104, 108, 134, 137-40, 141, 184, 189
  will, 10-21, 143
Shakespeare Action Committee, 2
Shallow, Robert, 33, 65-7
Shylock, 91, 92, 93, 94-7, 103, 104-5, 106-7, 108, 111-12, 113, 114, 116-18, 151, 167
Sidney, Sir Philip, 24
Silence, Justice, 67, 173
Simon of Glaisdale, Lord, 30-31, 43-4, 57, 86, 118, 139-40, 164-5
Sixtus V, Pope, 101-2
Slender, Abraham, 65, 67
Smith, Sir Thomas, 49
Somervell, Lord, 67, 79-80, 190
*Sonnets, The*, 3, 10, 24, 29, 30-31, 39, 43, 120, 126-8, 134, 135, 164-5, 183, 192
Southampton, 3rd Earl, 23-4, 25-6, 174, 189-90
Sprague, H. B., 103, 135, 137

Spurgeon, Caroline, 58
Steevens, George, 16, 119, 124, 142, 143, 147, 174
Stone, Harlan F. (Justice), 113-4
Stone, Julius, 171
Stopes, Mrs. C. C., 6
Stratford-upon-Avon, 1, 3, 35-6, 64, 66, 143-4, 148, 171
suicide, 77-8, 136, 147, 154, 169, 179

*Taming of the Shrew, The*, 28, 42, 62, 69, 124, 133, 168, 173
Tannenbaum, S. A., 12, 18, 109
Teller, J. D., 71
*Tempest, The*, 51, 153
terms, legal, 37-46, 119 *et seq.*, 148-50, 158-61
Theobald, Lewis, 18, 141-2, 146, 147, 173-4, 176
Thorpe, Thomas, 3
Thorpe, W. G., 172-3
Tillyard, E. M. W., 48
*Timon of Athens*, 47, 62, 136, 137
*Titus Andronicus*, 43, 47
Tonson, Jacob, 4-5
treason, 84-5, 87-8, 125, 134
trial scenes, 47, 84-118
*Troilus and Cressida*, 26, 28, 41, 43, 46, 51, 57, 129-30, 138, 163, 192
*Twelfth Night*, 17, 27, 40, 75-6, 80
*Two Gentlemen of Verona, The*, 63

Underhill, Sir Arthur, 6, 19-20, 120, 133, 134, 188-9
use, 117, 170
usury, 91

*Variorum*, editions, 130, 132, 144
  New, 91, 145
*Venus and Adonis*, 3, 23, 38, 155, 166
Verges, 46, 67-8

Wallace, C. W., 8
Warren, C. T., 127, 128-9, 159-61, 191
Washer, B. F., 186-7
Watts, P. R., 6-7
Wears, T. M., 19, 181
Webster, John, 169, 187
Wheler, R. B., 148
White, E. J., 103, 158-9, 160, 161, 180
White, R. Grant, 183-4
Wilkes, George, 185
Wilson, J. Dover, 77, 136
Windolph, F. Lyman, 77, 115-16, 190
*Winter's Tale, The*, 47, 62, 74-5, 87-8, 186
Wu, John, 163-4

Yeatman, J. Pym, 3, 11-12, 86-7
Young, G. M., 33, 36
Young, Lord, 166-7

214

Phillips, O. Hood          822.3
Shakespeare & the            P
lawyers